Woven
in the Womb

PEACE FOR THE
PREGNANT
AND POSTPARTUM
SOUL

By
Rachelle Keng, MD

©2024 by Rachelle Keng
Published by hope*books
2217 Matthews Township Pkwy
Suite D302
Matthews, NC 28105

www.hopebooks.com
hope*books is a division of hope*media

Printed in the United States of America by hope*books

All rights reserved. Without limiting the rights under copyrights reserved above, no part of this publication may be scanned, uploaded, reproduced, distributed, or transmitted in any form or by any means whatsoever without express prior written permission from both the author and publisher of this book—except in the case of brief quotations embodied in critical articles and reviews.

Thank you for supporting the author's rights.

First Print Edition
Paperback ISBN: 979-8-89185-039-2
Hardcover: 979-8-89185-040-8
Ebook ISBN: 979-8-89185-041-5
Library of Congress Number: 2023951508

Cover design copyright © 2024 by hope*books

Unless otherwise indicated, all Scripture quotations are from The ESV® Bible (The Holy Bible, English Standard Version®), © 2001 by Crossway, a publishing ministry of Good News Publishers. Used by permission. All rights reserved.

Scripture quotations marked (NIV) are taken from the Holy Bible, New International Version®, NIV®. Copyright © 1973, 1978, 1984, 2011 by Biblica, Inc.™ Used by permission of Zondervan. All rights reserved worldwide. www.zondervan.com The "NIV" and "New International Version" are trademarks registered in the United States Patent and Trademark Office by Biblica, Inc.™

Scripture quotations marked (NLT) are taken from the Holy Bible, New Living Translation, copyright ©1996, 2004, 2015 by Tyndale House Foundation. Used by permission of Tyndale House Publishers, Carol Stream, Illinois 60188. All rights reserved.

Scripture quotations taken from the (NASB®) New American Standard Bible®, Copyright © 2020 by The Lockman Foundation. Used by permission. All rights reserved. lockman.org

Scripture quotations marked CSB have been taken from the Christian Standard Bible®, Copyright © 2017 by Holman Bible Publishers. Used by permission. Christian Standard Bible® and CSB® are federally registered trademarks of Holman Bible Publishers.

Scripture taken from the New King James Version®. Copyright © 1982 by Thomas Nelson. Used by permission. All rights reserved.

For my late mother, Dr. Rita Huang, who carried me in her womb. You always knew I would write a book. I learned from the best. Thank you for parenting me by prayer. I miss you and always will. I love you more!

For my children, Maleia and Anya, who were woven in my womb. You both are the joy of my life and it is a privilege to be your mama. I love you more!

For you formed my inward parts; you knitted me together in my mother's womb. I praise you, for I am fearfully and wonderfully made. Wonderful are your works; my soul knows it very well. My frame was not hidden from you, when I was being made in secret, **intricately woven** *in the depths of the earth. Your eyes saw my unformed substance; in your book were written, every one of them, the days that were formed for me, when as yet there was none of them. Psalm 139:13-16 (ESV)*

Endorsements

"If you are pregnant, have a new baby, cannot get pregnant, or have had an abortion, feel overwhelmed and you just want to talk to a friend who will listen to the good, bad and the ugly, then curl up with this book for an understanding heart with biblical wisdom, practical tips and grace."

- **Ruth Graham**, Author of *Forgiving My Father, Forgiving Myself*

"Motherhood is a beautiful gift of joy, but it can also rock some of us to our core. Pregnancy, labor, delivery, and postpartum hold so many unknowns. That's why Rachelle does a great job of taking us by the hand through every part of a mother's journey. She holds our hand as someone who has experienced mothering a special needs child, is a sister in Christ, and has the medical experience of an OBGYN. Rachelle's heart for mothers bleeds out of the pages and becomes a compassionate healing balm for readers."

- **Liz Wann**, Author of *The End of Me: Finding Resurrection Life in the Daily Sacrifices of Motherhood*

"Woven in the Womb is a sensitively written, comprehensive guide through the wilderness of pregnancy and beyond. Find rest in the embrace of God's perfect love with this devotional treasure for the soul of every woman who is embarking on the amazing journey of motherhood."

- **Andrea Asher**, RN, Labor and Delivery Nurse, Mother of five, Grandmother, Global Missions Advocate

"Dr. Keng uses understandable terminology to explain the bodily and emotional changes one can expect through the progressive weeks of pregnancy and new motherhood. She uses the sufficiency of scripture to provide emotional buoyancy to the hormonal and cultural influences that assault the well-being of mothers and their relationships, showing how Jesus and our dependence on Him helps us navigate the turbulent waters of pregnancy and motherhood. Truly, a "must have" reference and devotional for every couple seeking to grow through the challenges of parenthood."

- **Peter Rothschild**, MD, Fellow of American College of Obstetrics and Gynecology, Director of Strong Dads Lifespring

"As a woman who has experienced the joy of being a mother and the heartache of pregnancy loss, this book truly means a lot to me. It reminded me that I am not alone, that I don't have to be perfect, and I will survive when tragedies come. It reminded me that I am truly loved by a Heavenly Father who holds me in the palm of His hand. As an OBGYN, I know that this book will help guide women through one of the most challenging times of their lives in a way that medicine alone cannot do. Anyone who wants to become a mother, is currently pregnant, or is navigating through the trials and triumphs of motherhood will greatly benefit from reading this book."

- **Erika Brandenstein**, MD, Fellow of American College of Obstetrics and Gynecology

"After years of serving as a perinatal psychotherapist, I have encountered a range of intense emotions occurring for women as they enter their reproductive years. In this work, I have longed for a resource like this to offer. Dr. Keng's words are a balm to a mother's anxious heart, a place of rest for a grieving mother's soul, and an encouragement for all of the in-between. She beautifully marries her medical knowledge with spiritual wisdom, helping women face realistic fears associated with pregnancy find rest in God's greater plan. Thank you, Dr. Keng, for the blessing of your writing."

- **Kristin Morgan**, Mother, Licensed Professional Counselor, PMH-C with a specialization in treating perinatal mood and anxiety disorders.

"Moms-to-be, this book will guide you week by week as you walk through the mothering journey. It is such a helpful guide as we embrace our call to motherhood!

- Shelby Dean, Mother of four (with two high risk pregnancies and two adopted children)

"I am a breastfeeding champion and also a realist. Motherhood is humbling to the core for many women. Since the very first page, I am convinced this is an inspired work of art. Dr.Keng's writing about pregnancy and postpartum is heartfelt and honest. The Lord's presence is so powerful through this book. I am humbled by His majestic creation."

Penny Merrell, Certified Lactation Consultant

Table of Contents

Forward 1
Prologue 3

Part I: Preconception 7
Chapter 1: The First Visit With Your Doctor 9
Chapter 2: Setting Expectations 11
Chapter 3: A Biblical Worldview Of The Womb 15

Part II: The Woes of the Womb 21
Chapter 1: The Griefs Of Miscarriage 24
Chapter 2: The Griefs Of Infertility 29
Chapter 3: The Griefs Of Abortion 34
Chapter 4: The Griefs Of Unexpected Diagnoses 39

Part III: Pregnancy 47

First Trimester 59
4 weeks: **Two lines!!** 52
    God Is Not Surprised (Isaiah 44:24)
5 weeks: **Sacrificial Love** 55
    God Understands Sacrifice (Hebrews 12:2)
6 weeks: **Morning Sickness** 57
    God Protects Us (John 15:4-5,12-13)
7 weeks: **Navigating Unplanned Pregnancy** 60
    God Is A Good Shepherd (John 10:10-15)
8 weeks: **Worry Is Normal** 63
    God Gives Us Peace (Isaiah 26:3)

9 weeks: **Facing The Fear of Miscarriage** 66
   God Is All-Knowing (Romans 8:28)
10 weeks: **Genetic Testing** 69
   God Is Sovereign (Psalm 139:15-16)
11 weeks: **When He Doesn't Get It** 72
   God sees (Psalm 139:1-4)
12 weeks: **A Symbiotic Bond** 75
   God Loved Us First (1 John 4:19)
13 weeks: **The Victim Vortex** 78
   God Said No To Self-Pity (Isaiah 53:7)

Second Trimester **81**
14 weeks: **The Roots Of Anxiety** 84
   God Is A Safe Shelter (Jeremiah 17:7-8)
15 weeks: **Mama Drama** 88
   God Remembers His Children (Isaiah 49:15-16)
16 weeks: **Finding Balance** 91
   God Gives Good Directions (Philippians 4:8)
17 weeks: **Learning To Self-Care** 94
   God Cares For Our Physical Needs (1 Kings 19:5-8)
18 weeks: **Stress Management** 97
   God Helps Us Cope (2 Corinthians 4:19-20)
19 weeks: **Am I Doing Enough?** 101
   God Is Already Enough (2 Corinthians 4:7)
20 weeks: **Perfectly Imperfect** 104
   God Does Not Make Mistakes (2 Corinthians 4:6-7)
21 weeks: **Cherishing the In-Laws** 107
   God Chooses Grace (Ruth 2:11-12)
22 weeks: **The Battle of Comparison** 110
   God Gives Contentment (Psalm 131)
23 weeks: **The Hormonal Roller Coaster** 113
   God Gives Self-Control (Genesis 8:9-15)

Table of Contents

24 weeks: **For the Fatherless** 116
    God Is A Loving Father (Psalm 68:4-6)
25 weeks: **Unity, the Best Gift** *119*
    God Heals The Impossible (Mark 10:7-9)
26 weeks: **What's In A Name?** *122*
    God Gives Us Our Identity (John 1:2)

Third Trimester **125**
27 weeks: **Unexpected Grief** *128*
    God Grieves With Us (Isaiah 53:3)
28 weeks: **Mothers at the Five o'clock Hour** *131*
    God Refills Us (Luke 8:43-48)
29 weeks: **Parenting By Prayer** *134*
    God Listens (Philippians 4:4-7)
30 weeks: **Redemptive Birth Experiences** *137*
    God Loves To Redeem (John 3:3-5)
31 weeks: **Assembling Your True Village** *141*
    God Provides Our People (Luke 1:41-45)
32 weeks: **Filtering The Filter-less** *144*
    God Defends Us (Luke 7:38-39)
33 weeks: **The Birth Plan** *147*
    God Plans The Detours (Proverbs 16:7)
34 weeks: **Something Always Hurts** *150*
    God Sustains Us (Lamentations 3:24-25)
35 weeks: **Learning To Laugh** *154*
    God Wants Our Growth (Proverbs 17:22)
36 weeks: **Pain Management** *157*
    God Is Our Hope (Romans 5:2b-5)
37 weeks: **Learning to Delight In Your Children** *160*
    God Delights In You (Psalm 37:4-7)
38 weeks: **Letting Go** *163*
    God Is Trustworthy (1 Samuel 1:27-28)

39 weeks: **The Imposter Syndrome** *167*
    God Knows The Truth (Matthew 11:28-30)
40 weeks: **On Being Held** *170*
    God Holds Us (Psalm 18:1-3)

Part IV: Labor and Delivery **173**
Chapter 1: **"Born Again Sanctification"** *176*
    A Devotion On Childbirth
Chapter 2: **Labor and Delivery Expectations** 180
- *The Truth About Labor* *181*
- *The Truth About Pushing* *183*
- *The Truth About Post-Delivery* *184*
- *The Truth About Cesarean Sections* *186*
- *The Truth About Pain Management* *188*
- *The Truth About Breastfeeding* *191*
- *The Truth About Postpartum Pain* *192*

    Myths about Labor and Delivery **194**
Chapter 3: QR Codes: Bible Verses From Pregnancy and
    Postpartum Devotions 199

Part V: Postpartum **201**
Week 1: The Mommy Expectations Redo **204**
    Day 1: **Feeling Like A Failure** 207
        God Is For Your Good (Psalm 42:5)
    Day 2: **When They Come Out Differently** 208
        God Is Trustworthy (Proverbs 3:5-8)
    Day 3: **Running On Empty** 210
        God Fills Us (Isaiah 40:11)
    Day 4: **Breastfeeding Idols** 211
        God Provides For Our Children (Matthew 6:25-27)
    Day 5: **Relying On Manna** 214
        God Knows Our Needs (Exodus 16:7-18)

Table of Contents

Day 6: **Letting Go Of Perfectionism** 215
    God Gives Us A New Song (Psalm 40:1-3)
Day 7: **Postpartum Blues Or Depression?** 218
    God's Perfect Power (2 Corinthians 12:7-10)

Week 2: Battling Discouragement 222
Day 1: **God's Mercy In Zoloft** 224
    God Helps Us (Isaiah 41:9-10)
Day 2: **Asking For Help** 226
    God Is Already There (Psalm 121)
Day 3: **Warring With Self-Doubt** 229
    God Has Called You (Nehemiah 6:15-16)
Day 4: **Surprising Grief** 231
    God Is A Compassionate Father (Psalm 103:8-14)
Day 5: **Comparing To Yourself** 233
    God Measures Differently (Galatians 5:22-23)
Day 6: **Fearing Worst Case Scenarios** 235
    God Is Merciful (Romans 8:38-39)
Day 7: **Lamenting For The Overwhelmed Mama** ... 237
    God Knows Our Colic Too (Psalm 22)

Week 3: Saying Hello to Guilt 240
Day 1: **Forgiving Ourselves** 241
    God Chose Us (Colossians 3:12)
Day 2: **Forgiving Others** 244
    God Forgives Us (Colossians 3:12-15)
Day 3: **The Art Of Boundaries** 246
    God Knows Our Limits (Proverbs 4:23-27)
Day 4: **Self-care Is Selfless** 248
    God Wants To Feed Our Roots (Jeremiah 17:7-8)
Day 5: **Trusting Others With Your Baby** 250
    God Knows Your Baby The Best (Exodus 2:2-4)
Day 6: **Everyone Needs More of You** 252
    God Rejoices Over Us (Zephaniah 3:17)

Day 7: **The "Good" Christian Mother** 253
God Embraces Us At Our Worst (Luke 15:20)

Week 4: Re-defining Your Identity **256**
Day 1: **Mommy Still Looks Pregnant** 258
God Re-defines Beauty (1 Samuel 16:7)
Day 2: **Mixed Emotion Mommy** 260
God Knows How We Feel (2 Corinthians 6:4,10)
Day 3: **Daddy's Identity Crisis** 262
God Loves Him Too (Hebrews 3:13)
Day 4: **Spouse Identity Crisis** 264
God Is Love (1 Corinthians 13:4-7)
Day 5: **Multi-tasking Mommy** 267
God Wants Our Attention (Luke 10:41-42)
Day 6: **Lonely Mommy** 269
God Understands Loneliness (Isaiah 53:3-5)
Day 7: **Enduring Rhythms** 271
God Is At The Finish Line (Hebrews 12:1-2)

Part VI: Epilogue **275**

Part VII: Acknowledgments **279**

Foreword

I have known the author, Dr. Rachelle Keng, for sixteen years. We met during our residency training in obstetrics and gynecology. We were bright-eyed and ambitious. We embraced life with the optimism that comes with pursuing a career that you truly love. We were filled with hope for an amazing and impactful future as physicians, wives, and mothers. We approached life without caution, believing that our own abilities and our faith would be enough to propel us into a quintessential future.

Like so many young women, I sought the ideal life with an ideal career, ideal husband, ideal children, and ideal home. I would soon discover my hopes for an ideal life were not real but only fantasy. Through life's journey, I have experienced extreme brokenness and seemingly insurmountable challenges. Rachelle has been with me through it all, and through her personal experiences with her daughter, she has shown me how to trust in God's sovereign plan, even when a dream dies. Her encouragement and example helped me to learn what it truly means to be loved by God. He knew the challenges we would face, and He had a plan for us all along, a good plan.

As a physician myself, I appreciate how this book includes a wealth of medical knowledge given in a very comprehensible and down-to-earth fashion, but it offers so much more. Through her writing, Dr. Keng has given women the opportunity to see and appreciate God's plan, even while enduring uncertainty and suffering. With a focus on scripture, this book will help guide women through the physical, emotional, and spiritual changes and challenges that go along with becoming a mother. Most importantly, this book shines a light on the all-encompassing love of God that will see us through.

Erika Brandenstein, MD, Fellow of American College of Obstetrics and Gynecology

Prologue

Congratulations! Your "baby" may still be an egg, you may be pregnant, or you're already running after your feral munchkins. You may already be aware of the great responsibilities of motherhood. Or it may feel like the most terrifying next step.

Wherever you are in your motherhood journey, I hope you will see God's beautiful plan of sanctifying women through motherhood.

This book is not your typical feel-good sunny pregnancy book nor your how-to pregnancy book. This book is also not a substitute for prenatal care with a physician or midwife. This book does not replace medical advice.

Instead, this is an honest and hope-filled book about the gospel truths found in the journey of the womb—in its triumphs and failures. I hope to share with you the wonder of our Creator and the miracle of pregnancy. I hope to remind you of God's great mercy and faithfulness, even in unexpected outcomes. As your bump grows, I hope to encourage you to be more focused on the Creator. As you grow horizontally, I hope you will also grow "vertically" in your relationship with God.

Keeping our eyes focused on the Creator instead of ourselves will keep our dreams, emotions, and fears in check. Focusing on our Creator gives us peace.

Peace. It seems like such a simple concept, yet it is so difficult to find. Especially during pregnancy and postpartum, when a mother's mind is usually anxiety-ridden with all of the things that can go wrong. Some fears are completely valid. But can we transform these fears into peace? How can we find peace while living in a broken world? How do we find peace even when our worst fears become true?

I am a Christian obstetrician-gynecologist trained to care for the medical needs of a mother and her baby. And yet, at times I find myself more like a grief counselor as parents reconcile their expectations with reality.

For the last seventeen years, I have cared for women through preconception, pregnancies, deliveries, and their motherhood journeys. I have the privilege of handing new life to happy parents. I am the first person to hold their squirmy baby. I have cried happy tears with a new daddy as he cuts his baby's umbilical cord, releasing his child into the world. I love the romance of childbirth. These are the highlights of my job.

But it is the woes of the womb—the lowlights—that have also caused me to draw on my relationship with Jesus. Because the truth is, pregnancy and motherhood are not all daisies. There are shadowed crosses amid the daisies. But amongst these crosses is gospel hope for all of us.

I have walked with women through infertility. Miscarriage. Unexpected pregnancies. Debilitating pregnancy symptoms. Unexpected diagnoses. Stillbirth. Postpartum depression. Motherhood isolation. Disappointing parenting journeys.

I, too, have walked through the woes of the womb. My postpartum experience kicked me in the behind. I felt betrayed by the books when my baby did not sleep. I was surprised at how difficult it was for me to bond with my baby when she had reflux and colic. But most of all, my motherhood story changed when my beautiful girl was diagnosed with Angelman syndrome. I learned (and am still learning) to die to my expectations of motherhood. I wrestled with a God I thought I knew.

Through my disappointment and heartache, He rewrote my story. He redeemed my broken heart through the perfectly blemished fruit of my womb.

If we understand a biblical worldview of the mother's womb before beginning our motherhood journeys, reality may be a little easier if life does not turn out the way we expect. And even if we do not have woes during pregnancy, motherhood itself is full of woes that need real answers.

You may be on a pregnancy endorphin high and have everything under control. You may have it all figured out, at least for now. But when your motherhood journey hits its first snag, I pray that this book can help you re-center your walk with God. We often do not lean into our faith until these woes become personal. We often do not ask questions until our motherhood journey is less than ideal.

Have you ever wondered if there is more to motherhood? Have you ever wondered whether your symptoms during pregnancy have an intentional purpose? Have you ever wondered why the postpartum period can be a dark cloud for some women and not others? We can better handle pain when we know the purpose behind it. This book explores these topics through a biblical lens. I hope to humbly share the truths I have learned from my journey as a physician and a mother.

This book is written from a Christian perspective for the disillusioned mother who needs to know there is more. It is also written for a woman dealing with infertility or miscarriage who is struggling to reconcile her biology with her desire. It is written for the woman adopting a child who is growing in her mother's heart even though her womb is empty. It is written for the anxious mother who believes her children's well-being depends entirely on her.

We will look at the beautifully crafted physiology of pregnancy, examining how God intentionally created women for the calling of motherhood. As your symptoms evolve through the dynamic changes of pregnancy, we will see an intentional design. Then, we will see how the lessons learned in pregnancy are the same lessons we carry into motherhood.

There are also some chapters written for pregnant women who are in crisis. Many women are in broken relationships at the time of their pregnancy, alone in their marriages, and in need of hope. Perfect "cookie-cutter" pregnancy situations are not a realistic view of what is happening in churches, schools, and families. Let us approach all pregnancies graciously, knowing that all mothers need encouragement. If a chapter does not apply to you personally, pray for the woman that it does apply to. We are a tribe that needs one another. Every mother has a different story but likely has similar aches as you do.

The Bible says that God has a purposeful order for marriage before sexual intimacy (1 Corinthians 6:18-20). Sexual intimacy without marriage can leave women susceptible to vulnerable situations. However, the reality is that many couples are entering parenthood unmarried. So, the terms husband and partner will be used interchangeably throughout this book.

If you are a single mother, this book is also for you. You are not spouseless when you know God. Your child is not fatherless when you know the Heavenly Father who cares for your child.

This book is still for you even if you are not a Christian. Sometimes, it isn't until pregnancy that you begin to question who is truly in control and what really matters.

This book is divided into the preconception, pregnancy, labor and delivery, and the postpartum periods. A mother's heart evolves through these different phases of motherhood, and this book addresses the different challenges mothers encounter in each phase. The tone of each section is different based on each unique season of motherhood.

Our dependence on God may not become a reality until our motherhood journeys diverge from what we expected. In these moments, we can have a hopeless grief or lean into God's Word so that He can fully make us like Jesus. Let us dig into the Bible to explore how God redeems our broken womb stories.

I pray that for whatever phase of pre- or present motherhood you are in, you will find God's hand holding you close.

> *For I hold you by your right hand—*
> *I, the Lord your God.*
> *And I say to you,*
> *"Don't be afraid. I am here to help you."*
> *Isaiah 41:13, NLT*

Part I:
Preconception

So you're ready to take the parental plunge.

Exciting or terrifying? You may have always seen yourself as a mother, or maybe you have not. Some girls have dreamt of this moment since they were little. And some women have never given it a thought. Wherever you are on this spectrum, the thought of pregnancy is usually a mixed bag of emotions.

There are so many expectations that go into pregnancy—expectations of your partner, expectations from your mother, expectations from your in-laws, expectations of God, and mostly, expectations of yourself.

Pregnancy will show you what you truly believe about God and what you truly believe about yourself. Motherhood brings us to our knees faster than anything else, so let us set the stage for realistic, hopeful expectations.

This preconception section may be read before considering pregnancy. It may also be read when you're pregnant or a veteran mother. The purpose of this section is to help us understand a biblical worldview of the womb. What does God say about the womb, and what should we expect in our motherhood journeys?

Chapter 1

The First Visit with Your Doctor

Many women go to their obstetrician-gynecologist (OBGYN) before getting pregnant to ask for advice on preparing their bodies for this new, exciting change. As a physician, it is a delight to see patients willing and ready to change their lives for a purpose greater than themselves. Many women have not seen a physician since their own pediatrician. There is excitement in the air when they come in for the preconception visit. Women are motivated to lose weight, quit smoking, and become a better version of themselves.

Your doctor or midwife may make specific recommendations about lifestyle or medication changes and recommend a daily prenatal vitamin before conception. There may be specific genetic tests to consider if you want to know more about yourself before getting pregnant. But most of the time, these tests yield limited definitive information about your future family.

Your doctor will also go over how to track your menstrual cycle so that you know the most fertile time in your cycle for intercourse. Some women get pregnant on the first try, while other couples try to get pregnant for many months and even years. If you are not getting pregnant after a year of trying, you should talk with your doctor. Every couple has a different journey. For some, this is a straightforward path. But for others, hearing their baby's first cry may be many years in the making.

There are also plenty of women who show up for prenatal care with no prior "preconception" visit. At least 40–51% of pregnancies are unplanned[1]. Therefore, almost half of the women who find out they are pregnant are not necessarily in the mindset of pregnancy when they find out their lives are going to change.

The preconception doctor visit is certainly not a requirement to have a healthy pregnancy, as we often see women who do not realize they are pregnant well into their second trimester (and sometimes even in their third). I have even seen women who show up to the labor and delivery department with abdominal pain, unaware they are about to deliver their full-term infant!

There isn't always time to prepare for the most significant transition of a woman's life. But if you're taking the time to prepare your body for motherhood, there are also ways to prepare your soul for motherhood. Motherhood is a spiritual experience that grows the soul.

Regardless of your spiritual beliefs, motherhood usually drives, humbles, and challenges women in ways that almost nothing else can.

We will examine the womb through a Christian worldview, which will help us reconcile the woes of the womb, the trials of pregnancy, and the ongoing challenges of motherhood. The more our souls are prepared with healthy expectations of how God cares for us, the more we will be able to laugh at the days to come.

For the Christian, this period of preconception is a vulnerable place because the created learns to trust God with her desires. The created must rely on the Creator to prepare her womb. It is a vulnerable time with the potential for paralyzing fear or incredible peace.

---

[1] Lawrence B. Finer and Mia R. Zolna, "Declines in Unintended Pregnancy in the United States, 2008–2011," The New England Journal of Medicine 374, no. 9 (March 3, 2016): 843–52, https://doi.org/10.1056/nejmsa1506575.

Chapter 2

Setting Expectations

It is easy to live in the romance of our expectations. I am a realist and a recovering romanticist. I began motherhood as an ideal romantic, but the harsh reality of my motherhood experience challenged my walk with God. When I found out I was going to be a special needs mother, I went into a dark place where no one could rescue me. I spent years trying to escape a pit that crumbled every time I tried to climb out.

My motherhood journey was not what I had imagined. I had stellar prenatal care, a healthy pregnancy, and a normal labor and delivery. My self-sufficient mind believed I had done my part to have a healthy baby. But the moment she was born, we knew something was different. I could not help my baby be comfortable no matter what I did. She began to miss developmental milestones. We became the outliers on the playground. I continued to believe we could catch up, but the gap between "normal" and disability only increased. When I was given a diagnosis, it was not a "heroic Christian" moment for me. It was a desperate moment of losing control over the perfect picture of my family. In these moments, I was disappointed with God. I was angry with Him for not "holding up His part of the deal."

And so I sulked.
I was not a resilient Christian with a faith-filled testimony.
I was bitter and hurt.

It was not until I had an honest conversation with God that I began to get it. If He wouldn't change my child, I needed Him to change me.

I had to reset my expectations to become resilient in this unexpected parenting journey. Thus, the faith-filled realist was birthed. My expectations for motherhood were recalibrated.

Our expectations affect the strength of our resilience when detours happen.

Read that again, my friend. If reality does not match what we expect, we either get back up again or spiral into despair.

Our ability to get back up after bad news reveals our true expectations.

There is no greater time of expectation than when expecting a new baby. Some expectations are apparent—growing a pant size and swollen feet. A new haircut. A pedicure before delivery. But it is the not-so-obvious expectations that rise to the surface when challenged.

We expect that we can get pregnant.
We expect healthy children.
We expect full-term deliveries.
We expect a birth that follows our birth plan.
We expect to be able to breastfeed.

It is not until we experience reproductive grief like infertility, pregnancy loss, an unhealthy child, a preterm delivery, or a cesarean section that we face the uncomfortable emotions of loss. Because we do not expect we will lose. We know that bad things happen—just not to us nor the ones that we love.

American prosperity can give the impression that we are immune to the brokenness of the womb. So when our plans are challenged, we are sometimes frozen in despair. What happens when pregnancy is different from what we expect? Do we feel slighted, disappointed, and even hurt that God did not provide what we expected?

Sometimes, I still spiral into despair. Resilience is the last thing on my mind when my worst-case scenarios unfold in front of me. But in these moments, I either curl up in the fetal position or resolve to get back up. I ask God to help me see His love for me. I pray for the eyes to see more than my limited vision. And then, I check my expectations.

If I expect a perfect and comfortable motherhood journey, I will be disappointed. Nowhere in the Bible does it say pregnancy or motherhood will be easy. Instead, the Bible says we will have many trials in this life (James 1:2), especially in the stories surrounding the womb (Genesis 3:16).

It's okay to pray for a perfect pregnancy and a perfect baby. But even if God's answer looks different from perfect, it is still okay. God's answer is Himself. When our wombs do not cooperate with our will, Jesus uses this place of brokenheartedness to reveal why He came. Our world is broken, and we need a Savior.

In this context, I am no longer expecting the perfect motherhood experience. Instead, I expect my motherhood journey will have many valleys in need of a Savior. I need Jesus to save me from every single one of them.

I climbed out of the pit when I finally released the idol of my "ideal child." And in this tender place, my bitterness melted into gratitude. God had given me a front-row seat to His gospel. Being a caregiver to a daughter with disabilities has taught me about my brokenness. I need a Savior to save me daily from my anger, impatience, and the idol of perfection. Jesus increased while I decreased. My difficult womb story brought me to the end of myself. I let go of what wasn't essential in this life, and now I cling to what lasts forever instead. In this honest, holy place, I have new expectations:

> *Even if we experience reproductive grief, we can expect Jesus to use the womb's brokenness for our good in this life (Romans 8:28).*

Christians can expect that God will use our difficult womb stories for the good of His people. At the end of ourselves, He can do more in and through us. We can be confident that His plan is for our good and His glory.

> *We can expect Jesus to redeem reproductive grief forever in heaven (Revelation 21:4).*

> *The pains of the womb will one day be a distant memory when we are made whole in heaven.*

These truths can hold us up in the moments of broken motherhood. Even when you do not have the perfect birth story. Even if you have a miscarriage. Even if you deal with infertility. Even if your child has been given a diagnosis that shakes your world. These truths will ground you when the emotions can be overwhelming. The stronger your theological view of motherhood is, the more you will be prepared for all the ways your children challenge you—inside the womb and outside of it.

Chapter 3

A Biblical Worldview of the Womb

The romance of pregnancy can sweep a woman off her feet faster than a man on bended knee. The woman is a tree. She is a goddess. She is a smoky silhouette with a beam of sunlight cascading off her baby bump. Instagram makes pregnancy seem easy and effortless. Her womb is a cozy cocoon with all things sweet, right?

But let's look at the reality of the womb. It is a powerhouse of an organ made of three layers of muscular tissue. The uterus looks more like a Thanksgiving turkey! It is one of the strongest muscles in a woman's body. It undergoes a dramatic increase from the size of a lemon to that of a watermelon at full term. The uterine muscle fibers act as a football offensive line to push a baby out of the birth canal. We will talk more about this birth process in chapters to come, but let's take a minute to marvel at the dynamic muscle fibers God created for this process.

The uterus is an autonomous organ. Unlike the muscles of our arms, whose movements we can control, women cannot control contractions whenever they want. The uterus cannot be toned with exercise. The uterus is at the mercy of its Creator.

God, the Creator of the womb, has ironed out every detail in the birth process. Yet in all of its miraculous wonder (like all other organs in our bodies), the uterus suffers the consequences of a broken world. Scar tissue, polyps, and fibroids can prevent an embryo from implanting. A blocked fallopian tube may prevent a sperm and egg from ever meeting. An embryo can stop growing and miscarry. The placenta, which should be the life-giver of oxygen-rich blood, can become diseased and cause growth restriction or preeclampsia. For all the normal births that occur, other babies get stuck in the birth canal, necessitating a cesarean section. Some wombs evict babies before they are ready to be born. Some wombs do not perform even when coaxed with induction.

The reality is the outcome of conception, implantation, gestation, and delivery are not under our control as much as we would like to believe. This is not meant to be discouraging but to give ourselves a realistic expectation of who controls the womb. My job as a doctor is managing and minimizing health risks. Not all outcomes are in my control. I wish I could help an infertile woman or someone with recurrent miscarriages have a normal pregnancy. I wish I could fix the birth defect that is diagnosed on ultrasound. I wish I could guarantee a vaginal delivery to every woman who wants one. But ultimately, I am not the Creator. The only One sovereign over the womb is God.

Where else, besides the Bible, will you find an infertile woman, a virgin, and a postmenopausal woman getting pregnant when it is physiologically impossible?

Consider Sarah, Rachel, Hannah, Mary, and Elizabeth—all women who should not have gotten pregnant. God is the one who "opened up their wombs." He calls the most unexpected women to be mothers. He is the God of surprise pregnancies.

The womb has been front and center since the Garden of Eden. God breathed life into Eve after removing a rib from Adam. Eve was given more than a rib—she was given a uterus.

But this privilege was distorted after Eve thought she could be like God.

The Lie that Eve Believed (And We Still Believe)

Eve lived in the paradise of Eden. She had everything she could have ever asked for: a ripe garden buffet next to a friendly petting zoo. The lion cuddled next to the lamb. Adam and Eve spent their days enjoying the goodness of creation. Most importantly, God was always near. Eve was secure in His love. She was protected from harm, unknowing of hatred and pain. She never had a heavy period. Nor a menstrual cramp. Nor a moody PMS day. Can you imagine that childbirth may have been as easy as picking up groceries at the store?

It would seem that Eve had it made.

But there was one caveat: "Do not eat anything from the Tree of the Knowledge of Good and Evil," God said. It was His only condition, and it became Eve's greatest temptation. But honestly, it wasn't about the fruit but whether Eve believed God knew best.

Eve became enamored with this tree. As her discontent grew, she doubted God knew what was best for her. Her restlessness with God's plan grew stronger. Eve believed the lie that she did not need God. So when the serpent convinced her she could be like God, Eve made her own way. In that one bite, Eve told the Creator of the universe that she was enough without Him.

If we are honest with ourselves, we have all been in Eve's situation. Do we believe we are enough without God? Do we choose God or ourselves?

In motherhood, we can easily believe that we do not need God and that we are enough on our own. We don't need to read the Bible since every parenting blog tells us how to do it right. We don't need to pray for help when we already have it figured out on our own. After all, we humans have figured out how to conceive babies in petri dishes. Surely, we can do things on our own if we have enough drive, resourcefulness, and will, right? This works until . . . until it doesn't. Mothering on our own power often leads to a disillusioned sense of control.

When Eve chose to eat the fruit, Eve chose herself. She decided she could do it on her own. But this decision brought out a new feeling: *fear*. She now knew what was right and wrong in this world. But she was helpless to fix it.

The "Eve complex" is knowledge of pain without the power to prevent it. This complex is why humans struggle with anxiety. Humans want to control everything that they fear to lose.

When Eve chose her way, God did not give up on her. But there were consequences for Eve's choice that would ripple into the generations to come. He told her, "I will surely multiply your pain in childbearing; in pain you shall bring forth children." (Genesis 3:16). We typically associate this curse with physical pain in labor and delivery. But the

Hebrew word for "childbearing" is herayon[2], which includes the physical conception and pregnancy.

The entire process of conception to delivery is now laced with pain.

The uterus is not a cozy cocoon, after all. It is not the picture of safety that we wish it would be. While we do not need to assume that all will go wrong in the womb, we must assume there are no guarantees of perfection. The womb was the very organ that was addressed after the fall of humankind. With the breakup, we lost God's protection from pain in the womb.

Indeed, we have knowledge of how to manipulate many of the outcomes of the womb. But ultimately, medicine has its limits. We cannot prevent every adverse obstetric outcome. We have knowledge on how to raise children. But motherhood has its limitations. We cannot mold every child into a perfect adult in society. We face the Eve Complex every day in motherhood, feeling powerless for all the "should-be" that we cannot control.

We could end the story right here and assume the worst. But the beautiful thing about the Bible, the gospel, and your motherhood is that there is more to the story.

> *Even the worst outcome of the womb can have a purpose in God's world.*

The story of the Bible is about beauty arising from unexpected pains. It is a story of God pursuing the very people who have rejected Him. No heartache in the womb is beyond the reach of redemption because there was another promise that day in the Garden of Eden.

The Offspring

Before God gave Eve her consequences for disobedience, He revealed the true battle by first addressing the snake. The snake, Satan, also believed a lie that he was better than God.

But God was not surprised by any of this and foretold the end of Satan's

---

[2] "Strong's Hebrew: 2032. וְיָרָה‎ (Heron or Herayon) – Conception, Pregnancy," accessed August 28, 2023, https://biblehub.com/hebrew/2032.htm.

fate. God cursed the serpent to a life on the ground. There would be a battle "between your (snake's) offspring and hers (human offspring); he will crush your head, and you will strike his heel" (Genesis 3:15). Ultimately, there would be a human offspring, Jesus, who would crush Satan when He hung on the cross and said, "It is finished" (John 19:30, NIV).

The womb was not doomed forever. In fact, God would use this broken womb to reestablish His connection to mankind. He intentionally used the immaculate conception to redeem this womb. Through a physiologically impossible conception, Mary would parent the offspring that would stomp out the snake.

Jesus frees the broken womb by entering the world through its very brokenness.

Through the humble beginnings of a little baby woven in Mary's womb, this child would grow up without sin. Jesus would rescue the very people who had rejected Him, dying on the cross as a sacrifice for sin. From the depths of the grave, breath would re-enter His body. In His new body, Jesus would walk the earth for forty days (Acts 1:3). He would then ascend to heaven with a promise to return someday to bring His people home (John 14:1–3).

Jesus did what Eve did not do in the garden. In the Garden of Eden, Eve chose herself. But in the Garden of Gethsemane, Jesus denied Himself and chose God.

Jesus paid a price on the cross so that the consequences of sin would not be the end of the story. Regardless of any pregnancy complication or grief of parenthood, we can now grieve with hope. Painful pregnancy experiences are not the end of the story in God's world. Instead, we can let our crosses tell His story.

Paul said in Galatians, "I have been crucified by Christ and I no longer live, but Christ lives in me" (2:20). Life is full of crosses. But if you are a Christian, Jesus carries your cross uphill with you.

Your imperfect womb story may be where your most worthy dreams are formed.

Every mother has a gospel story that intertwines with Jesus' story. Jesus does not save us from every woe of the womb. Instead, He saves us from ourselves. Our painful womb story can be redeemed for good.

The Redeemed Womb

What does this redemption look like? Perhaps it is a pregnancy that motivates an addict to fight for herself. Perhaps it is a miscarriage that brings us to greater dependence on the Creator of life. Perhaps it is an empty womb that hosts a home filled with foster children. Perhaps it is a disabled child that brings a family together. Perhaps it is a womb story that is still being written.

It could not have been easy to have been the mother of Jesus. Mary waited thirty-three years to see her womb story redeemed. Would she have considered her son dying on the cross a redemptive moment? It was not until Jesus ascended to heaven that she had the complete story of what God was doing through her son. Redemption stories often take years to write, and some endings are not solidified until heaven.

Ultimately, a redeemed womb story chooses God over herself. Because it is in this quiet cruciform that He does His most tender work. A redeemed mother makes a choice. She trusts in herself, or she relies on a trustworthy God.

God is good in healthy pregnancies and smooth deliveries.

God is also good in imperfect womb stories.

God is the perfect author regardless of where you are in your motherhood journey. And if you are willing, He has chosen your womb story to be woven into His.

Part II:
Woes of the Womb

This section on the woes of the womb is challenging but also vital to our understanding of God's purposes through pain. Maybe you have faced infertility, have lost a child, have dealt with the painful decision of abortion, or have encountered an unexpected diagnosis. Some of us have dealt with more obvious woes than others. And some woes seem more severe than others. But ultimately, for all of us who have been called to be mothers, the woes of the womb are inevitable. We will all experience broken expectations about our children—from the tiniest embryo to the adult child. Our recovery from these humbling moments is rooted in our beliefs about God.

You may also find yourself angry with God if you face the woes of the womb. Why do His purposes matter when you're in pain? Why does it matter if His intentions are for our good when it does not feel good? If we are honest with ourselves, when God's plan is not our plan, we are disappointed. Even hurt.

Like any genuine relationship, you can be honest with God. He knows your heart before you even say it. Have you ever cried out to God in honest desperation?

The Psalms are full of honesty with God. In some of the chapters, you can almost see the psalmist's tears on the page, blurring the letters from their trembling hand. Many of the lamenting psalms start with complaints of injustice. King David, the "man after God's heart," questions God's presence in Psalm 13.

> *How long, Lord? Will you forget me forever? How long will You hide Your face from me? How long am I to feel anxious in my soul, with grief in my heart all the day? (Psalm 13:1-2a, NASB).*

David is allowed to speak his truth. He asks honest questions of God. But then there is a turning point in the psalm when David claims God's truth over his emotions. The transition point is in verse five when David chooses to focus on the character of God over his circumstances.

> *But I have trusted in Your faithfulness; My heart shall rejoice in Your salvation. I will sing to the Lord, Because He has looked after me. (Psalm 13:5-6, NASB).*

David's circumstances did not change, but the strength of his faith changed. His relationship with God was strengthened by honesty.

If you are struggling in your relationship with God, it's okay. Tell Him how you genuinely feel. And then preach to your own soul about the truths of His character. Has God been faithful in the past? If you think God has abandoned you, ask Him to reveal Himself.

Cry out from your soul for God to meet you.

It's okay to cry. Tears wash away the fragile kingdoms that we have built around ourselves. Then, these tears water our roots so they become stronger foundations.

You can rebuild a new foundation when you read the Bible to understand the Giver rather than the gifts. A stronger foundation will be built on a relationship than one built on prosperity. Our darkest emotions can be sanctified by the truth of the Bible. The Bible can become the greatest comfort for your soul.

This section will be logical if you are rational, a realist, and in a balanced emotional state. But if you are experiencing reproductive grief from the woes of the womb, you may need time to cry, kick, and shout before you read these chapters. But please hang in there with me. When you have had a chance to be honest with God and yourself—there are truths that help your painful emotions make sense—and perhaps even become purposeful.

Chapter 1
The Griefs of Miscarriage

Most women do not think that a miscarriage will happen to them. But if you are part of the 15–20%[3] of women who have experienced a miscarriage, you are not alone.

Most miscarriages are a shock. We know they happen to other people—just not to us.

For many women, the early days after a positive pregnancy test are exhilarating. It does not take long to bond with the idea of a baby. But when the first ultrasound shows no heartbeat, the pregnancy dream quickly turns into a nightmare. It is earth-shattering.

But if you would allow me to speak into your pain, I hope you know:

No matter how long your child was here on earth (whether just hours as an embryo or years as an adult), your child's life matters. Your mother's dreams for your child matter, too. You will always be a mother even if you never held your child. A miscarriage is not something you get over quickly and just try again. A miscarriage is a lifelong loss.

The grief that women experience after a reproductive loss has many layers. Her body may not show signs of miscarriage until weeks after the loss has already occurred. Some of the most complex parts of miscarriage can be the physical effects. It is physically challenging to pass the pregnancy. Many times in my career, I have counseled women about their different options to help them through this process. But I know that true recovery happens after the physical passing of the pregnancy. The emotional loss often is not felt until after the physical passing.

---

[3] MJ Zinaman, ED Clegg, CC Brown, J O'Connor, and SG Selevan, "Estimates of Human Fertility and Pregnancy Loss," Fertility and Sterility 65, no. 3 (March 1996): 503–509, https://pubmed.ncbi.nlm.nih.gov/8774277/.

The Griefs of Miscarriage

I have seen women process their miscarriages very differently. Some are matter-of-fact about their loss. Some are completely devastated and depressed. Some women do not process their grief at all. They may feel triggered during the subsequent pregnancy when they reach the same gestational age. But the women who confront their grief come out stronger on the other side. Those who know Jesus find their faith sweeter after they go through a miscarriage. While still fearful of loss with the next pregnancy, their faith has been fortified.

Regardless of how women process their loss, they often experience triggers of grief. The triggers come in waves—women who have the same due date, children who would have been the same age, etc. There are unexpected triggers everywhere. The world becomes very small to avoid any reminders of loss. Even though a baby's life may have ended, the anniversaries live on. Life continues, although her world will never be the same.

The soul heartache is even more challenging than the physical recovery.

Self-blame is a common reaction for women who have gone through miscarriage. There is a disconnect between what she knows and how she feels. She may obsess about each possible misstep that could have caused a pregnancy loss. I have often heard women say after their miscarriage:

There is something wrong with me.
It was all my fault.

Was it too much stress? Didn't eat enough? Ate the wrong thing? The list of self-blame is endless. But this self-blame leads nowhere. Even when I tell my patients that it was not their fault that their miscarriage occurred, I know they still go home wondering what they did wrong. One of the lies women tell themselves is that their body is defective and a failure.

What you believe about your control over the womb is directly related to self-shaming. If you think that you can prevent every harm, you may be paralyzed by guilt after a miscarriage. But if you believe someone else is in control of the womb, you will be relieved that someone else is writing your child's story. Your miscarriage is not the result of incompetence. Instead, your miscarriage is a place where God wants to meet you.

Friend, you can be free from guilt because you do not need to carry what Jesus has already carried for you. Instead, you can pray, *Jesus, take away my guilt because I do not control my child's life. You knew all the days my child would live on this earth. You alone are sovereign over my child's life.*

If you believe this to be true, you will find His peace overpowers your guilt.

But I also understand if you want to refrain from praying.

You may not want to meet Him when you're hurting. Instead, you may be asking yourself, "If God is so sovereign and so good, why would He allow miscarriages?"

The womb was downtrodden by sin in the Garden of Eden. In the previous chapter, we discussed how conception is fraught with adversity. But what we know intellectually is not always helpful after loss.

Ultimately, the question women want to understand after their loss is: *Why, God? Why me?*

For many women, a miscarriage is the first time we are aware of our humanness. It may be the first time we recognize what little control we have over the womb and over our lives.

A miscarriage is humbling.
It is earth-shattering.
However, it is also heaven-facing.
How?

God wants to grow your heart for His heart. Your relationship with God can become richer when you trust Him with the most precious parts of your soul. God does not operate only in the confines of this world. His timeline extends past death. One day, there will be an eternal reunion not separated by a heartbeat that defines life.

God uses our loss in this lifetime to keep us focused on what truly matters. Loss reminds us that our lives are a mist (James 4:14).

God wants to give you a glimpse of His tenderness. God wants to comfort you. Meditate on this scripture to know His tenderness toward the brokenhearted: He holds all of your tears in a bottle (Psalm 56:8). He grieves death with you (John 11:35).

God wants you to know He understands.
At one time on the hill of Calvary, God was also separated from His child by the same heavens that separate you from yours. But the story did not end there. It ended with a reunion in heaven. Separation from our children is painful. But it is temporary. One day, heaven will be that much sweeter when you are reunited with your child.

God wants to rewrite your story.
The last line of your pregnancy story is not, "and they lived happily ever after." The last line of your pregnancy loss is "to be continued." He has a redeemed womb story for your loss and will bring beauty out of this loss. You will find a new camaraderie with women who have a story like yours because grief bonds strangers closer than blood. One day, your story will comfort someone else.

But maybe not today. And that's okay. But when the tears have brought you to the end of yourself, would you give your womb to its Creator? It can be something as simple as praying, *God, You made my body and have a purpose for my womb story. My children are Yours.*

When you surrender your children (born and unborn) to God, you will be filled with incredible peace. This state of surrender is where Jesus does His best work. New dreams are born, and gratitude is made anew. It is where we look at the snake, ugly in its face, and tell him that we do not choose ourselves, but we choose God instead. There is a power in this moment.

God is weaving the painful story of your womb in an eternal tapestry. The Bible describes heaven as a place where death will no longer separate mothers and babies.

> *Look! I am creating new heavens and a new earth, and no one will even think about the old ones anymore. Be glad; rejoice forever in my creation! And Look! I will create Jerusalem as a place of happiness. Her people will be a source of joy. I will rejoice over Jerusalem and delight in my people. And the sound of weeping and crying will be*

heard in it no more. No longer will babies die when only a few days old. No longer will adults die before they have lived a full life. No longer will people be considered old at one hundred!
-Isaiah 65:17–20, NLT

The Christian has hope that death is not the end.
One day, there will be no more weeping because every baby survives, every diagnosis is reversed, and every tear is wiped away.

Be kind to yourself, my friend.
And when you have time to breathe again, look up.
Our hope is in much, much more.

Precious Little One
(Author Unknown)

I'm just a precious little one,
Who didn't make it there.
I went straight to be with Jesus,
But I'm waiting for you here.
Many dwelling here where I live,
Waited years to enter in.
Struggled through a world of sorrow,
A world marred with pain and sin.
Thank you for the life you gave me,
It was brief but don't complain.
I have all heaven's Glory,
Suffered none of earth's great pain.
Thank you for the name you gave me,
I'd have loved to bring it fame.
But if I'd lingered in earth's shadows,
I would have suffered just the same.
So sweet family, don't you sorrow,
Wipe those tears and chase the gloom.
I went straight to Jesus' arms,
From my loving Mother's womb.

Chapter 2

The Griefs of Infertility

You are probably not expecting to see a chapter on infertility if you have picked up this book on pregnancy devotionals. But fertility struggles usually affect someone you know. And some women have fertility challenges even after having normal pregnancies. Discussing the woes of the womb would not be complete without addressing one of the toughest heartbreaks that women experience when they are told they cannot conceive.

You may be going through fertility treatments, have made peace with infertility, or perhaps it is still a lifelong grief.

If you have gone through infertility, I want to be careful with your heart. You may have a deep wound that is easily opened, and it may bleed more profusely in different seasons. Thank you for letting me share this space with you.

As an OBGYN, I see women in my office who have had unanswered questions about their fertility for decades. Sometimes there are obvious causes, and sometimes there are not. Sometimes, tests and procedures are pursued to improve fertility. Your doctor or midwife will probably have different suggestions for making your womb more "fertile friendly." You may need to meet with a fertility specialist to review all of your options. Sometimes medications are needed to sync menstrual cycles or injections to help women ovulate. And sometimes options are more involved, like embryo adoption and in-vitro fertilization. Regardless of the options you explore, the infertility journey is different for everyone.

If you are struggling with infertility, it may feel like you're going to endless appointments with no results. Getting pregnant and staying pregnant can be all-consuming as you wait for your next period. It may feel like a full-time job with daily injections and frequent ultrasounds.

To avoid "fertility burnout," it is important to set boundaries on how much getting pregnant will take over your life.

Are the majority of your conversations with your significant other about getting pregnant? Do you find that your desire to get pregnant is more important than your spouse's feelings? Is sex only for the purpose of conception? Are all of your savings going toward fertility treatments? It is not uncommon for infertility to become the catalyst for broken relationships. If getting pregnant matters more to one partner, it doesn't take long for resentment to build. To keep your relationship moving forward during this phase, keep pursuing each other by caring for one another's needs. Take time to encourage each other.

Both sperm and egg are needed to make a family, and both of their stories matter. When blame or ego get involved, sin taints the journey. But if you approach one another with a humble heart, it changes the entire experience.

If you are struggling with infertility, ask yourself if getting pregnant is a roadblock to worshiping God. It isn't uncommon that fertility brings up matters of the soul. Getting pregnant can become an all-consuming idol. If you have bought the lie that something is wrong with you, you are less blessed or less loved, it can paralyze your spiritual life.

So let's address it:

> *God loves you, regardless of your ability to have children.*
> *God loves you because Jesus said you were worthy (Ephesians 2:4–5).*

Your fertility does not define your purpose. The Christian's purpose is to love God and their neighbors (Matthew 22:34–39). This purpose can be accomplished regardless of having biological children.

But even when you know these truths, your heart may still ache. The Bible refers to children as a blessing. So, are childless women not blessed? If you have gone through infertility, you may have wondered if God has forgotten you. But let's talk about God's unconventional parenthood plans. He has not forgotten you (Isaiah 49:15). Your motherhood journey just looks different.

As discussed in the preconception chapter, when Eve decided she wanted her own way in the Garden of Eden, conception was no longer easy. But many generations later, God worked through a supernatural conception to prove a point. Jesus was not from typical human DNA. And while there is a unique experience of combining DNA and carrying a child, this is not God's only plan for parenthood.

God is creative in crafting atypical parenting journeys. Not all children are genetically related to their parents. Joseph was a "stepfather" to Jesus. Eli was an adoptive "father" to Samuel. Ruth birthed children that carried her dead husband's name because of Boaz. Pharaoh's daughter became an adoptive mother to Moses when a baby literally floated into her arms.

Family is not defined by blood. It is characterized by those who are covered by it.

The Bible speaks of an "adoption" that happens when God's children are welcomed into His kingdom. The apostle Paul says we are adopted the moment we accept Jesus. We become children of God (Romans 8:15–16) without even a single strand of heavenly DNA. We are adopted into God's family when we believe in Jesus. God's family is the most diverse DNA gene pool there is.

If you have the desire to be a mother, it is God-given. Motherhood is not defined by childbirth or by the ability to breastfeed. Motherhood is determined by the capacity to love, nurture, and care for the vulnerable. Motherhood may look different from what you may have imagined. You may be the spiritual mother to girls who do not have a mother. You may be a foster mother to children who need a home. You may be an older sister to someone who needs an encouraging presence in their life. You may adopt a son or daughter you would not have known otherwise. The title "mother" is not just for those who have birthed a child. The title "mother" is for women who want to love and give.

But even with this conviction, wounds still bleed. Motherhood is an inevitable part of female conversation. And every time it comes up, it can rub salt into a fertility wound.

Only God can comfort this wound and redeem it for something more. Not all womb stories end with your own baby in your arms.

Instead, God fills the emptiest places of our hearts with His presence. The journey from emptiness to fullness begins when our destination is more about Him and less about ourselves. God will fill you when you ask Him to meet you in an empty place.

In the Bible, Habakkuk paints a picture of emptiness during a famine:

> *Even though the fig trees have no blossoms,*
> *and there are no grapes on the vines;*
> *even though the olive crop fails,*
> *and the fields lie empty and barren;*
> *even though the flocks die in the fields,*
> *and the cattle barns are empty . . .*
> Habakkuk 3:17, NLT

Bare trees. Failing crops. Empty barns. Sometimes, an empty womb can feel like this famine. But Habakkuk made a conscious choice to rejoice even in famine.

> *. . . yet I will rejoice in the Lord!*
> *I will be joyful in the God of my salvation!*
> *The Sovereign Lord is my strength!*
> *He makes me as surefooted as a deer,*
> *able to tread upon the heights.*
> Habakkuk 3:18–19, NLT

At the eye level of the famine, the fields are empty. But when we choose to rejoice in the Lord, He gives us joy even in the emptiness. He gives us the strength to face the next dreaded conversation. And then He gives us the steady feet of a deer so we can see the land below.

From these heights, you will see things from a different perspective. You may even see all of the children who need a mama like you. He will show you things that no one else can see.

If you are not able to have biological children, God has a worthy purpose for you still. We can focus on the empty or we can rejoice with who is plenty.

My friend, you are blessed.

Plenty in Empty
By Rachelle Keng

The ache of a woman's soul—
is to nurture, make another whole.
But when the womb is empty, it's okay to grieve,
It's okay if you can't conceive.

He has a purpose, He has a plan,
All children from His hand.
Some are from our own womb,
Or the one who's facing her doom—
She's birthed a babe that needs a mama.
Your mother's story is at a comma.
Your child, birthed by another,
Needing your love, needing a mother.

He may be calling you to wait—
Or leading you to someone great
you would not have known otherwise,
If you let emptiness paralyze.

Our worth is not in our womb,
Rather by Christ who conquered the tomb.
He gave us all a second chance,
So that you too can enhance
The little life who needs your mercy,
To fill your heart and your nursery.

He is the matchmaker of all needs,
He is the gardener of all seeds.
The end is not infertility.
It is the start of a possibility—
For even when the womb is empty,
He fills the heart with more and plenty.

Chapter 3

The Griefs of Abortion

Pregnancy loss is always painful—even for women who have an abortion. The circumstances surrounding an abortion decision are never easy.

The decision to end a pregnancy is full of heartache for many women.

There are many reasons why women choose abortion. Sometimes, there is a complex medical situation that surrounds the pregnancy that makes pregnancy dangerous for mothers. Sometimes, the circumstances surrounding the pregnancy are not ideal. She may think abortion is for the child's good. She may not have ever seen herself as a mother. She may feel like she cannot care for a child in the way she has envisioned. Genetic tests tell her that her child will have a different path than she would have chosen. Ultimately, this is not the story that she has written for herself.

Afterward, there is initial relief. But then, for many, a deep hurt follows.

Parenthood with the wrong man, wrong context, and wrong timing is not for her. But it does not mean she will hurt any less afterward. For women who believe there is a baby involved in abortion, their grief is different. They mourn deeply and quietly. For women who were unsure if there was a baby involved, they may still have confusing grief they cannot explain.

A reproductive loss like a miscarriage brings casseroles and community. A loss like abortion brings silent grief and isolation.

Even when abortion feels justified by circumstance, there can be lasting grief from their loss. Women may feel that they cannot pray anymore. They may wonder if God still loves them.

If you are one of these women, there is good news today. The gospel story is about Jesus, who frees women in these imprisoned places.

Jesus came to restore women who have lost themselves. He came to do what earthly men could not. Unlike the men who have abandoned women after finding out they are pregnant, Jesus stayed. Despite having the power to leave the cross, Jesus' love kept Him there.

Just a few weeks before the cross, this same Jesus extended His love to a woman who had committed adultery in John 8. She had been dragged outside of the city with angry men surrounding her like hungry wolves. Each man was holding a mountain of stones, ready to throw them at this half-clothed woman. But then, amid the chaos, Jesus walked calmly into the middle of the circle and knelt beside the woman.

Jesus began writing something in the sand, ignoring the hatred around Him. Perhaps He was writing in the smallest font, so the stoners needed to lean in to see what He was writing. The trembling woman had a moment of reprieve so that she too could turn around to see her defender.

When He had all their attention, Jesus firmly uttered a statement that would echo into eternity: "Let any one of you who is without sin be the first to throw a stone at her" (John 8:7, NIV). At once, everyone dropped their stones as if they had suddenly become like hot coals. Jesus looked at the woman tenderly and told her, "Then neither do I condemn you. Go now and leave your life of sin" (John 8:11, NIV). And in that moment, she was healed from the bondage of shame. She was a new creation with a new purpose. She was freed to live a life for Jesus.

If you have gone through an abortion and feel that God cannot forgive you, look no further than Jesus. He can make your brokenness into beauty if you allow Him to change your life. When Jesus sees you, He sees your trembling hands and sits on the ground beside you. He defends you from the judgment of others. And then He takes your stones on Himself so that you can be freed from shame and made into someone new.

Your pregnancy loss does not need to be the end of the story. God loves to heal broken hearts. He wants to bring darkness into the light. The Bible speaks of this good news for the brokenhearted in Isaiah.

Isaiah 61:1–3, NIV says:

> *The Spirit of the Sovereign Lord is on me, because the Lord has anointed me to preach good news to the poor. He has sent me to bind up the brokenhearted, to proclaim freedom for the captives and release from darkness for the prisoners, to proclaim the year of the Lord's favor and the day of vengeance of our God, to comfort all who mourn, and provide for those who grieve in Zion.*

God sent Jesus to proclaim freedom for the woman imprisoned by her guilt.

Jesus took all the shame, embarrassment, and guilt on himself when He went to the cross so that you could be freed. Not only does He provide freedom, but He provides purpose. Your story can change the course of someone else's story.

God desires to give you a different ending to your story. In your loneliest places of grief, He wants to provide you with a new hope. Jesus came to this earth:

> *. . . to bestow on them a crown of beauty instead of ashes, the oil of joy instead of mourning, and a garment of praise instead of a spirit of despair. They will be called oaks of righteousness, a planting of the Lord for the display of his splendor. They will rebuild the ancient ruins and restore the places long devastated; they will renew the ruined cities that have been devastated for generations.*
>
> Isaiah 61:3–4, NIV

A crown of ashes is worn during times of grief. But God wants to give you a new crown of beauty. God can rebuild the ancient ruins of your loss into a new creation.

You don't need to hide anymore, for God still sees and loves you. Tell Him you want to come home. For when you recognize your need for restoration, God stands with open arms, waiting for you to return home.

If this is you today, tell someone who knows this grace herself. The ones who can hold your story are the ones who have experienced Jesus' grace themselves.

From Within
By Rachelle Keng

You wonder if forgiveness is possible yet,
For the choice that you cannot forget.
But here's the truth:
God's love is boundless and true,
And His mercy reaches out to you,
His grace can make brand new,
heal the pain you're going through.

And when our hearts in endless ache,
His love is unchanged by Christ's sake.
His love can make us whole again.
He is our defender and our friend.

So do not despair nor give into fear,
God's forgiveness is always near,
You do not have to carry shame,
When you call on Jesus' name.
When you ask Him to forgive
You will find a way to live.

Then forgive yourself and free your pain,
He wants your heart, not for you to explain,
Or justify or suppress what is on your heart,
Honestly, He already knows this part.

You are not defined by your past,
But by His love that will forever last,
There is no sin that can keep us away,
No sin that Jesus did not die for on that day.

He knows our hearts and loves us still,
even if we disobey His will.
Praise the Lord for the depths of His love—
For it is deeper than what we are capable of.
Praise the Lord that we are not alone,
For He can revive hearts of stone.

May we be soft to our need for Him,
May we be soft to our every sin,
For His forgiveness is where we begin.
And then His love changes us from within.

Chapter 4

The Griefs of Unexpected Diagnoses

Becoming a mother opens up a vulnerability to grief, especially when our children are different from what we expected. When my daughter was diagnosed with Angelman syndrome, I became vulnerable to the daily grief of motherhood. But as I died to myself and began to live for Christ, I learned how to grieve with hope.

Pregnancy loss is an obvious grief of the womb. But less obvious is the grief mothers experience when they receive an unexpected diagnosis for their children.

Perhaps your child is on a different developmental path or dealing with a chronic illness. Maybe your child has a disability or a birth defect diagnosed on an ultrasound. Or perhaps your adult children have gone wayward despite your efforts to bring them back. Many mothers grieve a dream for their children at some time in their lives.

Many griefs of motherhood are not part of the original parenthood signup. Unconventional children require supernatural parents.

But you know what?

God has a plan—especially for unconventional children. Mary, the mother of Jesus, did not sign up for supernatural motherhood either. She was chosen for impossible motherhood. No matter what she did right, her son would still be crucified on a cross.

In many ways, Mary was a "special needs" mother. She could not change the path that had already been given to her son. Mary lived a public parenting journey under the scrutiny of strangers who did not know the whole story. As she mourned her son at the cross, she must have wondered if this was indeed God's plan. It must have been so different from what she expected when she was visited by the angel Gabriel.

Thirty-four years prior, the angel Gabriel visited Mary to tell her she was with child. Young Mary was inexperienced, but she was also willing to carry the son of God in her womb. The precious babe was born on a romantic night in a stable under the twinkling stars. As she cradled her child, she saw the promise, not the cross.

Because how could this young Mary know that her son would be beaten and killed in front of her?

In His Mercy, God spared her from the details. In His love, God had a plan for Mary to raise an extraordinary son. God is sparing you of all the details for now but you can trust that He has a good plan. He knows your needs and your child's needs.

He may have given you a diagnosis, but He also has a plan.

> *It won't help you to know about tomorrow as much as it will help you to know who holds tomorrow.*

The moment you heard the news that your child had an unexpected diagnosis, did you feel numb? It is essential to recognize the trauma that occurred at this moment. It may have felt like God was far away, but He was not. He was in that room with you when you discovered your life would be changed forever. He continues to reach out His hand to hold you and your child. He is not finished with you. He is only beginning.

As you react to life-altering news, you choose how you will respond.

Mary's reaction and response to the news of an unplanned pregnancy teach us how we can navigate an unexpected diagnosis for our children. She is known for her prayer in Luke 1, the Magnificat, during which she praises God for this incredible blessing. However, was this prayer of praise her first reaction to the news of an unplanned pregnancy?

Mary's Initial Reaction:

1. Her first reaction to Gabriel was a question of logistics.

Mary was afraid when she was told she would give birth to a son. She asked, "How will this be since I am a virgin?" (Luke 1:34 NIV) Mary had been given a diagnosis, not a prognosis. The logistics were unclear, and Mary had a lot to lose. Would she lose her fiancé, Joseph? Would she be stoned for claiming a pregnancy from a supernatural source? The logistics were not straightforward during Gabriel's visit.

If you have been given an unexpected diagnosis, the first question parents usually ask is, "How can this be?" You may have had no risk factors to suggest that this diagnosis would happen. It's okay to wonder how this has happened. The typical reaction is to race through the "jungle of unknown diagnoses" with a machete in hand. You may be looking for a worn path with straightforward logistics. But sometimes you will not have a map. You will learn to trust your instincts. You will find God mercifully providing precisely what you need for the moment.

2. Mary took the time to get used to her new normal.

Mary had a few days to process her diagnosis of pregnancy before she met Elizabeth. The distance between their homes of Nazareth and Hebron was roughly one hundred miles, so she had "processing time" before she saw Elizabeth[4]. Although the Bible does not tell of Mary's emotions before the Magnificat, she may have worked through some of her feelings by the time she saw Elizabeth.

If you have received a diagnosis that has shaken your world, take some time to grieve. It is okay to be in shock, to deny it is happening, and to wonder where God is. It takes time to get used to the new normal. You will get there if you keep asking God to meet you.

3. Mary found a trusted friend who would see her diagnosis as a calling.

Mary had started her motherhood journey as a single mom. Unmarried, she went to stay with her cousin Elizabeth, who was pregnant with John the Baptist. John the fetus leaped in her womb to announce Jesus in utero. Fanfaring the messiah started in the womb. Mary stayed with Elizabeth during her first trimester. Mary would have had much to grieve in these few months: the loss of her own plans, the loss of her beautiful figure, the potential loss of her betrothed, Joseph. Mary needed to be around people who would encourage her with the honor

---

[4] (https://aleteia.org/2019/05/31/mary-traveled-a-highly-dangerous-path-to-visit-elizabeth/ accessed 12/25/23).

of the calling she had been given.

Surrounding yourself with positive people is very important as the news sinks in. Those walking with God will inspire you to see detours, not dead ends. They will help you see brokenness as an eternal treasure.

Mary's Response

After she held onto the news for a few days, Mary met with Elizabeth to tell her the news. It was during this time that she prayed the Magnificat. As we look at Mary's prayer in Luke 1:46–48, we have a better idea of how to navigate the shock of an unexpected diagnosis:

1. Mary chooses worship.

She recognized her posture when she called herself "his lowly servant girl." She did not think of herself as entitled to a perfect life. Instead, Mary saw herself as God's servant. She chose to praise God's character. She called on her God as mighty, holy, the one who had done great things for her, and the one who had shown mercy to those who fear him (Luke 1:46–50).

If you see yourself as God's servant, you will see His purposes as your own purposes—even when His purposes involve your brokenness. God can accomplish more through our brokenness than through our perfection. Your brokenness may be the most beautiful worship you will ever give when you let these pieces tell a greater story.

2. Mary chooses to focus on God's character over her circumstances.

Her circumstance was uncertain at the point that she prayed the Magnificat. Would she be a single parent? There were so many reasons to fear. But in Mary's moment of fear, she spoke of God's character (Luke 1:49–51). She described God as mighty, holy, and merciful. Mary recalled God's heart for exalting the lowly. She praised God for His justice and His mercy to the humble.

Becoming a special needs parent is humbling. The circumstances may seem senseless sometimes, which is exactly when we must call on God's character. Justice is important to Him. Mercy is His name. Remember who He is, and you will begin to see His daily fingerprints of justice and mercy in your life.

3. Mary knows God's Word and trusts His promises.

The Old Testament scriptures prophesied that the Messiah would be born by a virgin in Isaiah 7:14. So when Gabriel told Mary that she was the chosen one, Mary recognized that she was part of this covenant many generations later.

God has promises for special needs mothers as well:

> *His grace is sufficient for our daily weaknesses.* His power is made perfect in our childrens' weakness (2 Corinthians 12:9).
>
> *His mercies are new every morning* even when we live the same day over and over again (Lamentations 3).
>
> *Suffering changes where we place our hope.* Suffering leads to perseverance, and perseverance leads to character, and character to hope—a hope that is more profound than a cure (Romans 5:3–5).

We may want rescue from our unexpected diagnoses. Perhaps Mary did, too, when she initially feared the angel's message. But as we see in Mary's prayer, she embraces hardship. She chooses to be humbled by it instead.

Unexpected parenting weaves our hearts with God's. Our hearts are humbled in hardship as we empty ourselves so He can fill us. We may need Him in ways we never needed Him before. Our appetites may change as we hunger for heaven, where their bodies and minds will no longer be affected by disease.

A diagnosis is not the end of the world if we believe in a world outside of ours. The finale will be even sweeter for those who have needed Him the most in this life.

According to Isaiah, one day, in heaven at last:

> *Then will the eyes of the blind be opened*
> *and the ears of the deaf unstopped.*
> *Then will the lame leap like a deer,*
> *and the mute tongue shout for joy.*
> *Water will gush forth in the wilderness*
> *and streams in the desert.*
> *The burning sand will become a pool,*
> *the thirsty ground bubbling springs.*
> *In the haunts where jackals once lay,*
> *grass and reeds and papyrus will grow . . .*
> *But only the redeemed will walk there,*
> *and those the Lord has rescued will return.*
> *They will enter Zion with singing;*
> *everlasting joy will crown their heads.*
> *Gladness and joy will overtake them,*
> *and sorrow and sighing will flee away.*
> -Isaiah 35:5–7, 9b–10, NIV

In heaven, broken bodies will leap. Mute tongues will shout for joy. Harmony will be sweet. Hold on, my friend.

Perfectly Blemished
By Rachelle Keng

I thought I did everything right.
Ate well, slept at night.
My pregnancy was completely fine,
I followed directions,
stayed within lines.

But she was clearly different when I met her,
Sent by God to show me better,
Than what I thought I already knew,
Sent to make my faith anew.

The Griefs of Unexpected Diagnoses

My heart broke the moment of diagnosis,
It was a painful prognosis.
Wanted to fire the Boss for what He had given,
Didn't He see how I'd been living?
At first, I was angry, rejecting the gift.
But by His grace, my heart began to shift—

He wept with me in sorrow
And held me close, promising tomorrow
For He had created her every nucleotide,
In my womb, never left her side,
My life not mine as I thought it was,
It belonged to Him from up above.

My path is still filled with uncertainty,
But In His hands, my child will ever be.
And so I cling to faith, each day anew
Trusting God will see us through

My need for answers is less and less,
The peace has grown, and I am blessed.
I have an appetite for eternity,
For all of the things that will someday be.
When we are one day healed forever,

And I will see my greatest treasure,
Perfectly blemished to save my soul,
So those around her would also know:

He is a creator, who makes no mistake,
He uses all His creation for His sake
To know His heart for this broken world,
Restored one day new and unfurled,

So we yearn for heaven when we are whole,
With no more effects of sin to show,
No decay, no death, no disability,
But in the presence of God we will be,
Restored, redeemed, and free.

Part III

Pregnancy

The next part of this book is for those who are pregnant and looking to grow in their faith during their pregnancy. A positive pregnancy test is a life-changing experience. Some women are ready. Some women are not. Some women have dreamed of becoming a mother since they were little girls. And some women have not wanted to ever be a mother.

But regardless of where you have started, your pregnancy is not a mistake or an accident. Let's spend the next few months examining how God is an intentional Creator.

The Creator of your child also lovingly saw you inside your mother's womb. Cell by cell, He wove you as a masterpiece that is intentionally thought-out. And now He does the same thing for your baby inside your womb. As you think about the miracle God is doing in your body, may you be drawn to worship. Because worship is what will get you through uncertain days in motherhood.

We do not need to fear pregnancy worst-case scenarios. And we do not need to fear motherhood's worst-case scenarios. There will be anxious days, but we do not need to fear tomorrow. He is there no matter what. Saturating our minds with Scripture will provide us with a peace that surpasses all anxiety.

These devotions are written for each week of pregnancy. Each devotion is meant to be read at least twice each week. The sections also have a header to reflect on how God provides for us. Reflection questions will help you grow your mother's soul during this exciting time. Let's begin!

First Trimester

When I first found out I was pregnant with my daughter, we were living in Cleveland. I was a young OBGYN attending physician trying to live out what I had preached to my patients. And yet, the moment it was my turn, my brain turned to mush. My anxious heart trumped all I knew in my mind.

My husband and I had been trying to get pregnant. After having cared for so many women with infertility, I was convinced that it was going to take me a long time to get pregnant.

But the moment I missed a period, I took a pregnancy test and freaked out.

I realized that in all of my OBGYN training, I had never learned to read a pregnancy test. I had wonderful nurses who told me the results, and I took it from there.

But now I was the patient holding on to this stick as if it had not come into contact with my bodily fluids. And like I said, my brain had turned to mush.

I looked at the instructions pamphlet that came with the pregnancy test. I thought I saw two lines, but what if it was a fluke?

When my husband entered the door, I waved the stick like a frantic torch. "I don't know what this means!" I exclaimed. "I need to know what a negative pregnancy test looks like. Can you please give me a urine sample so that I can make sure mine is truly positive?"

I have the most patient and kind husband, who graciously complied. And it was in that confirmation of my positive pregnancy that my soul journey as a mother began.

We cried and praised the Lord for this gift. But right after the excitement came the terrifying fears of pregnancy.

What if I could not do it? What if my body wouldn't cooperate with my heart's desire to birth this child? What if my child was not as perfect as I was? (HA!) And more acutely, how was I going to make it through childbirth?

And the questions created a fear that I learned to give to God daily.

If you are on this journey with me and have just found out you're pregnant, you're going to make it. It is a supernatural calling to be a mother. Supernatural callings are usually impossible—at first glance.

Remember the pregnant virgin who also had a supernatural calling? Mary was in what we would call a "situation." She was engaged to be married and pregnant with someone else's baby. Can you imagine what was going through her mind the moment she found out she was pregnant? Supernatural callings don't always make perfect sense. But they are completely worth it.

You may be completely thrilled, depressed, or all the emotions in between with this thing called pregnancy. But as you process all your fears, God is present to process them with you. The Bible has so many rich encouragements for mothers, and I can't wait to share them with you!

Motherhood is a supernatural calling, and supernatural callings are impossible without God. But thankfully, God will equip you with what you need when you need it.

Your child is so blessed you are his or her mother.

Mama.

It is a precious name that takes time to grow into.

And if you already wear this name, then you already know its richness and heartache all bundled together. A true bundle of joy.

May God bless you on this journey!

4 weeks
Two lines! – God Is Not Surprised

This is what the Lord says—your Redeemer, who formed you in the womb: I am the Lord, the maker of all things, who stretches out the heavens, who spreads out the earth by myself.

Isaiah 44:24, NIV

Two lines?!

Okay, take a deep breath. I know it feels crazy. The plumbing actually worked?

Most women find out they are pregnant when they have a missed period and take a pregnancy test. The first time a urine pregnancy test may be positive is when the baby is approximately four weeks gestational age.

Finding out you're pregnant is either the best news in the world, the worst news in the world, or a mix of all of the above!

Pregnancy is not just about buying a minivan. It's a new mindset. A new mindset means change. And not everyone feels "ready" for change. It often means mourning what was and will no longer be and simultaneously experiencing flutters of excitement at all the possibilities. But what starts off as an ice cream sundae can quickly become an overwhelming melted mess. Excitement is garnished with fear. A lot of fear.

But you know what?

It is possible to have all of the above emotions simultaneously and still be a good mom. It is also possible to have all these emotions and still love God.

The strength of your faith is not dependent on how bravely you smile.
The strength of your faith is dependent on how honest you are with God about your fear.
Honestly, God already knows how you feel.

He is the maker who has stretched out the heavens and the earth by Himself.

And He has made you with the emotions you are experiencing today. He is not surprised about this pregnancy because He has already been weaving this little one in your womb. He is not far away in the heavens, unaware of what has happened. He is a tender Father who sits with His child while you tell Him how you genuinely feel about the pregnancy. You can be yourself, and He can handle it.

When you open your heart to Him, you will be empowered to do the supernatural.

The bond to our pregnancies strengthens when we let go of ourselves and let Him in.

Not all women bond with their pregnancy right away. And that's okay. Sometimes you may feel too sick to bond with this little person that is causing all your havoc. The bond grows as your body, heart, and soul finally sync. The problem is they just usually grow at different rates. Part of this mismatch is God's intentional design so that our journeys are more about Him and less about ourselves. When we are out of sync, we need the help of someone greater than ourselves.

Eventually, you will need to decide which emotion will win. On the hard days of pregnancy, it may be fear or frustration. On the best days of pregnancy, it will be excitement. Emotions are going to be all over the place in pregnancy. And this continues into motherhood!

Quite honestly, these mixed emotions are part of the growth of your mother's heart. This similar mix of emotions is experienced as our children go to kindergarten, as they choose their friends over parents and move away (or don't move away)—wait a second, I am getting ahead of myself—the baby is not even visible on ultrasound yet!

Your mother's heart is already growing amidst a positive pregnancy test, which is why you may feel all over the place.

Not an emotional person? It's okay. A rational person who can will feelings away? It's okay. But be forewarned: once your uterus has been primed, make sure you have a box of tissues the next time you watch the Hallmark channel.

Because emotional or not, motherhood brings out the feelings we may not have wanted to feel for years.

If you already have children, you may have days where it is entirely overwhelming and suffocating. I see these mothers in my office, and sometimes I am one of these mothers. But when I ask these mothers if it is worth it, they all say the same thing—they would do it all over again. These women show up in my office pregnant again two years later.

The best things in life require sacrificial love and patient endurance. The parents who come into my office the second time recognize the true gift of parenting chaos. They are seasoned from years of sacrificial love.

There are powerful spiritual lessons in pregnancy that will prepare you to be the best mother you can be. If He has called you to motherhood, He will empower you. God does not abandon those He calls. Hang in there!

Reflection Questions:

Are you honest with God about how you feel about this pregnancy? Tell him your real feelings about what you are most worried about.

If you are already on the emotional roller coaster, write down three truths about yourself and God. The Lord is the Redeemer and Maker. When fear threatens to take over, choose to meditate on truth.

Do you trust that God is intimately involved in the details of your life, including the formation of new life and the challenges that come with it?

5 Weeks

Sacrificial Love – God Understands Sacrifice

Because of the joy awaiting him, he endured the cross, disregarding its shame.

Hebrews 12:2, NLT

It starts. The waves of nausea that make chocolate cake taste like cardboard. The night awakenings from your bladder that remind you sleep is now a luxury.

One of the hardest things about the first trimester is that your body is no longer your own. Your taste buds have changed, your energy is gone by 3:00 p.m., and the emotional swings that make you feel cray cray? Yes, they're real. Women will sacrifice their time, bodies, and future plans for pregnancy.

Women bear the cost of motherhood. From the discomforts of pregnancy and the pains of labor and delivery to the sleepless nights and breastfeeding woes of postpartum, women carry a heavy cross. And yet, we are willing to take on this weight because of love. The Greek word for love, agape, is the laying down of one's life for another. It is an act of sacrifice.

Pregnancy is agape love.

The Christian sees Jesus as the most remarkable example of agape sacrificial love. Jesus was unjustly killed as a sacrifice for a broken mankind. But He knew what was on the other side of the cross. He knew that restoration, redemption, and a relationship with us was worth the pain. Jesus looked past the cross and saw you and me. Jesus suffered because of His love for you and me. Because of His love, He endured the cross

Jesus paid the cost for a life we could not earn by paying a debt He did not owe. You are giving Christ's sacrificial love to your unborn child. You are paying a cost for someone who cannot survive on his or her own.

Sacrificial love is denying ourselves for someone else. In this age, sacrificial love is hard to find. Because sacrificial love is difficult. Unnatural. Vulnerable.

One of the best ways to overcome our fears is to remember who is on the other side of the struggle. When we know *why* and *for whom* we struggle, we can endure more than we typically would be able to handle. For the joy of our children awaiting us, we can endure the cross of pregnancy. For the joy of our children, we can endure childbirth.

Sacrificial love is possible when we know that it is purposeful. Sometimes, the reward is the warmth of baby snuggles. But before that can happen, real sacrifices need to be made. We take on these risks because of what awaits us on the other side.

You are giving the most incredible gift by being a willing shelter for the little one that is being woven in your womb. The sacrifices of sleep, feeling crummy, and the emotional roller coaster are going to be worth it. You are amazing.

Reflection Questions:

Has there been a time that someone gave you agape (sacrificial) love? What was their cost, and what made it worth it for them to love you this way?

How is God providing for you even when you feel unwell? Spend some time thanking God for how He has provided for you today.

Do you believe sacrificial love has a purpose and meaning beyond the immediate sacrifices? How does this belief impact your willingness to make sacrifices?

6 Weeks

Morning Sickness – God Protects

Remain in me, as I also remain in you. No branch can bear fruit by itself; it must remain in the vine. Neither can you bear fruit unless you remain in me. I am the vine, you are the branches. If you remain in me and I in you, you will bear much fruit; apart from me you can do nothing . . . My command is this: Love each other as I have loved you. Greater love has no one than this: to lay down one's life for his friends.

John 15:4–5, 12–13, NIV

If you are one of the lucky ones, you may not have any first trimester symptoms. But many women experience nausea and vomiting during the first trimester. Tack on strange food aversions and odd cravings; your body may feel foreign to you.

This is because the little person growing inside you thinks he or she is the boss. This baby is telling you what to eat, when you can eat, and how to eat. The tug-of-war has begun, and there will be days when this child is the most powerful raisin-sized person in the world.

If you have always been in control of your destiny, then the first trimester can be incredibly suffocating. You may have days where it feels like you're barely surviving, and it's okay to wonder if you made the right decision about getting pregnant. But hang in there - it does get better!

A beautiful bond is already forming between you and your child. Your child already has a personality. Hangry? Impatient? This child wants to eat, and eat now! This personality may not get along with you during the first trimester. But don't worry, nausea is not a sign of your child's temperament, nor is an easy pregnancy a sign of an easy child.

If you are losing weight or getting dehydrated from vomiting, talk to your doctor about medications that can be helpful. The first trimester can feel like it lasts forever. But focusing on the small bites and the small wins will sustain you.

Focusing on what you are gaining rather than on what you are losing will keep you in a more positive headspace. There is a Creator's intention behind each of your symptoms of pregnancy. It does not make the days easier, but this thought should make the moments more purposeful.

When the embryo is implanted into the uterus, a hormone from early embryonic cells called HCG (human chorionic gonadotropin) is released at the implantation site. HCG causes nausea in women in the first trimester. A mother's nausea is protective for the well-being of her baby. The baby's development is most susceptible to toxins and environmental factors from 6 to 8 weeks of pregnancy. Nausea tends to be the worst during this time. Perhaps this is one of the reasons that women have food aversions to eggs, meat, poultry, and seafood, all foods that may have a higher risk of toxins if undercooked[5].

Not only are there food aversions, but there can also be strange food cravings. You may find yourself craving pickles, sour foods, and salt— this is God's amazing plan for providing for your baby's needs. As you increase your salt intake, your body begins to absorb more water[6], which increases the amount of blood your body needs to maintain the pregnancy.

The first trimester can deepen our relationship with Christ as we depend on God for everything we usually control. Food is no longer ours. Sleep is no longer easy. We may not have enough energy to care for our other children. We may be dealing with missed days at work with financial losses. We may be wading through our neglected homes. Each day is lived in survival mode.

---

[5] Samuel M. Flaxman and Paul W. Sherman, "Morning Sickness: A Mechanism for Protecting Mother and Embryo," The Quarterly Review of Biology 75, no. 2 (June 1, 2000): 113–48, https://doi.org/10.1086/393377.

[6] Ole Skøtt, "Body Sodium and Volume Homeostasis," American Journal of Physiology-Regulatory Integrative and Comparative Physiology 285, no. 1 (July 1, 2003): R14–18, https://doi.org/10.1152/ajpregu.00100.2003.

But at last, we are pliable and soft in the hands of God. Now, He can fill in the cracks we usually insist on holding together on our own.

Your growing baby depends on you the way you can depend on Jesus. You are the vine, and your child is a branch abiding via an umbilical cord. Jesus promises to be a vine that refills us when we abide in Him. God promises to give you a daily refill, so you have more to offer. Jesus is your vine who will feed you exactly what you need to bear fruit. Not too much. Not too little. Just enough.

You are not doing this pregnancy alone when you abide in the vine. The vine will supply you with what you need for the next meal. Keep connected to the vine, and you will find rest.

> **Reflection Questions:**
> *Can you think of a time when God used something challenging for your good?*
> *How can you spend more time attached to the vine this week?*
> *Have you noticed any patterns of growth in your relationship with God when you are forced to rely on Him more fully?*

7 weeks

Navigating Unplanned Pregnancy – God Is A Good Shepherd

The thief's purpose is to steal and kill and destroy. My purpose is to give them a rich and satisfying life. I am the good shepherd. The good shepherd sacrifices his life for the sheep. A hired hand will run when he sees a wolf coming. He will abandon the sheep because they don't belong to him and he isn't their shepherd. And so the wolf attacks them and scatters the flock. The hired hand runs away because he's working only for the money and doesn't really care about the sheep. I am the good shepherd; I know my own sheep, and they know me, just as my Father knows me and I know the Father. So I sacrifice my life for the sheep.

John 10:10–15, NLT

The second line on the pregnancy test is a gate that releases a flood of emotions. Do you skip excitedly to the yellow brick road, or do the lines resemble prison bars? How you feel about your pregnancy depends on your context. If you have your life together and want to be a mom, it will most likely be an exhilarating experience. But not all women are in this situation. Many women have mixed emotions the moment their pregnancy is realized.

It's more common to have feelings of dread, overwhelm, guilt, and fear. Will I be a good mom? Will my child have a good daddy that will care? Can I really handle another child right now?

Some women have partners that will walk with them through their pregnancy. But many women are alone and need to know there is someone who will provide the love and support they crave.

In the passage from John, Jesus says that He is the good shepherd who knows us, sees us, and pursues us. He claims that His purpose is to give a rich and satisfying life, contrasted with the one who takes and leaves.

The thief takes and destroys. Some fathers are like this thief who runs away when fatherhood is not their plan. A partner focused on his own needs may abandon his baby's mother when there is a cost to him. A husband who is not an active parent can be a very lonely marriage. True fatherhood requires sacrifice, but not all women have a partner who understands this.

If you are on this parenthood journey alone, the Good Shepherd knows you need encouragement today.

Jesus loves sacrificially by giving His life because He cares about His sheep. He does not abandon us in our moment of need. He stays with us. He understands the cost because He went to a painful cross to give up His life for you and me. He chose to remain on the cross because His love is sacrificial.

You and your child are treasured sheep in His flock. He does not abandon His sheep. He guides and protects mamas. Isaiah 40:11 says that He gathers His lambs in His arms, carries them, and gently leads those that are with young.

He will co-parent with you.

Jesus knows His sheep. He knows your name. He values you and does not abandon you in your most vulnerable moments. His love is not self-serving. Take a moment to revel in how this contrasts with many of the world's relationships. He understands what you will need to carry this pregnancy. He understands your fears. You can bring Him your weight—baby and all—He is strong enough to carry you both. Spend time reading about Jesus' interactions with women in the gospels. You will see how He tenderly cares for women who are in abandoned situations. Over the next few months of devotions, we will go through some of these interactions to grow our understanding of a caring Savior.

If you are doing motherhood alone, you will need practical help through this journey. Many nonprofit organizations provide practical assistance for mamas who are parenting alone. Pregnancy centers (www.care-net.

org) offer baby items free of charge. Some centers provide mentorship programs to help you succeed in your parenting journey. Your local Department of Social Services can help you get connected to programs like WIC (Women, Infants, Children). Churches focused on caring for the fatherless can be a great source of encouragement and practical help. Some maternity homes provide transitional housing until you are in a better situation. Some states offer childcare at subsidized rates. Check out your local Department of Social Services if you need health insurance.

Sometimes it is so overwhelming. But one thing is clear:

You are incredibly courageous for choosing to be a mama.

Reflection Questions:

What are some concrete ways you have seen God carry you this week?

If you are a single mother or are making this parenting journey alone, how can you build your village so that you have other women who understand what you are going through?

How can Jesus fill your desire for a partner in this parenting journey?

8 weeks

Worry Is Normal – God Gives Us Peace

You will keep in perfect peace those whose minds are steadfast, because they trust in you.

Isaiah 26:3, NIV

No matter how strong your faith is, worry is normal.

Pregnancy is one of the first times a woman feels out of control of her life. Without the power to control your baby's development, you may feel highly anxious. You can no longer eat what you want. You can't sleep anymore. Pooping is now a luxury. How can something the size of a sunflower seed create so much havoc?

In this world, we would like to believe that hard work pays off. It is only too easy to assume that this applies to pregnancy. We may have jobs, education, a bank account, and our health—all signs of prosperity that we may believe are the fruits of our hard work. But hard work does not necessarily guarantee a healthy pregnancy outcome in pregnancy.

And that is why pregnancy is so terrifying.

I wish we could guarantee healthy, full-term pregnancies with our diligence. But our wombs are at the mercy of their Creator. Pregnancy is all about waiting. Waiting for the next ultrasound, waiting for the test result, waiting for birth. It can be a time of extreme anxiety or extreme peace.

What we believe about the Creator's character will impact how we wait. Do you wait with perfect peace? Or do you wait with anxious anticipation? If you believe the Creator is trustworthy, you will wait differently.

God is an intentional creator. He knows the timeline of every life that He creates. He knows every bump, detour, pit that His children will encounter.

If you believe this to be true, none of the pain in your life will ever be wasted. No matter your pregnancy experience, He will equip you with exactly what you need.

If you have ever gone through a miscarriage before, the first few weeks of your next pregnancy are sometimes the most anxious time. Your previous loss will inevitably color the experience of your current pregnancy. It's okay to be scared. It's okay to not bond with your baby until you see your child's heartbeat.

The Bible promises perfect peace for those whose minds stay on Him because they trust Him. A perfect peace does not waver based on circumstance. We can still be afraid, but fear will no longer overcome us. We can have complete peace because we know who holds us for today's and tomorrow's drama.

Peace-filled motherhood brings our children to the altar when they are five millimeters long. We trust the Creator to start their heartbeats, grow them, and form their placentas. Giving our babies daily to the Lord sets the precedence for how we bring our toddlers, teenagers, and adult children to the Lord. Because, honestly, the anxieties of motherhood never end. They only morph with each season.

When He gives you more than you can handle, He wants you to trust Him. When we decide to trust Him no matter what, a true peace will be present regardless of circumstance. This true peace will keep your mind and heart safe even in your worst case scenarios of pregnancy.

Let's speak these truths out loud together:

God is good, and He loves me.
God is sovereign over my womb.
God created me in my mother's womb.
He knows what He's doing. He's got this.

Do you believe this?

If you do, these truths will carry you no matter your story. Whatever your womb story is, God has a purpose in it all.

Reflection Questions:

Is there an area of your life (and your child's) where you need to trust God with His plan over your plan?

How have you seen God use painful experiences in your life for your good?

Do you believe you have control over your child's development? There may be activities that you wonder if they are "safe" to do in pregnancy. After consulting with your healthcare provider, it is important to make choices during pregnancy that you will not regret later. Proactive and preventative care for a mother's mental health is important in this motherhood journey.

9 weeks

Facing the Fear of Miscarriage – God Is All-Knowing

And we know that in all things God works for the good of those who love him, who have been called according to his purpose.

Romans 8:28, NIV

Many pregnant mothers do not tell their friends and families about their pregnancies until they are out of the first trimester. Women are often afraid to bond with their babies until they can see a heartbeat.

If you have had a miscarriage before, any symptom will be interpreted with a heightened filter. You may wonder if you can dare to hope. Can you believe in the dreams you have for your children? It's okay to be afraid because in this place, you will choose where your true hope lies.

Hope that is based on perfect circumstances is fragile.
Hope that is based on God's perfect purposes is stable.

But if you have lost something or someone significant in your life, pregnancy can be a trigger for anxiety. The stakes are high, especially around the ones we love. If we don't work out these anxieties, our hope will be based on perfect circumstances.

How do we let go of our anxieties about loss?

- **Learn to trust in God more than yourself.**
  Like any relationship, digging into the relational file cabinet takes time to remember the occasions God has "shown up" for you. It often means asking yourself, "Do I trust God with the most vulnerable parts of my heart?" This may mean attending Christian counseling to understand why you may have difficulty trusting God. There can be traumatic feelings

of "abandonment by God," and it is okay to be honest about them. Tell a trusted pastor or mentor who will listen with compassion.

- **Fall in love with God's purposes over your own.**
  Romans 8:28 says that all things work out for His purpose—not our purpose, but His purpose. His purpose is to bless you and His church through your story. Part of falling in love with God's purposes over your own means that you trust in God over yourself (read point number one again).

- **Learn to grieve for the sake of the body of Christ.**
  Grief can make us feel weak, exposed, and mortal. There is nothing wrong with grieving privately. But what if we experienced grief for the sake of the body of Christ? Can the comfort we receive in our grief comfort someone else in the same struggle? Can the comfort that someone else has received during a miscarriage comfort you (2 Corinthians 1:3–7) if you were to go through a miscarriage? You may not know this comfort if no one knows what you are going through. One of the hardest parts of keeping a pregnancy under wraps is that if a miscarriage occurs, grieving occurs without recognition. When the body of Christ is allowed to grieve with you, deeper relationships will carry you. You will not be alone.

We can still be afraid of loss. But we do not need to live as if we are "waiting for the other shoe to drop." God loves you and wants what is best for you. He is not manipulating your womb like an evil mastermind. He is an intentional father who loves your soul.

May your hope be founded in His good purposes with your womb story.

> **Reflection Questions:**
> *What is your greatest fear in this pregnancy? Can you trust that God has a plan for whatever happens, even if this was to happen? Pray honestly to God to tell Him your fear. If you have unbelief in God's goodness, ask Him to change your heart.*

When you reflect on your life's worst-case scenarios, how did God show you His mercy? How has God provided for you in a painful circumstance? If you feel He has not provided for you, would you consider talking to someone about this tender place?

Have you seen God's purposes defined by your brokenness more than your successes? And if so, how?

10 weeks

Genetic Testing – God Is Sovereign

> *My frame was not hidden from you, when I was being made in secret, intricately woven in the depths of the earth. Your eyes saw my unformed substance; in your book were written, every one of them, the days that were formed for me, when as yet there was none of them.*
>
> Psalm 139:15–16

Your obstetrician will be talking to you about optional genetic testing in the next few weeks. There are many tests to consider, but the most common genetic testing is a screening test for Down syndrome. While no test can screen for every pediatric condition prenatally, the ability to screen for more medical conditions continues to grow as technology advances. It is important to understand what genetic testing tells you and what it does not tell you about your child.

If you want to know every possible bridge of your journey ahead of time, then prenatal genetic testing may be for you. But if you are content with crossing the bridge when (and if) needed, then you may not want to pursue prenatal genetic testing. Waiting for results may create anxiety, so you should know why you want the testing.

The decision to pursue genetic testing is a personal one. There are many reasons to pursue genetic testing. Some parents want the information so they may be prepared for a child with special needs. Some parents pursue genetic testing to abort the pregnancy if they have an abnormal result.

The truth is no one really knows how they truly feel about this topic until they receive an abnormal test result. No one is prepared to be a special needs parent. Special needs parenting is something we grow into, not something that most parents strive for.

Genetic testing can give us an illusion of control over our futures. But ultimately, it has its limits. Genetic testing will not tell you how your child will love you. Genetic testing will not capture the gifts of your child. An abnormal genetic test does not show the depth of a person. The result on a page is two-dimensional. But a person has more dimensions than any letters or numbers can capture.

Genetic test results are not a representation of your child's identity. Our intrinsic identity is in being the created.

If you believe God the Creator is sovereign over His creation in utero, then He lovingly pieces together your child's DNA. There are no mistakes. There are no surprises. There are no accidents. Children with unique genetics are also made in the image of God.

Psalm 139 says nothing is hidden from God while He creates your child. Your child is being intricately woven in the depths of your womb. He is intentionally crafting each nucleotide next another nucleotide on your child's DNA ladder.

An ultrasound during the time of a positive pregnancy test at four weeks shows a black circle called a gestational sac that is a sign of an early pregnancy. You cannot see a formed embryo on ultrasound until around six to seven weeks of gestation. At four weeks, on ultrasound, the gestational sac appears to be empty. But the baby's chromosomes have already been replicating—all before an ultrasound can detect the shape of a baby! Down's syndrome and other genetic conditions have already been determined when the embryo is still formless.

In Psalm 139, God sees "the unformed substance" during this intricate weave. He sees the embryo before it has formed during its most critical time of chromosomal development. Therefore, gene deletions and mutations are known by God before they ever become detectable to the human world.

Every day of our children's lives is already known from conception, while they are formless.

If you have received an abnormal genetic test, it is okay to be afraid. You may be tempted to escape. But God has chosen special needs parents to have the best seat in the house to His work. He invites you to see miracles in your children and yourself. God did not make a mistake in choosing you to be your child's mother.

Your story is not over - it is only beginning. See the section on "When your child has an unexpected diagnosis."

Reflection Questions:
Would knowing a diagnosis change your desire to parent your child?
What defines the personhood of your child?
Spend some time reflecting on whether you trust God with your child's future no matter what.

11 weeks

When He Doesn't Get It – God Sees

You have searched me, LORD, and you know me. You know when I sit and when I rise; you perceive my thoughts from afar. You discern my going out and my lying down; you are familiar with all my ways. Before a word is on my tongue you, LORD, know it completely.

Psalm 139:1–4, NIV

You are the first one who feels like a parent. Is it the first wave of nausea? The unwelcome nighttime potty breaks? Or the emotional roller coaster that you have just signed up for?

His hormones haven't changed a bit. He's sleeping like a log while you spend your nights in the bathroom. He hangs off the pillow cliff comfortably every night, while you struggle to find a comfortable crevice.

But honestly, pregnancy is also difficult for men. They see their partners crying, vomiting, and in pain. And there is little they can do to help besides be present. They are the Taco Bell chauffeur, the crib fixer-upper—navigating it all with a resilient temperament to ride the wave of an emotional pregnant woman.

Men do not bond with the baby the same way women do. Women are bonded with their children at the minute of implantation. Motherhood is real the moment their bodies are taken over. Men often do not bond with their children until they feel the first kick (usually not until after twenty-four weeks). Sometimes, fatherhood does not feel real until they are fearfully cradling their newborn in their arms.

It can be lonely when he doesn't get it. Or he doesn't want to get it. Because when men are not interested in fathering, it is even harder to bond with this little being. But when men are willing to develop a dad bod with your ever-growing figure, it is truly a gift.

Their presence means more than they will ever know. But even with the most present husband, pregnancy can still be a lonely experience. No one sees the twenty-four-seven sacrifice you are putting into this new job except the One who is there twenty-four-seven.

In the same Psalm that says God is weaving the little one in your womb, He also has promises for mamas as well. The beginning of Psalm 139 says God knows everything about you. He is ever-present. He knows your disrupted routines because of this pregnancy. He knows the details of your life, even down to the timing of when you sit or lie down. He is familiar with all of your ways.

God knows what you're thinking, how you feel, and what you are truly trying to say.

God knows your heart.

Your partner may not always get it. Or if you are doing this alone, it may comfort you to know that even a supportive partner is not able to fill the void that women need. Only God can fill this void.

God, the creator of your child, understands you and is with you. He has time to listen, for He never sleeps (Psalm 121:3–4). You can tell Him how you feel because He understands suffering (Hebrews 4:15). He sustains those He calls (Isaiah 41:10, Psalm 55:22).

Take some time this week to look up these scriptures and write them on Post-it notes to remind you on a daily and nightly basis. Even if no one else recognizes what you are doing for your baby, God sees you.

Reflection Questions:

How can you pray for your partner/husband today? What kind of encouragement can you give him for how he is supporting you?

How does knowing that God sees you change your confidence in carrying this pregnancy?

In what ways can you encourage your partner to participate in the pregnancy? Can you both come up with a list of what you each need to be encouraged this week? Start the conversation by asking your partner, "How can I encourage you to be the best father?" And then gently talk about how you would feel encouraged. For example, "If you would help with the other children so that I can get a nap, that would really help me feel loved." or "I would be encouraged if you help me with the baby registry."

12 weeks

A Symbiotic Bond – God Loved Us First

We love because he first loved us.

1 John 4:19, NIV

In the world of biology, the fetus has a parasitic relationship with his or her mother. By definition, the baby is an "organism that lives within another organism by deriving nutrients from the others' expense[7]." The parasitic relationship is one-sided. In contrast, a symbiotic relationship has benefits for both the parasite and the host.

Most adults like relationships with symbiosis, where there is a give and take. Conflicts arise when relationships are parasitic rather than symbiotic. But the relationship of mother and child, by nature, is a parasitic one. The baby lives off the mother's nutrients, sometimes at the mother's expense! The relationship may feel one-sided until there are more tangible physical ways that children give back: their first smile, their first soccer game, the first time they set the table, and the tender care they give to their aging parents. However, would you believe that your child may already be giving back to you in the womb?

Fetal microchimerism is the concept of baby "souvenir cells" that cross the placenta during pregnancy. The baby's cells stay inside the mother's tissues even after the baby is born. Fetal microchimeric cells can persist for decades after pregnancy. There is still much research going on to understand the benefits and risks of these cells on the maternal immune system. However, we know that fetal microchimeric cells have

---

[7] "Oxford English Dictionary," Accessed 5/4/2023, https://www.oed.com/.

been found inside mothers' cesarean scars after delivery[8]. Amazingly, the baby's cells were responding to the mother's need for healing! The baby's cells were "stem-cell-like" and also "signaled" other repair cells to come and heal his mother's cesarean scar.

Additionally, women who have birthed children have a decreased risk of breast cancer[9]. Women with children have protective fetal microchimeric cells in their normal breast tissue. In contrast, women without children do not have fetal microchimeric cells in their breast tissue. Emerging research is still needed to confirm this link, but perhaps the baby is sending protective cells to his or her mother before they even see one another!

So maybe babies are giving back to their mothers in utero. But the daily reality for a pregnant woman is that she is giving more to her child. It is truly a parasitic relationship. So why would anyone ever want to be pregnant? Why does she keep on? Because of love. Parasitic relationships are possible because of love.

The relationship between God and woman is not symbiotic. In this "spiritual, biological" relationship with God, humans are the true parasites. We need Him, yet He is self-sufficient as a host.

This is the gospel story: He loved us first—even when we did not love Him and even when we had nothing to offer Him (1 John 4:19). He paid a cost on the cross anyway. This is the beauty of God's love for us. When we marvel at this grace, we have the strength to do the impossible - like carrying a pregnancy that feels heavier every day. Like caring for our "forever-parasitic children." When we remember our true spiritual state, His love gives us the endurance to press on.

---

[8] Uzma Mahmood and Keelin O'Donoghue, "Microchimeric Fetal Cells Play a Role in Maternal Wound Healing after Pregnancy," Chimerism 5, no. 2 (April 1, 2014): 40–52, https://doi.org/10.4161/chim.28746.

[9] Vijayakrishna K. Gadi and J. Lee Nelson, "Fetal Microchimerism in Women with Breast Cancer," Cancer Research 67, no. 19 (October 1, 2007): 9035–38, https://doi.org/10.1158/0008-5472.can-06-4209.

Reflection Questions:

In what ways do you expect God to provide for you? Are the things you ask of God true or fair? If you have seen yourself as higher than God, take some time to ask God for forgiveness and then spend some time worshiping His mercy.

Spend time thanking God for the ways He cares for you. And then ask yourself who in your life also needs to be a recipient of this mercy.

If you already have children, what is the most exhausting part of having children? And what are the surprising ways they have given back to you?

13 weeks

The Victim Vortex – God Said No To Self-Pity

He was oppressed and treated harshly, yet he never said a word. He was led like a lamb to the slaughter. And as a sheep is silent before the shearers, he did not open his mouth.

Isaiah 53:7, NLT

By now, you may know every curve and contour of your toilet bowl. You can still squeeze into your jeans—as long as you choose not to breathe, right? You may pat your "bloat bump" that is already showing (which your obstetrician sadly tells you is gas, not your actual baby yet).

If pregnancy and motherhood are going well, this week's devotion may not make sense. But for those who are dealing with the continual trials of the first trimester (while everyone else is feeling better around you), it is easy to quickly spiral into a "Why me?" complex. The victim vortex is not unique to pregnancy. It is a temptation to spiral downward for any suffering person.

Diving into the victim vortex is a temptation that many mothers face lifelong. Why is her pregnancy so much easier than mine? Why does breastfeeding look so easy for her? Why doesn't my child do what everyone else's child does? The questions and comparisons can be endless.

We must beware of the dangers of the vortex:
- *The victim vortex is full of lies.*
  Have you ever heard yourself say, "I deserve better?"
  Lies will tell you that you deserve more. (Genesis 3:1)

But truth will tell you He has given you everything you need. (1 Kings 17:13–16)

- *The victim vortex enables destructive behavior.*
  Have you ever told yourself, "It's okay to (smoke, lie, cheat, etc.) because my life is so unfair?"
  Lies tell you that you deserve whatever feels good. (Genesis 3:4–6)
  But truth will tell you that sin grows. (James 1:15)

- *The victim vortex breeds miserable company.*
  The victim vortex is where we find other commiserators. Commiserators tell us what we want to hear—not what we need to hear.
  But truth will tell you even when you are wrong. (Proverbs 27:5–6)

- *The victim vortex leads us to self-centeredness.*
  Check out your self-talk. The question we need to ask is not "Why me?" but "Why not me?" None of us (including Christians) are immune from the woes of the womb. Yet sometimes we are surprised by suffering as if it couldn't or shouldn't happen to us (1 Peter 4:12–13).

If you are going down the victim vortex, remember where the vortex ends. It is usually dissatisfying and dark. But if you know the One who can redeem the woe into something that has worth, then you will be empowered to get off the spiral before it disappears into the depths.

Jesus, who was led to the cross like a lamb led to the slaughter, did not open His mouth. There were so many things He could have said in that moment. He could have justified himself and fought those who were cursing Him. It took more strength to keep His mouth closed than to say what He deserved to say. He could have been in a "victim-vortex" at the cross, but Jesus let go of revenge. He loved us more than He loved being vindicated.

Obviously, we are not Jesus. Our sin causes us to ride the victim vortex. If you are stuck in the vortex, finding help from a counselor is important. Your thought patterns may be teetering a slippery slope and may need evaluation by a professional. Talk with your medical professional, especially if you are having days where you feel so low you cannot get out of bed.

And most importantly, pray for God to change your heart. If you feel like you have gotten the short end of the stick, let God show you His mercy. If you are dealing with injustice, let God be the judge. If you are always right and everyone else is always wrong, then make sure there is not a log in your eye (Matthew 7:3–5).

God transforms victims into victors when they choose Jesus over justice.

Reflection Questions:

Have you ever experienced the victim vortex? Do you have any unhealthy behaviors or self-harm habits as a result of the victim vortex? Will you let yourself get help?

Check your self-talk when you are facing suffering or struggling. Do you ask yourself, "Why me?" or do you ask yourself "Why not me?" Are you surprised by suffering or do you see it as part of God's plan to reveal His glory in you? Reflect on 1 Peter 4:12–13.

Where in your pregnancy are you feeling sorry for yourself? Can you give that frustration to God this week?

Second Trimester

He bought the wrong toilet paper.

How dare he!

My poor husband sat there with arms full of a mountain of cheap toilet paper rolls. It was the scratchy kind where you needed to use a whole roll to be clean. And so I flipped out on him. I knew it was being an irrational pregnant woman. I knew I was being hormonal. But I couldn't stop myself.

Don't you know that this cheap toilet paper is not good enough for a pregnant lady who is running to the bathroom every two minutes? I fumed.

I remember thinking that this cheap toilet paper roll was a depiction of inconsideration (and my husband is the most considerate person I have ever met). I jumped to that conclusion like a mad bull. The entitlement I experienced in pregnancy was incredible.

It was only too easy to think that I deserved special treatment because I was pregnant.

But in doing so, I was pushing away my greatest support system.

The problem with pregnancy is that when women need the most support, we can become the most difficult people to be around.

When something hurts all the time, and you aren't getting a full night of sleep, problems seem gargantuan. But when you have a minute to step back and re-evaluate, you might be able to see where things have gone askew. Pregnancy is hard for everyone else as well. They may need to be more gracious to us. But maybe we need to become more gracious to them as well.

It's okay. We all have been there.

Some women love pregnancy. They are high on endorphins. Good for them.

But for the rest of us who had labile emotions during pregnancy, I see you.

And it's okay.

If you are taking your emotions out on others, take time to recollect yourself. You probably need a heart check-in. Then, start to look around at all the people who are supporting you the best they can. There are changes that are happening to you and everyone around you.

After my emotions diffused, I apologized to my sweet husband and asked for forgiveness. I knew his heart's intentions were good. He was thinking about cost-efficiency for the faucet of a woman he was now married to. I was taking it way too personally. Sometimes you can see the irrational freak-out right after it happens . . . and sometimes you can't.

Let's just say he still buys the Charmin Ultra Soft even though I'm no longer pregnant. He probably doesn't want to risk testing a crazy mama. My husband is considerate, and he isn't dumb either.

14 weeks

The Roots of Anxiety – God Is A Safe Shelter

Blessed is the man who trusts in the Lord, whose trust is the Lord. He is like a tree planted by water, that sends out its roots by the stream, and does not fear when heat comes, for its leaves remain green, and is not anxious in the year of drought, for it does not cease to bear fruit.

Jeremiah 17:7–8 ESV

The first-trimester anxieties of "Will I have a miscarriage?" and "Is my baby going to be okay?" tend to diminish by the second trimester. But for some, the anxiety gets worse. Do you find yourself waking up in the middle of the night with anxious thoughts? Are you unable to fall asleep because you're worrying about all the what-ifs? Or are you obsessing about all the things that need to happen before the new baby arrives?

Mamas want to feel like they have everything under control before the baby arrives. Routines, childcare, job transitions, housing situations, and the other siblings being settled are just a few. Usually, pregnant mamas tend to do all of the above transitions - at the same time! So of course, pregnant women are anxious! Throw in hormones, poor sleeping patterns, and physical pain, and the anxiety can be paralyzing.

These new depths of emotions can extend into postpartum and then even into motherhood. Quite honestly, the anxiety never ends. We just learn to live with it. Anxiety is difficult even for the Christian. So, let's look at the roots that feed anxiety to understand the type of fruits that result.

Why are we anxious?
  Your anxiety is the result of love.

As your pregnant belly grows, your mother's heart also grows with it.

As the power to love grows, the room for hurt also grows. It is a new vulnerability that we experience as mothers. There is so much love for this helpless being that we fear loss in a new way. We are afraid to lose something that we love so much.

But anxiety is also the consequence of the Garden of Eden. We discussed the Eve Complex in the preconception section. After the fall, Eve could understand good and evil, but she did not have the power to do anything about what she knew. Unlike God, who was all-knowing and all-powerful, Eve was neither of these. She knew just enough to make her scared about pain without the power to protect her loved ones from pain.

The Eve Complex is the inability to control the loss that we fear. The Eve Complex gets amplified in pregnancy and follows us into motherhood. The combination of a mother's love with the Eve Complex is the perfect recipe for anxiety.

Anxiety can become a true medical concern in pregnancy. Our intellect is not always connected to how we feel. Intellectually, the Christian knows who is in control of their baby's development, but anxiety is not rational. When anxiety is at a decibel that drowns out the truth, we need to get help.

Sometimes, faith, will, and resolve are enough. But sometimes they are not. We need to acknowledge that just as our wombs are susceptible to the woes of Genesis 3, our minds are just as susceptible to brokenness.

While some healthy anxieties are protective, other anxieties can become unhealthy obsessions.

Unhealthy anxiety cannot see the truth. Unhealthy anxiety needs to control every possible variable of pregnancy. Unhealthy anxiety shows up with physical symptoms (heart palpitations, trouble sleeping, emotional outbursts).

Healthy anxiety experiences fear but can still choose truth. Healthy anxiety is protective, but understands who holds our children. Healthy anxiety causes more dependence on God and less on ourselves.

Unhealthy anxiety is like a tree that has been fed by the wrong fertilizer. Over time, the fertilizers of perfect performance and people-pleasing grow anxious fruits.

But when the roots are fed by a trust in God, the fruit of the spirit is peace.

You will not be fazed by the weather when there is a drought. Your fruit-bearing is not based on the environment's ability to cooperate. Your roots are in the word of God and what He says about you.

Anxiety about your children's safety is normal. But if you are experiencing unhealthy anxiety about your children, take a moment to define the meaning of "safety." Most women believe that the baby is "physically safe in the womb."

However, the safest shelter is not inside an amniotic cocoon.
The safest place for your child is inside the center of God's will.
God knows what your children need and how your soul needs to grow.

If fear has become the driving force of your actions, take a moment to step back. It may be important to understand why you fear loss. A counselor can help you understand how your past traumas have given you unhealthy coping mechanisms. Talk with your obstetrician to decide whether counseling or medications may help you. Medications may help filter extreme emotions so that you can see the truth.

The healthier your mental state as a mother, the more your children will thrive.

Dealing with our anxiety and getting over ourselves is one of the hardest trials of this motherhood journey. But when we finally trust God to carry us no matter what, anxiety no longer has power over us. And our children no longer need to carry this burden with us.

Reflection Questions:

How can the Eve Complex contribute to anxiety during your pregnancy and motherhood experiences?

Where do you have healthy and unhealthy types of anxiety in your life? Make a list of the unhealthy anxieties, and then each morning this week, give this individual anxiety to the Lord. He already knows them, but when you write them down and pray them out loud, you will experience a different kind of freedom.

How does anxiety affect your relationships during pregnancy and motherhood, and what can be done to prevent it from damaging them? Richard Rohr, a Franciscan friar and author, once said, "Pain that is not transformed gets transmitted."[10]

Does this ring true for you, and where do you see the pain in your life that needs to be transformed so that you can be a better mama?

---

[10] (https://cac.org/daily-meditations/transforming-pain-2018-10-17/ Accessed 12/29/23)

15 weeks

Mama Drama – God Remembers His Children

> *Can a mother forget the baby at her breast and have no compassion on the child she has borne? Though she may forget, I will not forget you! See, I have engraved you on the palms of my hands; your walls are ever before me.*
>
> Isaiah 49:15–16, NIV

Many women have complicated relationships with their mothers. Often, it is not until women become pregnant that they finally have an understanding of their own complicated mothers. You may find yourself sounding more and more like your mother, for better or worse! Your mother influences the mama that you become. You may want to be exactly like her, nothing like her, or somewhere in the middle.

Pregnancy brings out the mother-daughter history—with all of its baggage tested in a new way. A promotion to grandma often comes armed with advice. Some advice is helpful, and sometimes it's just plain overwhelming. Most mothers are excited about their daughters becoming pregnant, but the context is very important. Does she like the father of the baby? Does she believe her daughter is ready to be a mom? These factors either cause her to celebrate or perseverate.

Our mothers come in all flavors of sweet and sour.
And sometimes a mix of both.

Perhaps you had an overbearing mother. Perhaps you have had an absent mother. Perhaps you never knew your birth mother. Or perhaps you had a mother who knew exactly when to challenge you and when to encourage you. Even so, no mother is perfect.

Mothers are sinners, trying their best with what they have.

When you become a mother, you often discover your heart growing in grace or festering in bitterness toward your own mother. God has a plan for how He will use this relationship for your good and His glory. He has known all the mountains, chasms, and cliffs that would occur in this relationship. Whatever your childhood relationship was, your current pregnancy may help to redeem and solidify your relationship with your mother.

Pregnancy can be terrifying when you have a mother who has not set an example of love for you. Pregnancy can be a trigger for mamas who have been abandoned by their own mothers, especially if they experience the fierce love for their child that they know their mother did not possess for them. Pregnancy can harden your heart toward your mother even more if you have had a difficult relationship.

Or…pregnancy can be a time when you grow in grace.

For the first time, you may understand why your mother was overwhelmed. As you become a mother, you may understand how difficult it was for her to do everything. Your compassion for her inadequacies may grow as you realize how hard it was for her to carry you. You may even be prompted to forgive her for the sake of bringing generations together.

Regardless of your adversities with your mother, you were also chosen to be your mother's daughter. God can use both generations to sharpen one another for His glory.

If your mother feels absent now, it makes carrying this little one even harder. It is sometimes difficult to continue if she is not celebrating this milestone with you. Perhaps she is no longer with you. Or perhaps she has a critical spirit that makes you feel like you are doing this alone.

> *Even if you do not get your mother's approval, you can still get God's approval.*

As we seek God's approval, the need for approval from other family members becomes less central. Most of us have a desire for approval from our mothers. We want them to trust us with our decisions.

We want them to celebrate this milestone of pregnancy with us. But sometimes, it may not be possible to get her approval, and she may feel absent.

God cares for you in these moments of not having a mother's care.

In Isaiah 49:15, the Israelites had just been exiled to Babylon. They felt abandoned and forgotten by God. God responded to them with a promise of presence. He gave them an image of an intimate relationship of a mother breastfeeding her child. But in this passage, even this mother had forgotten her child. In contrast, God told them that He never forgets His children.

Even if you feel like your mother has forgotten you, God has not forgotten you.

In fact, He has your name permanently engraved into his hands (Isaiah 49:16). His palms are strong enough to endure the piercing of a nail yet gentle enough to hold you.

When God fills your "mother" wound, you will hurt less and love more.

Ask God to use your pregnancy to help you understand your mother better. Ask God to give you a heart of forgiveness.
God may use your pregnancy to restore this relationship.
For out of new life comes a new beginning for all.

Reflection Questions:

How has your relationship with God influenced your relationship with your mother? How has your relationship with your mother influenced your relationship with God?

Are there any unresolved issues or hurts from your childhood with your mother that you need to address before becoming a mother yourself? If so, find a trusted friend, pastor, or counselor to help you process these areas.

How do you feel about the idea that God sees and understands you even when your mother may not?

How can your pregnancy be an opportunity for a new beginning in your relationship with your mother?

16 weeks

Finding Balance – A God Who Gives Good Direction

And now, dear brothers and sisters, one final thing. Fix your thoughts on what is true, honorable, right, pure, lovely, and admirable. Think about things that are excellent and worthy of praise.

Philippians 4:8, NLT

There is much to think about these few weeks as you prepare for the upcoming big transition. If you are a student, should you still apply for school? If you have a job, should you work full-time or cut down your hours after the baby arrives? Who will help with childcare?

The questions are overwhelming, and the logistics seem endless. How do we find calm in these moments of panic?

Multitasking and balancing priorities are new skills that your pregnancy is teaching you. Yes, you are officially a grown-up. But sometimes, it can be so overwhelming that we can shut down.

But fortunately, God has given mothers a measuring stick for our priority lists in the book of Philippians 4:8, NLT:

> *Whatever is true, honorable, and right.*
> *Whatever is pure, lovely, and admirable.*
> *Whatever is excellent and worthy of praise.*

If we measure our priorities against this list, we can quickly sort through what needs to be shredded. And the answers to these questions will be different for each mama.

Where should you spend your time so that you can stay true and honorable to who you are? You will need to know your priorities in order to make decisions that reflect the time spent on each of these priorities.

What do you want your children to remember about you? Will you choose the most admirable thing? Perhaps this is being a stay-at-home mom. Your children may need you to be more present at home. Perhaps this is being a working mother. You may need to be a working mom to survive financially. Sometimes you may not have a choice. But your children will remember how you spend time with them after work. There are different callings for each woman with their unique gifts and circumstances. If God has called you to work outside of the home, He will provide a way to care for your home and work. The best salary that you may ever receive may be quality time with your children.

What is worthy of praise in your motherhood? Proverbs 31 talks about the woman who is praised by her children. She is present at home and resourceful with her family's earnings. What will your children say about you on a Mother's Day card? Will they say that you were present or that you were always distracted with the next thing?

These verses from Philippians help you focus your priorities so that the time you have available for your children can be purposeful.

To improve your time management, remaining grounded in your priorities will help you know what is important to accomplish for the moment. The dishes can wait. The report may be less polished. And it's okay. Because your role as your children's mother is irreplaceable.

Ask yourself:
Do you have good things or worthy things on your schedule?

> *Good things give temporary happiness, but worthy things last forever. Good things are expendable, and worthy things are laced with regret if lost.*

You are replaceable at any job except for being your child's mommy. The quicker you realize this, the sooner you can say no to the good things and save your "yes" for your worthy things.

Often, we know which events on our schedules are right, admirable, and worthy, but we still try to do everything. We are usually over-confident in our multitasking ability and so we keep going until we crash. But if we take the time to pause, we can evaluate if worthy things are getting compromised by all of our commitments. Pregnancy is often a mandatory pause to re-evaluate these commitments. Learning to balance the good things with the worthy things is a lifelong dance.

When you seek His kingdom first, God will show you what you need to do (and what you don't need to do). He will fill in all the cracks if you keep His purposes the center of your life.

Reflection Questions:

What are my current priorities, and how do they align with these qualities listed in Philippians 4:8?

How can I balance the good things in my life with the worthy things with eternal value?

Fill out the below chart with the things that are "good" in your life and decide whether or not they add eternal value to your life.

Good Things	Worthy Things

Am I over-committed or over-confident in my ability to multitask? How can I evaluate my commitments to ensure that worthy things are not being compromised?

What is God calling me to do in this season of life, and how can I seek His kingdom first in all that I do? How can I trust Him to fill in the gaps and bring to completion what He has called me to do?

17 weeks

Learning to Self-Care – God Cares For Our Physical Needs

Then he (Elijah) lay down and slept under the broom tree. But as he was sleeping, an angel touched him and told him, 'Get up and eat.' He looked around and there beside his head was some bread baked on hot stones and a jar of water! So he ate and drank and lay down again. Then the angel of the Lord came again and touched him and said, 'Get up and eat some more, or the journey ahead will be too much for you.' So he got up and ate and drank, and the food gave him enough strength to travel forty days and forty nights to Mount Sinai, the mountain of God.

1 Kings 19:5–8, NLT

One of the hardest parts of motherhood is learning your limits. We want to believe we can sacrifice endlessly for our children because we love them. We want to believe our energy is enough to keep up with them. We can tough out a vaginal delivery, push through breastfeeding barriers, and discipline our children to ensure they are well-behaved. Determination accomplishes all goals, right? But the conviction we may feel during the day often comes out as anxiety at night.

Do you lie awake at night, perseverating on what you must do to prepare for the baby? Or do you shame yourself with what you haven't done for your other children?

Every mother realizes sooner or later that there is a limit to how much she can push herself (and those around her). Mothers tend to run on empty until the engine completely breaks. There is a hamster wheel to buy the newest fad, to make organic baby food, to be enrolled in the Harvard preschool—it is no wonder mothers go to bed exhausted, wondering if they have accomplished enough for the day!

In 1 Kings, Elijah was running for his life. He finally sat down under a tree and wished to die. It was too much for him, and he was in his victim vortex.

At that moment, God did not lecture him. He did not ask Elijah why he was of little faith. God was not angry with Elijah for his inability to push through his exhaustion. God did not demand obedience at this moment. Instead, He cared tenderly for his crying child, like a mother comforting her newborn.

God cared for his physical needs by encouraging Elijah to rest. The Angel of God then made him not just any bread but bread baked on hot stones. It was fresh bread with a crispy crust and a warm, soft inside. God encouraged Elijah to drink a jug of water. And then He let Elijah sleep some more. God knew Elijah needed both restorative and preparative rest. The journey of forty days and forty nights was about to begin, so God nurtured Elijah like a baby.

It is not a coincidence that pregnancy is forty weeks long, and Elijah was about to go on a forty-day journey into the wilderness.

Pregnancy is a forty-week wilderness. There is no comfortable position to sleep in, so you might as well be sleeping in the bush. Temperature regulation is a challenge. And the path is not always clear in the wilderness.

But God will care for you during the forty weeks of pregnancy. He knows this is a long journey for you. And He will continue to provide for you after your baby arrives.

He loves to restore those who ask. Unfortunately, we often don't ask until we finally crash.

Knowing the warning signs of your exhaustion is an important skill. Being aware of your cues for exhaustion helps you be aware of when you need to take a physical rest from the demands of motherhood. An exhausted mother is resentful, impatient, and irrational. But a rested mother is resilient, patient, and clear-minded.

What are the cues of exhaustion? Trouble focusing, getting anxious and depressed, and feeling burned out all the time. If you find yourself exhausted, it will be important to prioritize your basic needs. Take a nap instead of having a clean house. Spend time reading your Bible intentionally and praying purposefully. Eat balanced meals with small snacks consisting of fiber and protein to steady your blood sugar. Choose an earlier bedtime. If being with people energizes you, spend time with them. If being with people exhausts you, take a social rain check. Learn to trust a babysitter so that you can take the respite needed from overwhelming motherhood.

You can prepare for motherhood by accepting a more inefficient you. It's okay to have limitations.

We know our children have limitations, right? When your frazzled toddler acts out in an overtired or a hangry tantrum, you know what he needs. A nap and a snack can give you a completely new child.

If we can read our children's limits, God can also read our limits as well. If you are getting overstimulated in this motherhood journey, you may need to take a break to focus on your basic needs. Please rest, my friend. He wants to feed you. He wants to fill you. He will give you strength for the journey when you rest.

Reflection Questions:

Have you ever found yourself pushing past your physical or emotional limits? What were the consequences of doing so?

Are you able to recognize your cues for exhaustion? If not, what can you do to become more aware of them? Are you an exhausted mother, or are you a rested mother?

How can you incorporate intentional rest and self-care into your daily routine?

Have you ever experienced God's provision for your physical or emotional needs during a difficult time? How did it change how you processed your circumstance?

18 weeks

Stress Management – God Helps Us Cope

We are hard pressed on every side, but not crushed; perplexed, but not in despair; persecuted, but not abandoned; struck down, but not destroyed. We always carry around in our body the death of Jesus, so that the life of Jesus may also be revealed in our body.

2 Corinthians 4:8–10, NIV

Children are pros at pushing buttons on their parents' last nerve. How many shades of red can mommy turn today? Like oxygen to a flame, they feed off their parents' stress and vice versa. Our maternal stress is palpable to our children in utero and out of the womb. Have you seen children act out more when their parents are stressed? Our children are mirrors to our stress management, whether we like it or not.

This connection begins in the womb. The maternal stress hormone, cortisol, crosses the placenta[11]. During maternal stress, the baby receives a rush of adrenaline, which can cause the baby's heart rate and sometimes cause the baby to be more active than usual.

Mamas and babies are connected starting in utero. I have observed the mother/baby mind-body connection on ultrasound. An anxious mother, pregnant at thirty-two weeks, arrived at the hospital in a panic when she was sent in for elevated blood pressure. Initially, both her and the baby's heart rates were elevated. As the mother listened to quiet music in a dark room, both her heart rate and the baby's heart rate calmed down. When I placed the ultrasound probe on her abdomen,

---

[11] Birthe R. Dahlerup et al., "Maternal Stress and Placental Function, a Study Using Questionnaires and Biomarkers at Birth," PLOS ONE 13, no. 11 (November 15, 2018): e0207184, https://doi.org/10.1371/journal.pone.0207184.

the effects of the classical music were astounding. Not only did the baby's heart rate calm with music, but the baby turned to his mother's voice—specifically, her singing voice - which calmed the baby's movements. Her pulse and blood pressure came back to normal.

Our stress amplifies our children's stress.

So, let's come up with some wise ways to manage our stress, because stress management skills are needed for the rest of motherhood!

Here are few techniques to consider:

- *Mental health specialists teach "grounding" to help with anxiety surrounding the unknown.*
  Grounding keeps us engaged with the present time rather than focusing on future hypothetical disasters. Grounding enlists the five senses to help us recognize the here and now, affirming that there is no danger in the present. By redirecting our minds to the present, grounding diffuses the fight-or-flight body response, bringing down heart rate and blood pressure. This physical calming allows our thoughts to slow down and the panic to decrease[12].
- *God grounds us when we bring the focus of our five senses to His creation.* Changing your context is one of the best ways to manage stress in pregnancy and motherhood. Take a walk outside where you can feel the sun, smell the flowers, hear the birds, and run your feet through the grass. As you focus on His provision for even the birds and the lilies, you will be amazed at how this same Creator cares for you and your pregnancy.
- *Take time to diffuse your emotions so that you can hear the truth.* If you don't take the time to reset your mind on the truth, emotions will win. In the pressure cooker of pregnancy, emotions are extreme. But when you have had your chance to shout at the wind, you will be able to think more clearly.

---

[12] Crystal Raypole, "30 Grounding Techniques to Quiet Distressing Thoughts," Healthline, September 15, 2023, https://www.healthline.com/health/grounding-techniques#soothing-techniques.

- *Be aware of how "black-and-white thinking" can create unnecessary stress[13]*. Black-and-white thinking occurs when thought patterns are extreme. Everything is all good or all bad. Do you worry about all the worst-case scenarios that can occur in the future? Extreme emotions give us extreme thoughts. But for most life stressors, we will see our true reality when we have time to regroup. Extremes are not as severe as we may have thought initially. Most situations are gray rather than black and white.

The next time you feel like you are getting stress overload, take a minute to regroup by trying the above methods. A counselor can help you understand your thought patterns and how to diffuse your stress.

But even with the best stress management techniques, it is important to address *why* we are stressed. Ultimately, the best stress-management is being aware of the spiritual issues that surround the unknown.

Can you trust God with your worst-case scenarios? If you are currently going through your worst-case scenario, reflect on Paul's approach to his trial. Paul was in prison and in chains when he wrote his letter to the church in Corinth. He had just gone through shipwreck and abandonment, but somehow, his spirit was still strong.

> *We are **hard pressed** on every side, but not crushed; **perplexed**, but not in despair; **persecuted**, but not abandoned; **struck down**, but not destroyed. (2 Corinthians 4:8-10 NIV, Emphasis added).*

An outsider looking in would describe him as hard-pressed, perplexed, persecuted, and struck down. Paul was in a worst-case scenario. And yet Paul described his situation as *not* crushed, *not* despairing, *not* abandoned, *nor* destroyed.

Where did the strength of his faith come from?

---

[13] Rebecca Joy Stanborough Mfa, "How Black and White Thinking Hurts You (and What You Can Do to Change It)," Healthline, January 14, 2020, https://www.healthline.com/health/mental-health/black-and-white-thinking.

The answer lies in the following verse 10:
We always carry around in our body the death of Jesus, so that the life of Jesus may also be revealed in our body. 2 Corinthians 4:10, NIV

There will be "scars" in our hearts that reflect Jesus' death. But those who hope in Jesus will have a new life that is revealed through these scars. There is always life after wounds. In God's kingdom, wounds are not the worst-case scenario.

There are always unexpected stressors and wounds we may not anticipate. But if your life is grounded in being like Jesus, you will not fear the same things you may have feared before. With your perspective rooted in eternal things, you will stress less!

Reflection Questions:

How can you change your context when you feel overwhelmed and stressed?

How does reflecting on 2 Corinthians 4 help you gain perspective and hope in difficult situations?

What steps can you take to prioritize your stress management, especially during pregnancy and motherhood?

How can you model healthy stress management for your children?

19 weeks

Am I Doing Enough? God Is Already Enough

But we have this treasure in jars of clay, to show that this all-surpassing power is from God and not from us.

2 Corinthians 4:7, NIV

There is restlessness at this stage of the mid-second trimester. The big change feels so close and yet so far away. Nausea has usually improved, and energy is back. Many women wonder if they should be doing more for their pregnancy. But unless your health care provider advises you otherwise, there are more passive than active requirements of a pregnant mother at this stage.

You may have noticed that you feel like your breathing is more shallow and more frequent. You may feel more winded going up stairs, and exercise routines take more effort than before. You may need to use the bathroom more frequently as the baby dances on your bladder. Your appetite may be back with a vengeance after the first trimester fast.

All of these changes are God's intentional, intelligent design.
Let's marvel at the miracle of the placenta.
Your placenta is a multi-organ system all in one.

Your placenta is your baby's lungs. As you breathe more frequently during pregnancy, you release more carbon dioxide, which keeps the body at a perfect pH level. This pH change is needed for the placenta to transfer oxygen to the baby.

Your placenta is also your baby's kidneys, filtering the baby's wastes. She gives it all back to your kidneys to deliver to its proper receptacle.

Your placenta is also a digestive system. Your gut breaks down the food you eat into fatty acids and amino acids that are passed through the protective sieve of the placenta. The placenta absorbs the nutrients and sugar, passing them through the umbilical vein to become the building blocks of the baby's organs. The miraculous placenta acts like a train station, as a mastermind conductor coordinating the timetables of all arrivals and departures.[14]

You are eating for two, breathing for two, peeing for two—and I am sure you feel it more days than not! You are a vessel, now carrying a precious child of God. Your child will thank you for being the vessel (someday, hopefully!).

So, what can you do in this second trimester? Unless your doctors say otherwise, you are already doing enough by being "the vessel."

What is a vessel in the kingdom of God?
The vessel that is in 2 Corinthians 4:7 is a jar of clay.
It is fragile and breakable.

We can do our best to make our vessel the most hospitable place for a baby to grow. But what happens inside the vessel is up to the Potter. Our child's development is ultimately in the hands of the Potter, who makes a beautiful creation within the vessel.

This is why pregnancy is so terrifying: there is no formula, no exact protocol to follow, and no measure of hard work that can determine the ultimate outcome with one hundred percent certainty.

But there are some decisions you have to make repeatedly during pregnancy.
You decide:

> *Whether or not you trust the Potter in all things.*
> *Whether or not you will let God's power be shown through your vessel.*
> *And whether or not you will allow yourself to be the clay.*

The vessel in 2 Corinthians was once a moldable piece of clay, soft in

---

[14] Graham J. Burton and Abigail L. Fowden, "The Placenta: A Multifaceted, Transient Organ," Philosophical Transactions of the Royal Society B 370, no. 1663 (March 5, 2015): 20140066, https://doi.org/10.1098/rstb.2014.0066.

the Potter's hand for whatever purpose it was made for. Will you be a pitcher or a vase, or will you contain oil? Every vessel is made differently for its unique purpose. Will you be open to whatever motherhood journey God gives you?

God has designed you to be a vessel that holds His treasure. He knows what He is doing. His miraculous placenta is likely already doing enough for your baby.

It is not whether we are doing enough.
It is whether we believe He is enough.

Reflection Questions:

How can I trust God's design and plan for my pregnancy, even when there is no exact protocol to follow?

How can I let God's power be shown through my vessel during this time?

Am I willing to be moldable, like the vessel in 2 Corinthians, and open to whatever motherhood journey God has in store for me?

20 weeks
Perfectly Imperfect – God Does Not Make Mistakes

> *For God, who said, 'Let light shine out of darkness,' has shone in our hearts to give the light of the knowledge of the glory of God in the face of Jesus Christ. But we have this treasure in jars of clay, to show that the surpassing power belongs to God and not to us.*
>
> 2 Corinthians 4:6–7, ESV

Your healthcare provider will be ordering an anatomy ultrasound of your baby during this time of your pregnancy. Ultrasound can detect many things, such as risk factors for preterm labor or if there is an issue with the location of the placenta. The second-trimester ultrasound also looks at the baby's anatomy. Many parents do not sigh in relief until they see their baby on this ultrasound. I have often heard parents say, "I don't care if I'm having a boy or a girl. As long as it's healthy." But how does the Christian define health?

Ultrasounds detect patterns of normal and abnormal fetal development. Your anatomy ultrasound illuminates what your baby has been doing the last few months. Most of these anatomy ultrasounds are normal, but sometimes ultrasounds will detect abnormalities. If there are any abnormalities, your doctor will likely recommend more ultrasounds during the pregnancy. But in many cases, your doctor may not know how this ultrasound abnormality will truly impact the baby's function until the baby is born.

Sometimes, the course is clear, and sometimes, it is unclear. It can be a long wait for many parents when they receive diagnoses that have unknown long-term significance. Furthermore, a normal ultrasound does not guarantee a healthy child. Many developmental concerns cannot be diagnosed until after a child's birth and will not be seen on ultrasound. For example, autism is not detectable by a blood test. Addiction does not have a prenatal screening test. There is not one test that guarantees perfect children.

Ultimately, there are limits to what these tests tell us about our children and their adult lives. Many details are uncertain at the time of an abnormal ultrasound.

But what is certain for the Christian is that God is creating your little one for His purpose. Sometimes, His purpose requires your child's perfect health. And sometimes His purpose does not.

When an imperfect ultrasound arises, a mother is quick to blame herself as the cause of her baby's different development. The initial reaction is that her womb is broken. I have seen women apologize to their partners when there is a birth defect or when there is a stillbirth. Women take on both the victories and the self-blame for their wombs.

The passage from 2 Corinthians 4 is worth repeating this week. When pregnancy is going well, women struggle with doing and being enough. But when women are facing the woes of the womb, the guilt magnifies even more.

In verses 1–6, the light of the gospel is contrasted with darkness. Jesus shines out of the darkness. Verse 7 describes a cracked jar of clay with light inside. The beams of light stream through its broken edges, illuminating the silhouette of its cracks. A perfect jar cannot show this light - it is only a broken vessel that allows God's power to shine through it. The treasure of light inside the vessel is not a perfect baby but a relationship with Christ.

Broken vessels are treasured in the kingdom of God. If you find yourself dealing with pregnancy loss at this stage of pregnancy, a cervix that is dilating when it shouldn't, or a birth defect seen on ultrasound, it may feel like your body is betraying you. You thought you were already doing enough. Or maybe you believed the lie that you should have done more. Regardless, God is still doing good work through your vessel.

God works through all of His perfectly imperfect creation. And He can still do good work in your vessel through its imperfections. A vessel's responsibility is not to be perfect but to be pliable. A broken vessel is perfectly imperfect.

Let's change "as long as" to "even if."
Even if your child is healthy or is not healthy,
even if you have a normal or abnormal ultrasound,
even if you are dealing with a late miscarriage in the second trimester-
None of these scenarios are outside of God's tender arms.
He blesses us in surprising ways in our "even if" scenarios.

Do you believe this? Then, whatever happens at this ultrasound, you will be okay, my friend.

Reflection Questions:
How do you view imperfection? Do you see it as something to be ashamed of or something that can be used for God's purpose?

How can you practice being pliable amid imperfection and allow God to work through you?

How can you change your mindset from "as long as" to "even if" and trust God's plan even in difficult circumstances? Write down the phrases that are determining your happiness for this pregnancy. For example, is a healthy baby the only way you can be happy about motherhood? If so, ask God if He can give you a deeper love and great peace for the "even if."

21 weeks

Cherishing the In-Laws – God Chooses Grace

> *All that you have done for your mother-in-law since the death of your husband has been fully told to me, and how you left your father and mother and your native land and came to a people that you did not know before. The Lord repay you for what you have done, and a full reward be given you by the Lord, the God of Israel, under whose wings you have come to take refuge.*
>
> Ruth 2:11–12, ESV

Will your child have dimples like mommy? A strong nose like daddy? Her grandmother's musical abilities? Or his grandfather's knack for cracking jokes? Some traits of your baby are genetically determined the moment egg and sperm dance—blood type, eye color, hair color, and whether he will be bald (at forty years old, that is, no guarantees about birth[15]).

However, your child's character traits are more likely influenced by your nurturing. How secure is his relationship with his parents? And how will the extended family support this new person?

A baby is bonding two families together whether they like it or not. Combined genetic pools have now intertwined two families for the rest of their lives. Your spouse's family will be intimately connected with yours, for better or worse. Children are a beautiful bond of unity for some families. But for other families, the next generation exposes the fragile cracks. The politeness fades when children are at the center,

---

[15] Lumen Learning, "Heredity and Chromosomes | Lifespan Development," Accessed 7/31/2023, https://courses.lumenlearning.com/wm-lifespandevelopment/chapter/heredity-and-chromosomes/.

and boxing gloves come off. So, how do we have in-law relationships centered on unity rather than dysfunction?

Ruth and Naomi are the most well-known in-law relationship in the Bible. Ruth was married to Naomi's son, Mahlon, for ten years before he died. During this decade, Ruth was childless and had not taken on the faith of Naomi's family. Instead, she was a Moabite, a foreigner who had married into a family with a different religion than hers.

Her mother-in-law, Naomi, permitted her daughter-in-law to go back to her family and start over. It would have been easy and almost expected for Ruth to leave her mother-in-law at that moment. After all, Ruth was grieving herself. She had lost her husband. Ruth had every right to care for herself now rather than someone else.

Yet, Ruth chose to stay with this embittered woman in this tempting exit strategy. Despite Ruth's loyalty, Naomi called herself "Bitter," focusing on the emptiness in her life instead of the love of her daughter-in-law by her side.

So what would prompt Ruth to stay?

- *Ruth was able to stay with her embittered mother-in-law because she had great compassion for her.* She saw Naomi's suffering, and it broke her heart. Ruth did not see a critical or an embittered woman. Instead, she saw a hurting and grieving woman.

- *Ruth went into the relationship not expecting her mother-in-law to change, but instead, Ruth made the decision to change herself.* "Your people will be my people and your God my God." (Ruth 1:16). It was Ruth's kindness and loyalty that began the healing of Naomi's broken heart.

The story continued with a wedding and a redemptive birth. By God's divine, sovereign plan, Ruth remarried a family member impressed with her loyalty. Boaz and Ruth had a son that restored Naomi's joy. Ruth became the great-grandmother of King David and part of Jesus Christ's lineage. God used this important in-law relationship to bring about the greatest kings of all time.

Pregnancy brings out tension with the older generation whether we like it or not. They may have had different parenting methods. They may preach at the most inopportune times. But we are still called to honor them.

Honoring our parents and in-laws is different from pleasing them at all costs. Honoring parents means that we respect their opinions even when we do not agree. Honoring parents means we don't have to convince them we are correct. Honoring parents means that we remain open and teachable to their wisdom.

We honor our parents not to receive from them but because we honor God. He chose to love us even when we had nothing to offer Him (Romans 5:8). Even when our in-laws have opinions contrary to ours, we can accept their advice graciously. For we honor God when we honor our in-laws. When honoring God is first and foremost, we will demand less of our in-laws and ask more of ourselves. The relationship becomes sweeter when we give it to God.

Reflection Questions:

How can you respect your parents or parents-in-law's opinions and wisdom while making decisions that align with your values and beliefs?

Think about a challenging relationship with an in-law or any person of authority in your life. How might your perspective change if you could see them as a hurting and grieving person rather than a critical or embittered one?

Reflect on the story of Ruth and Naomi. What lessons can you learn from their relationship about compassion, loyalty, and healing in difficult circumstances? How can you apply these lessons to your own relationships with in-laws?

22 weeks

The Battle of Comparison – God Gives Us Contentment

> *O Lord, my heart is not lifted up; my eyes are not raised too high; I do not occupy myself with things too great and too marvelous for me. But I have calmed and quieted my soul, like a weaned child with its mother; like a weaned child is my soul within me. Psalm 131:1–2, ESV*

From here on out, there will always be a mother who has it more together than you do. She will have a blog showing her perfect pregnancy with her perfect baby bump and perfect hair. It does not take more than thirty seconds on social media to feel like something is missing in your life. Comparison is a robber of joy. Because everyone has it together for a millisecond snap on the internet.

A mama's comparison to others begins while the baby is still in her womb. A baby's growth percentile is charted on a growth curve against the averages for each gestational age. These growth charts continue with a child's pediatrician. These charts can become the bane of a mother's existence when her children fall off or exceed the growth curve. Some comparisons are good in healthcare because they help doctors care for the outliers. But there are also some comparisons that can be damaging to a mother's spirit.

You will need to be aware of your triggers to survive social media (and the playground). There are many minefields in motherhood, so being aware of your triggers is half the battle. Your friends may have more disciplined, smarter, or more talented children than yours. Protecting yourself from these triggers may mean a social media break. Surrounding yourself with friends who are not competing against you is important.

How do we find contentment in a world that looks better than ours?

- *Finding contentment with what is rather than what isn't.*

    You will need to make a choice whether contentment is relative to those around you. How has God provided for your needs for today? And if it is unclear today, how did He provide for your needs yesterday? Clinging to God's unique provisions for your unique situation is how your glass remains half full.

- *Knowing your worth is absolute and not relative to others.*

    If your worth is defined by how close you are to the norm or how much better you are than the norm, you will find yourself in a dizzying maze with no end. Comparison either drives you crazy or drives you to your knees. What God says about you needs to define your worth because this does not change. You are chosen (1 Peter 2:9) and saved by grace (Ephesians 2:8–9).

- *Redefine the purpose of your race.*

    How do we find peace amid all the competition? We must get on our knees first if we want to leave the race. We must believe that the goal is not to win. The goal is to know our tender and all-knowing Coach. Our victories and failures fuel our pride when the race is about us. But when the race is to know our Coach, we can run through any hurdle with endurance. The best part of the race is that He is running alongside us.

King David, one of the greatest kings of ancient Israel, recognized his true identity. His heart was "not lifted up," nor his eyes "raised too high." David recognized who he was in relation to God, not in relation to others.

In a few months, you will know the cry of a newborn hungry for his mother's milk. It is a frantic cry that is soothed only by his mother. In contrast, while still dependent on his mother, a weaned child is content being in her presence. The weaned child in Psalm 131 is calm and quiet with his mother. We can have this same relationship with God—dependent and content in His presence.

Comparison is self-centered.
But contentment is God-centered.

Tell someone if you struggle to see the good in your life. You may need the eyes of someone else who can see God's faithfulness to you. Ask God to show you His fingerprints of mercy. You will see things you have never seen before when He opens your eyes.

Look up and then look down at the grass under your feet.

The grass on your side is very, very green.

Reflection Questions:

What triggers me to feel inadequate or not good enough compared to others?

How do I define my worth, and is it based on how I compare to others or on my relationship with God? You are chosen (1 Peter 2:9) and saved by grace (Ephesians 2:8–9). These things do not change based on how much weight you gain, how many stretch marks you have, and how many friends you have. This week, spend time thanking God for how these absolute truths change everything.

How can I cultivate a relationship with God where I am content in His presence, regardless of my circumstances or how I compare to others? Are there friendships that I need to invest in that are more positive influences? Are there friendships that I need to have careful boundaries so I do not go to a place of envy in my heart?

23 weeks

The Hormonal RollerCoaster – God Gives Self-Control

For God gave us a spirit not of fear but of power and love and self-control.

2 Timothy 1:7, ESV

Pregnancy is a hormone soup. While some love the endorphins, most women are riding the emotional rollercoaster of pregnancy. Some emotions are well-founded. After all, there is a big change happening. You may be grieving how your life will change while also excited about what your life will become. But sometimes, emotions are so extreme that pregnant women can become almost impossible. Pregnancy is so hormonal that even the most rational person becomes a hot mess of emotions.

So, while you melt, let's discuss the hormones causing this meltdown[16]. You are experiencing a surge of estrogen, progesterone, testosterone (especially if you're having a boy), prolactin, relaxin, and human chorionic gonadotropin, to name a few[17].

These hormones are changing your body's capacity to carry a growing baby. These tiny molecules can create incredible havoc in your body, mind, and heart. They have purposeful functions, but they also can cause much drama.

---

[16] Lily Wan et al., "Reproduction-Associated Hormones and Adult Hippocampal Neurogenesis," Neural Plasticity 2021 (September 10, 2021): 1–20, https://doi.org/10.1155/2021/3651735.

[17] Sathish Kumar et al., "Androgens in Maternal Vascular and Placental Function: Implications for Preeclampsia Pathogenesis," Reproduction, November 1, 2018, R155–67, https://doi.org/10.1530/rep-18-0278.

While your mother's heart grows, your brain is shrinking from all the hormonal changes. A mother's brain matter shrinks in the prefrontal cortex, the temporal cortex, and right ventral striae when comparing pre- and post-pregnancy brain structures[18]. These areas of your brain give you a rational filter, regulate your emotions, and interpret if something is good.

Thus, your ability to control your emotions is physically affected by your brain changes. You may have more trouble staying calm, crying at the drop of a hat, and feeling like you're not thinking as clearly.

But please do not be discouraged by this. Interestingly, the women who have the most brain shrinkage are more likely to bond better with their infants. In this case, less is more! The brain changes persist even six years after the baby is born[19]. So yes, "placenta brain" and "mommy brain" are real! The more your brain shrinks, the better connection you may have with your child!

These changes in mothers' brains are part of God's way of preparing us for motherhood. A mother's emotional brain is awakened because mothers are being prepared to comfort their young[20].

Her brain's filter is changing to become more defensive and more easily angered. God is giving mothers a protective instinct with these brain changes. Officially, the mama bear is born.

This is a beautiful brain change! But our emotions must be held carefully, especially when they have warpath potential. When you become a mama, you may have difficulty controlling your emotions. Suddenly, you may have become aware of everything that can go wrong.

---

[18] Hoekzema, E., Barba-Müller, E., Pozzobon, C. et al. Pregnancy leads to long-lasting changes in human brain structure. Nat Neurosci 20, 287–296 (2017).

[19] Elisa Rehbein et al., "Shaping of the Female Human Brain by Sex Hormones: A Review," Neuroendocrinology 111, no. 3 (March 11, 2020): 183–206, https://doi.org/10.1159/000507083.

[20] Elseline Hoekzema et al., "Becoming a Mother Entails Anatomical Changes in the Ventral Striatum of the Human Brain That Facilitate Its Responsiveness to Offspring Cues," Psychoneuroendocrinology 112 (February 1, 2020): 104507, https://doi.org/10.1016/j.psyneuen.2019.104507.

Fear causes mamas to react, behave, and parent differently.
Fear can also cause mamas to become defensive and abrasive.

If you are driving life on your own, fear may feel powerful. Filling the tank with fear keeps the car running, but it is a stressful drive . . . for everyone.

For the Christian, there is a different driver. The Holy Spirit drives the Christian with power, love, and self-control.

> *For God gave us a spirit not of fear but of power and love and self-control.* 2 Timothy 1:7, ESV

Our spirit does not need to be controlled by our fears because God has given us a spirit of power so that we do not need to be afraid. The Holy Spirit can give us love for even the most obnoxious person in our lives. And the Holy Spirit can give us self-control even when we want to freak out.

With all the hormonal brain changes of pregnancy, we are susceptible to irrational responses in our relationships. Recognizing and owning the irrational outbursts is how our relationships can thrive during pregnancy. When it is clear that we have hurt someone, we should own our actions. Because ultimately, we are still accountable to God even amidst our brain changes.

Recognize the "irrational" love that is being woven in you. Your brain is going through the necessary changes to become a mother. Your soul is also going through the necessary changes to thrive in motherhood. When you let your soul be driven by the Holy Spirit rather than your fears, it will be a much easier ride.

Reflection Questions:

How have the hormonal changes of pregnancy affected your emotions and relationships?

Have you experienced any irrational outbursts or defensiveness during pregnancy? How did you handle those situations?

How can you recognize and own your actions when you have hurt someone during pregnancy?

How can you preserve your support system during this time, and why is it important?

24 weeks

For the Fatherless: God Is a Loving Father

> "Sing to God, sing praises to his name; lift up a song to him who rides through the deserts; his name is the Lord; exult before him! Father of the fatherless and protector of widows is God in his holy habitation. God settles the solitary in a home; he leads out the prisoners to prosperity, but the rebellious dwell in a parched land."
>
> Psalm 68:4–6, ESV

Are you experiencing little foot flutters? Invasive jabs? Daddy may be feeling more of the baby's movements now. He has seen you growing in love with this little person inside you over the last few months. But his connection to this little being has been formless. That is until he begins to develop his dad bod. The midnight cravings of mommies are consumed by dutiful daddies as well. Next time you're at the doctor's office, ask the nurses to weigh him too!

For men who want to become fathers, supporting their partner is an exhilarating experience. They can't wait to hear their baby's heartbeat at the doctor's appointments. They come armed with a notebook of questions, proudly holding their wife's purse and belongings. An involved father makes an astronomical difference in a woman's pregnancy experience.

You can help him succeed as a father if you let him care for you. You can help him feel useful if you let him protect you.

You can help him feel a part of the baby's life by involving him in the baby's name selection or the nursery decor, just to name a few ways.

But not all women have men who know how to support them. Not all men know how to be fathers. They may have been fatherless. Or the father they knew provided a meal on the table and not a relationship. Men may want to become better fathers than the ones they had, but they may not know how to break the cycle. It takes determination, mentorship, and the mercy of God to reset his course.

If you are in a lonely marriage, a new child layered onto a broken marriage accelerates the pressure cooker. But God can transform even stubborn hearts if you both have teachable spirits. Be willing to "go there" with your spouse and a marriage counselor, for better or worse. You may need to heal individually before you can heal as a couple.

Some women believe that a baby will change their partner or hope that he will grow up when he becomes a father. While this is sometimes the case, having a baby does not always accelerate his maturity. If you find yourself excusing his abusive behavior or accepting mistreatment, it is important to be honest with yourself. Then, tell someone who will listen without judgment. Tell someone who knows how to advocate for you. If this is not a family member, tell your healthcare provider. If you feel unsafe in your relationship or believe your children are in danger, you need to get help. Maternity homes and other support services exist to walk alongside you (https://natlhousingcoalition.org). Finding a church that cares for heartbroken mothers can help you feel less alone. It takes courage to admit this isn't okay and you need help.

No child is born to a perfect mommy and a perfect daddy. Even the best marriages struggle with parenthood. Even the best earthly daddy is flawed.

But we can trust God is a perfect Father who protects and provides for His children.

Psalm 68 says God is a Father of the fatherless and a protector of widows. God settles the solitary in a home. He leads the prisoners to prosperity, but the rebellious dwell in a parched land. He is a responsible Father who will ride through the desert with us when no one else will. For the single mother who knows Him, He will provide a holy home. For the woman who feels imprisoned by her situation, God can free her heart. For the man who rebels against the responsibility of fatherhood, he is choosing a parched land for himself.

Pregnancy can be an isolating and lonely experience. Even a supportive partner cannot completely understand all the physical discomforts and emotional swings of pregnancy. But if you have a partner who is willing to partner with you, take the time to thank him today for caring. Let him know the specific ways you appreciate him. Your appreciation will go a long way in helping him become the best father he can be.

But even if he does not protect you, your Heavenly Father will. It may look different from what you expect, but He will send others to care for you. Even if you are a single mother, your child is not fatherless. God loves your child. He will send other relationships to fill in this role for your children. And even if your partner does not provide for you, you can trust God to provide for you. For He is a Father who protects His children who call on Him for help.

Reflection Questions:

Have you communicated your needs and desires to your partner regarding his involvement in the pregnancy and fatherhood?

If you are in a lonely marriage or facing challenges with your partner, are you open to seeking help and counseling to benefit your relationship and child? If he is not loving you as Christ loved the church, will you talk to wise counsel from your church?

How does the description of God as a Father of the fatherless and a protector of widows resonate with you? Can you trust in His provision and care for you and your child, even if your earthly circumstances are challenging?

How can you express appreciation and gratitude to your baby's father for his support and involvement during this pregnancy?

25 weeks

Unity, The Best Gift – God Heals The Impossible

Therefore a man shall leave his father and mother and hold fast to his wife, and the two shall become one flesh.' So they are no longer two but one flesh. What therefore God has joined together, let not man separate.

Mark 10:7–9, ESV

In a few weeks, your doctor will be recommending a blood test to screen you for gestational diabetes. You will be given a syrupy drink and then will wait one hour before your blood is drawn. This will measure how well your body metabolizes sugar. If your blood sugar is too high, you may be diagnosed with gestational diabetes. Pregnant women are more susceptible to diabetes because of their placentas[21]. Your placenta is releasing a hormone called human placental lactogen (hPL) that causes your body to be resistant to insulin. With increasing insulin resistance, sugar remains in your blood rather than being taken up by your body's cells, which can cause diabetes.

God made hPL so that mothers' bodies could make sugar more accessible to their growing baby. Some insulin resistance is helpful because it allows babies to receive more sugar for growth. However, with rising rates of obesity, insulin resistance has become too resistant, causing blood sugars to be too high. And now gestational diabetes affects approximately 2–10% of all pregnancies[22].

---

[21] Rafał Sibiak et al., "Placental Lactogen as a Marker of Maternal Obesity, Diabetes, and Fetal Growth Abnormalities: Current Knowledge and Clinical Perspectives," Journal of Clinical Medicine 9, no. 4 (April 16, 2020): 1142, https://doi.org/10.3390/jcm9041142.

[22] "Gestational Diabetes," Centers for Disease Control and Prevention, March 2, 2022, https://www.cdc.gov/diabetes/basics/gestational.html.

Something that was meant to be good has now become pathologic.

Similarly, there are relationships outside of the expecting parents that are good. Still, these relationships can also become pathologic if not handled wisely. Relationships without boundaries can damage marriages.

Young parents often struggle with how to say no to a well-meaning village. But a true village will empower you and your spouse to become your family unit. A true village should not demand you meet a need for them. A true village will understand when you need space.

For many couples, their extended families are their village. While family means well, it does not always strengthen the new parental unit. You and your spouse may need to establish good boundaries that work for both of you.

Good boundaries honor your spouse.
Good boundaries allow your spouse to step up because he knows no one else will.

You can honor your marriage by recognizing how your other relationships affect your family unit. Be honest with how his village affects your self-worth. Be honest with how your village is affecting his manhood. It's not easy because we want to be "nice." Still, a discussion about boundaries may ensure the unity of your family.

The Bible discusses the relationship change that must occur between adult children and their parents in Mark 10. In marriage, the husband leaves his family to become a new family with his wife. The Bible describes a "leave and cleave" that happens as the next generation grows. Some families do this well, and others struggle to set these boundaries.

Your "mommy and daddy" unit is vital to your growing child. Unity in the home is one of the greatest gifts you can give your child. The strength of your bond is what gives your children their security. Unfortunately, more things pull marriages apart than keep them together. Small problems in marriage can become colossal if not addressed while the problems are still fixable.

Awareness of the cracks in your relationship will allow you to fix them before they widen. Children do not make cracks better but tend to put more stress on a broken foundation. Sometimes, you may need a new foundation. When you think about it, two sinners have their own ideas of how to parent and how to live. This is a challenging strain on even the strongest relationship. Sometimes, a mediator is needed from a non-biased party. An honest counselor who is willing to see every angle of the relationship can help with forward momentum.

But ultimately, cracks are not repairable by human effort alone. Pray for God to grow your heart for your spouse. Only He can give you the grace to forgive your spouse's shortcomings. Only God can unify two very different people with different families. But for the sake of your child—and ultimately, for the sake of Christ—you owe it to yourself to work on your marriage before your motherhood.

When this baby arrives, the distractions will increase even more. The chasms become easier to ignore until it is too late. But if you commit to pursuing one another now, you will protect your marriage with the boundaries it deserves.

> **Reflection Questions:**
>
> Reflecting on the concept of boundaries, how am I navigating the relationships outside my immediate family? Are there any relationships that may require boundaries to protect the unity of my marriage?
>
> In what ways am I honoring and empowering my spouse in our relationship? How can I ensure that external influences do not negatively impact his self-worth and manhood?
>
> Am I aware of any cracks or vulnerabilities in our relationship? How can I address and repair these issues to ensure a solid foundation for our family?
>
> Can my husband and I commit to work on our marriage even after we have children? This may mean weekly dinner dates, intentionally seeking connection, or putting the phones away.

26 weeks
What's in a Name? God Gives Us An Identity

But to all who did receive him, who believed in his name, he gave the right to become children of God.
John 1:12, ESV

One of the most common questions you hear when you're pregnant is, "Have you picked a name yet?" You may already know the baby's name. A family name? A name that you chose when you got engaged? Certainly, everyone else has an opinion about what the baby's name should be. All the opinions can be overwhelming.

It is an important decision because names are attached to identities.

Names mark a rite of passage in life's different identities. Daughter, friend, sister, girlfriend, wife, to name a few. The Bible often marked a changed life by a change of name. For example, when Abram received the covenant, he became Abraham (Genesis 17:5–6). Saul became Paul after his conversion (Acts 13:9). When you become a mama, you will begin referring to yourself as "mama" when you speak to your children.

The new name of "Mommy," "Mama," or "Mom" can be exciting or jarring when you try it out for the first time. You may wear the new identity proudly by buying every possible t-shirt that announces your new title. Or you may not see yourself as a mother, even if your belly declares it so. Not every woman sees herself as a mother.

The transition to the identity of "mama" is one of the most drastic changes women experience. It takes time to grow into this role. Sometimes, we choose our "mama" label, and sometimes, the "mama" label chooses us. Regardless of how you feel about your new name, a deeper core identity defines who you are.

What's in a Name? God Gives Us An Identity

When a woman recognizes that Jesus saves her from sin, she becomes a daughter in God's world. John says (1 John 3:2) that when you know Jesus, your core identity is a daughter of God.

As a daughter of God, you are a child of the King.
You are a princess in the kingdom of God.

As princesses of another world, we interpret our experiences, successes, and failures differently. Your identity in Christ changes everything.

How does our identity in Christ help us face our challenges as mothers?

- *When we see the world falling apart around our children, Jesus understands.*
  God has a plan to restore this world once and for all. (Revelation 11:15)

- *When we (or our children) experience rejection, Jesus understands.*
  He was rejected too. (Matthew 21:42)

- *When we see our children grieve, Jesus understands.*
  He is well acquainted with grief. (Isaiah 53:3)

- *When our children disobey, Jesus understands.*
  He forgave us so we can forgive them. (Ephesians 4:32)

Jesus understands your challenges as a mother. So many of the motherhood woes are the very woes that Jesus died for on the cross. Let the cross be your core identity—even more central than being a mother. If your core identity is being a follower of Jesus, no challenge of motherhood will be too much.

Whatever defines your core will determine how you cope, how you live, and how you laugh. The names you accumulate in this lifetime are secondary to the core identity that grounds you always and forever.

You are precious, dear daughter of God.

Reflection Questions:

Reflect on the different roles and identities you have assumed throughout your life. How have they shaped your sense of self?

How do you feel about the name "Mommy" or "Mama"? Are you excited, hesitant, or unsure about embracing this new identity?

Reflect on your identity as a daughter of God. How does this new label and relationship with God change your perspective on life, experiences, and your role as a mother?

Third Trimester

The third trimester is the start of appointments every two weeks. The slow beginning sometimes accelerates into a full range of panic. There is usually a renovation or move that occurs during pregnancy. Working women clock more hours in to prepare for maternity leave. Siblings wonder what their new roles will entail. The amount of transitions can be overwhelming. The delicious excitement and simultaneous freak-outs are real.

Sleep usually gets more difficult at this time of the pregnancy. Besides the frequent bathroom wake-ups, mamas' minds are racing in the early morning hours. The nesting instinct that happens for birds happens for human mamas as well. There are many things to prepare and complete before the baby arrives!

And then, of course, all the baby gear.
What to buy, what is safe, what is the best?
Which baby monitor do I buy that is reliable?
Cloth diapers? Disposable diapers?
Baby-food makers?
Which breast pump works like a dream but is small enough to fit in my purse?
Is there a diaper bag that has the swag of a purse?

The list is endless.

When I was pregnant with my first child, I went into a Babies R Us and pretty much had a panic attack. An aisle for just bottles. An alley full of cribs. A wall of diapers. So many well-meaning advertisements tell me how to have the perfect baby experience. Pictures of sleeping babies, idyllic images of breastfeeding, and all things sweet and syrupy.

I was overwhelmed. The internet wasn't much better. Every Amazon baby product had five-star and one-star reviews. Every blog offered conflicting advice to the other.

The number of things to buy and the information overload creates incredible anxiety for a new parent. But is there really any way to prepare enough for parenting?

I spent my entire first pregnancy reading, nesting, and researching. The OBGYN residency taught me how to deliver babies, not how to care for them. My husband, on the other hand, was busy with his oncology fellowship. He was unable to attend most of my prenatal appointments. But when my contractions began, my husband grabbed the nearest Baby411 book. He began flipping through the book like the propeller of an airplane! He has always been a crammer as long as I have known him. He read the entire book by the time I began to push.

When my firstborn arrived, we were ready.
Or so we thought.

I had spent so much time reading information, but when it was time to implement the knowledge, none of it applied. From day one, I had to read my child, not the book.

The third trimester can be overwhelming with all of the information that has been trail-blazed by the mothers before us. But the reality is your motherhood experience will be unique. Your birth experience will be different from everyone else's. Your baby's temperament is going to be different from all other babies. There is no way to prepare for every possible scenario that may occur.

But this doesn't mean we stop reading and preparing. We just do not need to be anxious about whether or not we will know what to do. We can have confidence that He who created our children will give us wisdom on caring for the little one woven in our wombs. Some of these insights will come from books, some will be from other mamas' experiences, but most of it will come from your God-given instinct.

God will give you wisdom to know what to do. Most of the true motherhood lessons you will learn happen on the job anyway. There will be overwhelming days. Celebratory days. Frustrating days. Compliant days. Non-compliant days. It will be all the things.

But God will not abandon you. He will strengthen and sustain you. And it will be beautiful.

You are going to figure it out!

27 weeks

Unexpected Grief – God Grieves with Us

He was despised and rejected—a man of sorrows, acquainted with deepest grief. We turned our backs on him and looked the other way. He was despised, and we did not care.

Isaiah 53:3, NLT

There are so many beautiful, wonderful, happy moments in pregnancy. Baby showers, exciting kicks, and a palpable excitement in the air. But as with every milestone, pregnancy can also be a trigger for grief.

Have you lost someone in your life that you expected to be present for your pregnancy? Often, God gives families a new baby as another life finds closure. This does not make the loss easy, but hopefully, it provides comfort as you say goodbye to a loved one.

Pregnancy is a milestone attached to certain expectations: a present mother, a vital marriage, or the perfect situation before the baby arrives. The grief can be paralyzing when these expectations do not come to fruition.

Fathers also grieve as they learn to share their wives with their children. A couple's relationship before children is exclusive. During pregnancy, a woman's focus shifts toward her baby. Fathers may find themselves trying to understand where they fit in the picture. They can feel useless when they are not experiencing the physical effects of pregnancy. Unexpected grief can deepen further when the baby arrives, and all of her affection is no longer just for him.

Pregnancy is a dream machine. Wonderful for those who get their dream and devastating for those who face a dying dream. Pregnancy is an unexpected trigger for grief.

For those who have gone through childhood trauma - pelvic exams and doctor's visits add to white-coat hypertension. For those who have been abandoned by a parent, pregnancy brings up the question of what kind of mother she will become. For those who have gone through a stillbirth, the anniversaries of each gestational week bring up the previous pregnancy's experiences.

If you are struggling in grief this week, you are not alone. God understands your grief (Hebrews 4:15–16).

Jesus knew grief well. Isaiah 53 describes how Jesus carried grief on his back to the cross. He experienced the cross so that our grief would not be the end of the story. His blood flowed down as the promise of a limited number of tears that would flow for you and me.

In some ways, Jesus gives us grief as a gift because grief changes what we value, what we treasure, and what we give. Even though time heals wounds, the scars remain. The weight of grief is still there. The only difference? The capacity to carry grief grows with time.

If grief is causing you to justify self-destructive behavior, please get help. Grief can flush someone down the victim vortex with ripple effects for years. Grief can enable generational sin.Getting help early can change a person's entire life trajectory. Grief can destroy, but it also has the power to build you up.

Grief can make you into a deeper, more intentional mother.

Grief will change how you teach your children about heaven, for grief is actually homesickness for heaven. It is grief's sting that recalibrates our journey's ultimate destination. Without grief, we would love this world more than the cross. We would be more world-obsessed than heaven-bound. Grief teaches the heart to hope in the cross. Those lumps, pits, and tears are reminders of a God who is not satisfied with brokenness. He does not abandon us in these moments but takes our crosses on his own back, nailing them to his hands.

Grief focuses our view and deepens our palate for the hope of heaven. This homesickness for security, permanence, and belonging, with satisfying answers for "why," will all be met in heaven.

And this is why we grieve with hope.

That heartache you experience from something or someone you have lost? It is the best reminder of where your true citizenship lies. It will make you a more grounded mother.

Those never-ending cycles of tears? We will know we are in heaven when our Father tenderly wipes them away for the last time. You will see your children with even more compassion.

The healing that did not occur the way you wanted? Brokenness makes heaven that much sweeter when He heals all wounds forever. You have been given this perspective of grief to help your children process a broken world and their need for a Savior.

Although grief during pregnancy may be amplified, may your joy be amplified even more. May you grieve with hope and may your child bring you joy amidst sorrow.

Reflection Questions:

What has been a surprising grief during your pregnancy? How have you acknowledged this loss?

How has your grief story intersected with Jesus' grief on the cross? How does knowing that Jesus understands grief help you process your grief?

Is there an unanswered prayer that has caused grief for you? How can you allow the grief of this unanswered prayer to bring you to a heavenward focus? How can this help you teach your children about our world?

28 weeks

Mothers at the Five o'clock Hour

A woman in the crowd had suffered for twelve years with constant bleeding, and she could find no cure. Coming up behind Jesus, she touched the fringe of his robe. Immediately, the bleeding stopped. 'Who touched me?' Jesus asked. Everyone denied it, and Peter said, 'Master, this whole crowd is pressing up against you.' But Jesus said, 'Someone deliberately touched me, for I felt healing power go out from me.' When the woman realized that she could not stay hidden, she began to tremble and fell to her knees in front of him. The whole crowd heard her explain why she had touched him and that she had been immediately healed. "Daughter," he said to her, "your faith has made you well. Go in peace."

Luke 8:43–48, NLT

When pregnancy is added to all the other motherhood duties, the ability to give is limited. Some days are successful. But many times, as a mother lays her head on the pillow, she wonders if she has done enough. Guilt sinks in. She begins to believe if only she was more involved, her child would be doing better academically. If only she worked harder, they could afford his hockey season. The "if only" list goes on and on for all the things that she is not doing for her children.

In these moments, we need to ask ourselves, what are the most important needs of our children? How do we make sure we address their most significant needs?

There are so many different needs to balance for all of our children. Their needs can easily get lost in the shuffle, especially at the five o'clock hour. A mother at the five o'clock hour can become overwhelmed quickly as she makes dinner for her needy children.

Jesus was constantly surrounded by needy people. He was always teaching, healing, and leading. In Luke 8, we see the story of Jesus at the five o'clock hour. Having already experienced a busy day, Jesus walked through the crowds when He felt His power leave Him. A woman who had been on her period for twelve years crawled through the crowd to touch Jesus' robe. With a simple touch, she was healed. It would have been more efficient for Jesus to heal her without acknowledging her. Instead, Jesus paused His busy schedule and turned around. He gave her value. After years of being told she was unclean, Jesus called her "daughter." He must have been exhausted from His day, but Jesus still paused to acknowledge this woman's spiritual need. How did He still have more to give when all of the needs around Him were so great?

Jesus had taken time earlier to refill Himself so He would have more to give at the five o'clock hour. Jesus would go to lonely places to pray (Luke 5:15–16) and be filled by His Father.

As mothers, do we start our day in lonely places, acknowledging only God can fill us? Too often in motherhood, we are running on our own power. Yet the more we are filled, the more we have to give our children. And the more our children are filled, the more they have to give to one another. They listen better. They are more gracious to our mistakes. And they are more resilient to disappointment.

We know our children's most important needs when we are powered by the Spirit of God. And then we will also have the wisdom to respond.

Okay, but how do we apply this to real life?

The alarm has just gone off, and the snooze button is much more important. The morning takes off like a roller coaster.

If you don't have time in the morning, you can still make intentional pit stops throughout the day to be filled by Jesus daily. The next time you tie your child's shoes, reflect on Jesus washing the disciple's feet. Sing a song of worship as you race out the door to the car. The next time your child has an ungrateful tantrum, pray quietly in front of your children. When children hear you praying, they stop bickering and listen. If you graze on God's Word throughout the day, you will be filled continually. It may be scripture on a sticky note or snippets of audio Bible when you're in your car. Finding intentional ways to fill yourself throughout the day will keep you focused and faithful.

Children thrive when their mother thrives.

A thriving mother recognizes when she needs to slow down so that she can be filled herself. When you tap into your source of strength, you will have more bandwidth, even at five o'clock. You will be able to pause your multitasking to affirm your child's worth. Your patience will be deeper. Your joy will be richer in the mundane.

Because in these quiet moments, when Jesus turns around and calls you "daughter," you will be refilled.

> **Reflection Questions:**
>
> *How often do you pause and affirm the worth of your children? What are your children's spiritual needs? (Are they dealing with issues of pride, low self-worth, impatience, or jealousy?) How can you pray for your children about these spiritual needs so that you are intentional in shepherding them?*
>
> *How can you go to lonely places and pray throughout your day? If you can't go to lonely places, are there certain "pit stops" in your day when you can build a habit of spending time with God?*
>
> *Are you thriving or surviving this motherhood journey? If surviving, how can you build margins in your schedule so that you prioritize what matters most?*
>
> *As you prepare your children for the arrival of their new sibling, how can you encourage your children's gifts? For example, if your daughter loves to make up stories, can she draw a story for her new sister? If your son loves trucks, can you help him decorate a diaper truck that will carry diapers to you when the baby needs one? If your teenager likes to paint, can she paint the nursery with you? Check out www.rachellekeng.com and subscribe to receive access to "The Sibling Promotion," a list of ideas to help your children become big brothers and big sisters using their love languages to bond with the baby.*

29 weeks

Parenting by Prayer – God Listens

> *Rejoice in the Lord always. I will say it again: Rejoice! Let your graciousness be known to everyone. The Lord is near. Don't worry about anything, but in everything, through prayer and petition with thanksgiving, present your requests to God. And the peace of God, which surpasses all understanding, will guard your hearts and minds in Christ Jesus.*
>
> Philippians 4:4–7, CSB

As you near the thought of laboring and delivering a tiny human out of your body, you may be more anxious! You may be nesting to prepare a perfect home, scrambling for the last vacation (babymoon, yay!), and tying up job responsibilities before maternity leave. With all of the hectic loose ends, how do you protect your peace?

In Philippians, Paul gives us a clear roadmap of how to protect this peace with prayer. The peace of God is what guards our hearts and minds from anxiety. We must remain in connection with Him to receive this peace.

Yet, how often do we treat prayer as the last resort instead of the first resort?

How often do we barrel through the obstacles for our children, trying to fix them ourselves, only to find ourselves discouraged? Or how often do we mom-shame ourselves when we cannot fix them?

> *Prayer changes the outcome.*
> *The outcome may look different from what we initially thought.*
> *Because, ultimately, prayer changes us.*

Prayer as a first resort keeps our minds focused on who has created our children. Prayer as a first resort will give us strength to endure whatever comes our way.

Prayer as a first resort protects our peace. When we remember our children are His, we stop holding on so tightly to our plans.

Instead, *we begin parenting by prayer.*

Philippians 4:4-7, CSB gives us a roadmap to parent by prayer.

- *Rejoice in the Lord always. I will say it again: Rejoice! Let your graciousness be known to everyone (4:4).*
  Starting with praise keeps you in the correct posture when you approach God. You don't have to be happy in all circumstances. Rejoicing means that you are confident in the ultimate end of the story.

You can pray:

> *Jesus, You are gracious to me and my children. I rejoice in your goodness and faithfulness to me! Despite the crazy life going on over here, I rejoice in You!*

- *The Lord is near (4:5).*
  How often do you worry about your children—their growth, safety, and emotional well-being? Philippians says the answer to this anxiety is God's presence. "I am near." God's presence is near the anxious heart. There will be unexpected stories in our parenting journeys and chapters that we would not have written for ourselves. But we know the Author who is nearby. He writes the ending to our stories (Hebrews 12:2).

You can pray:

> *Jesus, you are near me. I do not need to be afraid for myself or my children because you go before me and are next to me. You are the one writing the story for my children.*

- *Don't worry about anything, but in everything, through prayer and petition with thanksgiving, present your requests to God (4:6).*

Too often, we spend more time worrying (praying to ourselves) rather than praying to God. Worrying is circular, and prayer is linear. Keep your eyes on God, and you can break the cycle. When we pray, we remember who has the power and knowledge over everything. It resets a perspective of how big God is and how small we are.

You can pray:

> *Jesus, forgive me for praying to myself! I can't fix it anyway. Thank you for letting me pray to you instead! Thank you for taking care of my children so I do not need to worry about what is happening.*

- *And the peace of God, which surpasses all understanding, will guard your hearts and minds in Christ Jesus (4:7).*

If you believe the above truths, you will receive a supernatural peace guarding your heart and mind. Anxiety keeps our hearts and minds into fight-or-flight mode. But the peace of Christ is supernatural and often does not make sense. Jesus is your defense against the powers of the anxious human mind.

You can pray:

> *Jesus, protect my heart and mind from my anxious thoughts. Your peace trumps my anxiety because I believe my life is yours.*

We can pray with confidence that He holds our stories. No matter the outcome of our parenting journeys, He is the true Author. Our detours are His intentional design and for our good. Let us be freed from anxiety because of our hope in Jesus.

Reflection Questions:

What worst-case scenario for birth or motherhood do you need to give to God and affirm that He is sovereign over? For example, it may be, "God, I am most anxious about a C-section. Will you help me trust you? You are near. Protect my mind from anxious thoughts about all the worst-case scenarios."

If you are already a parent, how much time do you spend lecturing your children, and how much time do you spend praying for their hearts to change?

Where do you need to turn your parenting over to prayer? Can you turn your "I need to fix this for my children" into "I trust you, Jesus, to write their story, and you are doing a good work in them?"

30 weeks

Redemptive Birth Experiences – God Loves To Redeem

Jesus answered him, "Truly, truly, I say to you, unless one is born again he cannot see the kingdom of God." Nicodemus said to him, 'How can a man be born when he is old? Can he enter a second time into his mother's womb and be born?' Jesus answered, 'Truly, truly, I say to you, unless one is born of water and the Spirit, he cannot enter the kingdom of God.'

John 3:3–4, ESV

This may be your first pregnancy, or it may be your fifth. You may have had dream deliveries. But many of us have had a birth experience we did not expect or plan.

The first experience may be a long labor with unexpected grief. Sometimes, it is a marathon induction that ends in a c-section. Or, perhaps you have a memory of your baby being transferred to the neonatal intensive care unit (NICU) after birth. Or, maybe there was a breastfeeding experience that did not work as expected. For those of you who have had regrets or felt unheard during your last labor experience, this chapter is for you.

Approximately one-third of babies born in this country are born by cesarean section[23].

There are usually two reasons an obstetrician may recommend a cesarean. First, your doctor may think the baby is safer outside the

---

[23] "Total Cesarean Deliveries: United States, 2021," March of Dimes | PeriStats, Accessed 8/4/2023, https://www.marchofdimes.org/peristats/data?reg=99&top=8&stop=86&lev=1&slev=1&obj=9&dv=ms#:~:text=Delivery%20Method&text=In%20the%20United%20States%20in,live%20births%20were%20cesarean%20deliveries.

womb. A c-section is the quickest way to help you and your baby. Second, the baby may not fit through the birth canal. A cesarean is indicated to protect both you and your child from further harm.

Every woman who has had a bad experience with her previous labor usually fears a repeat of their first experience. For those who have had a c-section, your doctor will counsel you on whether you should consider a TOLAC (Trial of Labor After Cesarean). Talk to your provider to tell him or her of your concerns from your last birth experience. The frustrations from the previous experience are often due to miscommunication between the staff and the family. Sharing your frustrations with your current birth provider can help you know how to advocate for yourself during your next birth experience.

If you are looking for a "birth do-over," I am praying that you have a redemptive birth experience. Sometimes traumatic birth experiences need a "do-over" for a mama to move on from the grief of her previous labor experience.

But regardless of whether this is your first or fifth baby, the reality of birth is very intimidating. Not all things are predictable. Birth is full of uncertainties.

But there are a few certainties you can claim when the anxiety starts to rise. Meditating on these truths now will keep you grounded during pregnancy and in the delivery room.

- *God will bring to completion what He has already started in you in Christ Jesus.*
  "Being confident of this, that he who began a good work in you will carry it on to completion until the day of Christ Jesus" (Philippians 1:6, NIV). If He has called you to be pregnant, He will not leave you at the moment you need Him the most.

- *God is in the whisper.*
  Labor can be an incredibly loud experience. If we get focused on all of the noise around us, we get distracted. "After the earthquake came a fire, but the Lord was not in the fire. And after the fire came a gentle whisper" (1 Kings 19:12, NIV). There is a rest between contractions, the "quiet" before the

next fire. Meditate on God's presence during this whisper to give you strength for the next contraction.

- *God is trustworthy.*
  Will you trust Him no matter what? Do you trust God has given your birth care providers the knowledge to care for you and your child? "Trust in the LORD with all your heart and lean not on your own understanding; in all your ways submit to him, and he will make your paths straight. Do not be wise in your own eyes; fear the LORD and shun evil. This will bring health to your body and nourishment to your bones" (Proverbs 3:5–8, NIV).

- *There is a birth story that doesn't have to be uncertain.*
  If you have accepted Jesus as your Savior from your sins, you have already experienced the most important birth story that exists when you were "born again" (John 3:3–4). This is the true birth story that ultimately affects your motherhood journey most of all.

The uncertainty of motherhood changes with every season. But God does not change. He is the same yesterday, today, and forever (Hebrews 13:8).
His character is certain:
He loves to save.
He loves to redeem.
He does not abandon us in our darkest hour.

My friend, He will be with you in that delivery room.
These things are certain.

Reflection Questions:

Have you had a birth experience that didn't go as expected or planned? If so, what were the specific challenges or regrets you faced during that experience? Check out www.rachellekeng.com to subscribe and receive a birth plan template that helps you have this conversation with your healthcare provider.

Have you communicated your concerns and frustrations about your previous birth experience with your healthcare provider? If not, how would discussing these issues with them help you in your next birth experience?

What are the uncertainties that you are most afraid of in motherhood? What are the certain truths that can ground you?

31 weeks

Assembling Your True Village – God Provides Our People

> *When Elizabeth heard Mary's greeting, the baby leaped in her womb, and Elizabeth was filled with the Holy Spirit. In a loud voice, she exclaimed: "Blessed are you among women, and blessed is the child you will bear! But why am I so favored, that the mother of my Lord should come to me? As soon as the sound of your greeting reached my ears, the baby in my womb leaped for joy. Blessed is she who has believed that the Lord would fulfill his promises to her!"*
> *Luke 1:41–45, NIV*

This is a good time to start thinking about who you will want at birth, who you will want to visit in the hospital, and who will aid you at home after you bring your newborn home. The first few weeks are best served by a support person who will take care of the leftover duties (groceries, cleaning, cooking) while you and your partner nurture your new family. So much of your energy will be used in keeping the little person alive that you will need a true village.

If you are a people-pleaser, you might worry more about other people's feelings than your true feelings. Acknowledging how you truly feel does not make you a selfish mother. Instead, it is the start of healthy boundaries that allow your family to grow to its greatest potential. Those who truly love you will understand you are the boss—a boss who may make mistakes but still needs to make them on her own anyway. But establishing healthy boundaries can be difficult if you're used to being nice.

Can you give yourself permission to be inhospitable?

There are so many things to learn about your baby in the first few days that managing other people can become another exhausting layer. Learn to say, "Thank you, I'll consider that," and "I appreciate your care, but no thank you." Your true village will understand.

Mary, the mother of Jesus, had a true village in her cousin, Elizabeth. A double fertility miracle occurred when the virgin Mary found out she was pregnant with Jesus. Elizabeth was in her old age (postmenopausal) and infertile. But when the angel Gabriel visited Mary, Elizabeth was already twenty-four weeks pregnant. When Mary came to Elizabeth, Elizabeth's baby (John) leaped in her womb. In utero, John the Baptist was already preparing a way for Jesus by announcing His arrival. Fetus acknowledged fetus. The two pregnant mothers lived together during Mary's entire first trimester. These two women spurred each other on in their faith and pregnancies.

Elizabeth was Mary's first true village that helped her grow into her calling. Her first village was not Joseph! Mary went to her cousin Elizabeth (instead of her immediate family or Joseph) when she found out she was pregnant. It was Elizabeth and her husband, Zachariah, who ended up being the first village to shelter Mary (Luke 1) before Joseph took over. After this time with Elizabeth, Mary went to be with Joseph.

This story helps us understand the unconventional village:

- *Our villages often end up being surprising.*
  God's villages are not always connected by blood, and that is how you know that God has orchestrated it. God will show you who your people are if you ask Him. Your village will make itself known with meals that show up on your door, baby clothes that are handed down, or a text from an acquaintance who is praying for you.

- *Our villages don't always understand boundaries.*
  The village is a vital part of growing a family. But sometimes the village can move into your house and stay past their welcome. There is a balance of remaining teachable to their wisdom while trying out your new parental muscles. Making a plan for how long someone will stay will set clear expectations.

- *Our villages will make mistakes.*
  No village is perfect. Villages can be too overbearing or not attentive enough. But as you grow into parents, you will also have a greater understanding of what you need, when you need it, and how you need it. You will learn how to ask for help.

- *Even when human villages fail us, God always provides for us in different ways.*
  God's power is your ultimate village. Even if you don't have someone to give you a break, God can multiply your energy. Even if your spouse does not give you a break, God can make twenty minutes of sleep feel like four hours. God works in many different ways to sustain His people. Let your faith grow deeper in how He provides for you through the little (yet significant) things!

Reflection Questions:

How have you already seen God provide unexpected relationships as a village in your pregnancy?

Prepare how you will say "no" while also humbly acknowledging the support of your village. For example, "We appreciate your care and will certainly call you when we are ready for a visit. We can't wait for the baby to meet you."

Are you more worried about how others feel or about how you feel? Start thinking about who you want around you after your delivery. There may be someone whose feelings are hurt if they are not included in your list of postpartum visitors. Still, setting a clear boundary for when you will be ready for visitors is okay. Clarity of expectations is kindness.

32 weeks

Filtering The Filterless – God Defends Us

> *... weeping, she began to wet his [Jesus'] feet with her tears. Then she wiped them with her hair, kissed them and poured perfume on them. When the Pharisee who had invited him saw this, he said to himself, "If this man were a prophet, he would know who is touching him and what kind of woman she is—that she is a sinner."*
>
> Luke 7:38b–39, NIV

Oh, the filterless are many. Have you had strangers in the grocery store pat your belly yet? And how about those well-intentioned friends who share their traumatic birth stories? It breeds fear rather than camaraderie. As if pregnant women do not struggle enough with body image, they are told their baby looks too big or too small. And if you are around someone with a critical spirit, it can be exhausting.

Unless your doctor tells you that your baby is dealing with growth concerns, it will be important to wear a "filter" when interacting with the rest of the world's opinions and jarring stares.

In Luke 7:38–39, there was a woman who knew how to filter well.

Mary came onto the scene while Jesus was talking with other men. Without saying a word, she wept at Jesus' feet. She broke a jar of expensive perfume onto His feet and wiped His feet with her hair. She kissed Jesus' feet because she knew her need for a savior. But in this moment of worship, the Pharisee spiritual leader began to say nasty things about her. Without any care for her dignity, the Pharisee proceeded to shame her publically for using an expensive perfume that could have been used to make money for the poor.

But in this moment, Jesus defended Mary. And Mary was unfazed by the criticism around her.

Why?

Her need for Jesus to rescue her was more important than her appearance to others.

She knew who she owed. Ultimately, she knew her posture in front of a king.

You don't owe an explanation about your pregnancy to anyone. There will always be traumatic birth stories that women want to tell each other, but these stories are not helpful for your spirit. God is the only one who knows how your birth story will unfold. Your birth story will be your own unique birth story.

If you are doing what God has called you to do, you can filter out all the opinions that are not helping you with your calling. Wearing your "filter" will help you interpret and receive critical comments.

Consider which filters you use to sift through the comments that come your way:

- *Security Filter:*
  Who is your defender? (Psalm 91:1–15) If it is Jesus, you don't need to live defensively.

- *Worth Filter:*
  Who defines your worth? Is it based on what people say about you, or is it based on who Jesus says you are? (Ephesians 1:13–14). If you know your value in the kingdom of God, then God's word will be louder than your inner critic.

- *Approval Filter:*
  Whose approval do you need the most? Is it God's approval or the approval of man? (Galatians 1:10) If you answer to Jesus, you may look "strange" to the world, but you know whose opinion matters the most.

The woman who wiped Jesus' feet with her hair was unfazed by the critics around her. Mary knew who her defender was. Her worth was based on who Jesus said she was. Mary knew her identity—she was a sinner in need of a savior. Nothing else mattered to her more than her Savior's approval.

If you learn how to interpret criticism through these filters, you will be focused on what truly matters. Finding your security, worth, and approval in Jesus changes everything. If your confidence is in God, you will not be fazed by the critics on the motherhood path. You can even have mercy on the offensive Pharisees because their words will have less weight. Your worship for your Savior will drown out the other noise.

So let them talk.
You're at the feet of Jesus. And He knows your heart.

Reflection Questions:

Have you experienced when you felt judged or criticized by others during your motherhood journey? How did those encounters make you feel, and how did you respond to them?

Reflect on the concept of wearing a "filter" when interacting with the opinions and judgments of others during motherhood. How do you currently navigate and filter out the external voices that may affect your self-image and confidence?

In the story of the woman who anointed Jesus' feet, how do you relate to her posture of recognizing her need for a savior? Are there moments in your pregnancy journey where you have felt a deep reliance on Jesus?

How does knowing that Jesus defends, forgives, and loves you impact your response to filterless individuals or those who may criticize you during pregnancy? Are you able to extend mercy and patience to them? Ask Jesus to grow your heart for these people, and you will see them differently.

33 weeks

The Birth Plan – God Plans The Detours

In their hearts humans plan their course, but the Lord establishes steps.

Proverbs 16:7, NIV

With birth around the corner, women often dream of their perfect birth experience. You may be thinking about your birth plan and have done extensive research into your preferences. Will you hire a doula? Will you get an epidural? Will you breastfeed?

Women face tremendous pressure (society-induced and self-induced) to always do everything correctly. But if the birth does not go as planned, women experience feelings of failure after their delivery. While it is good to have some idea of your preferences, the best birth plan is to be flexible and to hold your plans loosely.

If we dig past the surface, most mothers are navigating a barrage of lies in the world. There are many well-intentioned voices that mothers must filter daily. Blogs that tell you what you need to do, be, or have to be a good mother. There is pressure to deliver a baby vaginally or else you're a "weak" woman. Breastfeed or else your child will have deadly infections. Be perfect so that your child will be perfect.

In this information age, while some knowledge is power, it is also a hamster wheel for the restless mind. Dr. Google says there is an answer for everything, so we should lack nothing. It is no wonder that women are feeling like they are not enough.

The truth is you do not need to be enough. You were never supposed to be. It is only through God's mercy that we are enough for our children.

There is a refreshing relief when we expect less of ourselves and more of God.

But the reality is, we expect a lot of ourselves. We try to perfect our formulas. If we eat the right things, exercise enough, and follow all the doctor's suggestions—we will have the desired outcome. This lie follows us into parenthood. If we homeschool with the "right" household rules, our children will become Christian adults. But the problem with pregnancy and the rest of parenthood is that there is no formula. Motherhood is not mathematics. Motherhood is a foreign language with changing grammatical rules that do not always make sense.

You don't have to have everything figured out. Micromanaging itself is not a bad thing, but when it becomes obsessive, it can quickly become unhealthy. Micromanaging gets to a point where you must ask yourself: Who is God? And who is not? Your daily peace will help you determine if you have this balance correct. If you are micromanaging without peace, ask yourself whether God is truly the authority of your life. If you are micromanaging with peace, then you will not be fazed by the plans that fall through despite meticulous planning.

Because sometimes, it is good for us to have plans that fall through.

The plans that fall through often seem to be the good ones. But they aren't always God's plan for us or our children. It is intensely humbling to let go of our plans for our children. But only God can determine our children's steps.

Our dependence on God's mercy changes how we pray, how we parent, and how we let go.

Often, it is not until our plans fall through that we start to remember whose we are. The Bible does not define our worth based on our performance. Jesus does not accept us based on how well we fare pregnancy or how well we parent. While we were still imperfect, God sent Jesus to die for us (Romans 5:8) because He loved us.

When we experience this love personally, we have this same grace to give to our little ones, teenagers, and adult children. They will fail in their performances, but as their parents, we can be the first examples of

God's grace in failure. We can love them not because of how well they perform. God's mercy given to each of us is the same mercy we give to our children.

Your child doesn't need a perfect parent.
Your child doesn't need a perfect birth experience.
Your child needs a humble and gracious mother most of all.

From birth to motherhood, we will have many opportunities to fall short in our parenting. The birth experience may be the first time your limits will be tested as a mother. But may it not be the last time you show grace to yourself as a mother.

Some women have a dream birth experience. Some do not. I truly hope you have your birth plan fulfilled. I hope you see God's mercy in your experience. But even if you don't have your perfect birth plan, I hope you see the provision of God regardless. Because regardless of failed birth plans, epidurals, C-sections, or bottle-feeding, God is determining your steps. He knows all the terrains—over the hills, through the valleys, and into the jungle. He will carry you through them all.

Reflection Questions:

Reflect on the idea of being flexible and holding your plans loosely when it comes to your birth experience and motherhood. How open are you to adapting and adjusting your expectations if things don't go as planned? Ask God for the faith to be flexible.

Consider the statement that you do not need to be enough as a mother and that it is through God's mercy and grace that you are sufficient. How does this perspective bring relief and a shift in your mindset?

How does the understanding that God determines your steps and knows the map for your children's lives with all its detours impact your trust and dependence on Him? How can you embrace detours as growth opportunities and rely on God's guidance?

34 weeks
Something Always Hurts – God Sustains Us

> *The Lord is my portion; therefore I will wait for him. The Lord is good to those whose hope is in him, to the one who seeks him; it is good to wait quietly for the salvation of the Lord.*
> Lamentations 3:24–25, NIV

When we think about how much more there is to go, the journey can feel overwhelming, especially if you are in pain. Have you been visited by varicose veins and hemorrhoids yet? At this stage, the baby is compressing your bowels and bladder and giving you lower back pain. And the swelling? It's no joke. Cankles are the new normal, right?

Why does swelling happen in pregnancy? First, there is a temporary plumbing problem in your cardiovascular system: the baby sits upon the pipes that bring blood back to your heart, so the blood pools at your feet, causing more swelling in your legs. Second, the pregnant body is in a low protein state, which squeezes more blood toward the baby (the intentional design of the Creator to give your baby more nutrients). But the mother's low protein state[24] also squeezes fluid into the path of least resistance—your feet, face, and hands. So it's no wonder you feel like a water balloon!

The reality is that every week, something else hurts. At first, it is back pain; the following week, it is heartburn, and then constipation moves in. As the baby grows, new growing pains arise. We don't get much time to be comfortable with our symptoms before a new set of aches and

---

[24] Monika Sanghavi and John D. Rutherford, "Cardiovascular Physiology of Pregnancy," Circulation 130, no. 12 (September 16, 2014): 1003–8, https://doi.org/10.1161/circulationaha.114.009029.

pains arrives. If you have had a baby before, chances are you already feel like you're full-term. The back pain and pelvic pressure start earlier in subsequent pregnancies.

Pregnancy is a time when we learn to get used to being in pain and anticipating pain.

And of course, we anticipate labor and delivery, the grand finale of pregnancy pain.

Something always hurts.

But if you really think about it, pregnancy pain is an allegory of the story of our lives. Like the never-ending symptoms of pregnancy, there is always something brewing in our broken world.

Mountain after mountain, living in this world is a marathon of mountain climbing. Have you ever felt like you can barely breathe because there is no respite between trials? This world is a challenge even for those who know Jesus. The trials can feel never-ending. Some trials have no quick fix, so we learn to adjust our baseline. Our tolerance and resilience to trial become stronger in order to survive.

When you go to labor and delivery, the nurses will strap your belly to two different monitors. One of the monitors measures your baby's heartbeat. The second monitor shows how often you have contractions. When you are set up, look at the paper recording your contractions. They literally look like "mountain after mountain" of squiggly lines.

Each peak symbolizes our resilience. Each valley symbolizes our resolve to keep showing up. Every decade of mothering has new challenges and heartaches. There are new bridges to create and new fears to conquer.

But despite all the mountains, we can continue the journey because we know the destination.

For the Christian, our heavenly birthday is a celebratory reunion with our Father in heaven. For the laboring mother, it is the earthly birthday of her new precious child.

So, how do we get through a life marked by trials? One day at a time. And how do we get through labor? One contraction at a time. Each mountain has a peak and then a release, followed by a rest in between. There will always be another peak. There will always be another rest.

God's provision is enough for each mountain of the journey.

Lamentations 3 says that the Lord is our portion. A portion is not an overindulgent buffet. A portion is just enough to satisfy and be good for us. He will give you enough strength to scale this next mountain. It may be as simple as an anti-hemorrhoid prescription, or it may be the miraculous relief of an epidural during labor. It may be the support of a friend who delivers you a meal. God gives us a boost to get to the top in so many ways. He will sustain us.

During the last few weeks of pregnancy, it is hard to wait. Especially when something always hurts. Reflecting on how far you have come instead of focusing on how much more you have to go will get you through the last few weeks.

Because let's say it out loud:
Pregnancy is hard.
Labor is a labor of love.

But the hardest, most laborious things are followed by the most amazing joy.

The moment the baby cries, there is relief in the room. First, the obvious relief of a tired mama. The relief from the new daddy (if he has not fainted yet). And then, if you look at your obstetrician, there is also relief in his or her eyes. Labor is a challenging journey, and watching pain evaporate into joy is a relief for all. I imagine that this look is how God the Father will look at us someday when we join Him in heaven, relieved that we are rescued from the pain of the contractions of this broken world once and for all.

And as we cradle in His arms, we will already know His voice. For He is the one who has comforted us while we were in the womb. What a beautiful moment of salvation it will be for all!

Reflection Questions:

How do you see God sustaining you this week on your pregnancy journey?

As you anticipate labor and delivery, what are you most afraid of? What part of the process do you need to trust the Creator God that He will provide what you need?

How does the hope of heaven change how you approach your trials in this life?

35 weeks

Learning to Laugh – God Wants Our Growth

> *"A merry heart does good, like medicine, but a broken spirit dries the bones."*
>
> *Proverbs 17:22, NKJV*

There's nothing really glamorous about the last few weeks of pregnancy. In fact, there's a lot to laugh about if you're secure enough to talk about it. Can you roll over in bed without a crane? Is your water breaking, or did your baby just kick your bladder? Who needs the diaper now?!

If you feel like you're waddling like a duck, it's because you *are* waddling like a duck. Your body is making relaxin[25], a hormone that relaxes all of your joints in your pelvis so that a baby can fit through. Relaxin also affects your core stability, making you less stable on your feet. Relaxin relaxes your pelvic floor and is the source of more bathroom accidents. So thank you, relaxin, for giving us our childbearing hips.

There is no pregnancy glow. There is only a pregnancy sweat. Pregnancy isn't glamorous. It is sometimes downright embarrassing! You may have lost control over your bladder or bowels. You may have had an increase in acne. You may have hair growing in places you don't want. And although you knew she always existed, getting to know Gravity is different when it's personal. She is not nice.

Pregnancy is awkward, up close and personal. And if there is any romantic boundary you have been trying to maintain with your partner, it is about to be crossed big time.

---

[25] A MacLennan et al., "Serum Relaxin and Pelvic Pain of Pregnancy," The Lancet 328, no. 8501 (August 1, 1986): 243–45, https://doi.org/10.1016/s0140-6736(86)92069-6.

But it's going to be okay!

We can either own it, or we can be embarrassed by it. Your doctor doesn't care/remember/judge if you have a pedicure or you have waxed. Your nurses don't care if you poop during labor. If you have a healthy marriage, your husband will still find you romantic after birth. This is truth.

The quicker you let go of the need to be perfectly put together, the quicker you will experience the freedom of motherhood. Learning to laugh at yourself is one of the greatest gifts you can give to your partner and your children.

The quicker we admit imperfection (and even savor it), the more resilient we will become.

In Proverbs 17:22, a merry heart is the medicine. You may not feel merry. But this verse says, be merry. Laugh even if you don't feel it. The feeling will come when you let go. Laugh at how gross pregnancy is! Let go of having it all together. If you don't, pregnancy can feel more like the second part of verse 22, a broken spirit with dry bones. Which attitude do you want? A merry heart or a broken spirit?

"Gross growth" is important in the kingdom of God!
Because gross growth creates a vulnerability that is for our good.
Sometimes, we need "gross growth" to become more delightful to God.

God is using your child as sandpaper for your soul. As you watch your weight on the scale rocket into unknown atmospheres, your child teaches you to confront your true body image. As your body parts stick out of areas they shouldn't, your child is teaching you to let go of vanity. As you let go of performance, your worth will no longer be in perfection.

If you can learn to laugh at yourself, you will bring others (and your children) joy with your merry attitude.

So what does this look like?
Can you laugh at the hemorrhoids by naming your unwanted guests?
Can you have a duck walking contest with your family to see who does it the best? (Make sure there are sound effects.)

Can you use body paint to make stretch marks on your partner's belly similar to yours?

The faster you let go of your image, the more fun you will have with this motherhood roller coaster. The rest of motherhood continues to have hilarious twists and turns. Our children want us to be imperfect. They want to laugh with us.

Learn to laugh, and you will find freedom to be a kid again.

Reflection Questions:

Reflect on the idea of embracing imperfection. How does this mindset contribute to the freedom of motherhood?

How can you incorporate laughter, trust, and relaxation into your daily life as a mother? What practical steps can you take to maintain a positive mindset and gracefully embrace the uncertainties?

Where do you believe God is challenging you with "gross growth?"

36 weeks

Pain Management – God Is Our Hope

> *"And we boast in the hope of the glory of God. Not only so, but we also glory in our sufferings because we know that suffering produces perseverance, perseverance, character, and character, hope. And hope does not put us to shame because God's love has been poured out into our hearts through the Holy Spirit, who has been given to us."*
> Romans 5:2b–5, NIV

By now, you have likely thought about whether or not you will want pain medication in labor. There are usually three different approaches to epidurals. The first woman says, "I will have my baby naturally without pain medication, no matter what." The second woman says, "I will want an epidural the moment I feel a contraction." And the last woman says, "I will see what I need when I get there." (Truthfully, the second and third women usually get an epidural during labor.)

There is no way to prepare for labor pains because there are not really any other equivalent levels of pain to contractions. What you may believe about your pain tolerance may be very different when it comes to actual labor.

I often hear women say, "I have high pain tolerance." And some women truly do have high pain tolerance. But have you ever thought about the strength of your emotional pain tolerance?

Our emotional pain tolerance is the ability to rebound when we are disappointed or hurt. As we age, our emotional pain tolerance usually gets stronger. For example, I was much more easily offended in my younger years. But motherhood helped me get over myself. Because, quite honestly, my ego was left at the hospital with my placenta. As I have gotten older, my emotional pain tolerance has gotten stronger.

God is growing your heart through motherhood to show you a new perspective. You will find that the things that seemed so important in your relationships or past experiences may not be as important as they once were.

Our emotional pain tolerance becomes stronger the more times we rebound from our motherhood woes.

There are so many moments in motherhood that require a mama to dig deep. What if your baby rejects breastfeeding? Your toddler doesn't meet his or her developmental milestones? Your child is bullied? Your teenager chooses their friends over you? Your children reject your faith? How do you rebound from all of these detours?

In Romans 5:2b–5, Paul writes this letter after having gone through shipwrecks, imprisonments, and disappointing relationships. Paul describes suffering as having a progression. Suffering leads to character and then to a new hope. For those who desire the character of Christ, suffering trains us to have a different hope. The focus will no longer be on ourselves but on God. Hope will be in the unseen and the eternal (2 Corinthians 4:16–18).

Mothers who know Jesus have a strong emotional pain tolerance even in the detours of motherhood.

Those who know Jesus have a different hope in their motherhood journey. Their hope is not based on their children's achievements. Their hope is not based on being the most well-rounded mother. Their hope is in God's love, no matter the detours.

You decide where your hope lies so that when the detours come, they do not derail you.

Labor and delivery are full of many detours. Sometimes, a strong pain tolerance is enough to get there. But if there are any prolonged detours, pain medications may be an important part of surviving this journey. You will need to find the pain management plan that makes the most sense for your delivery experience.

Everyone's pain experience is different. But the ability to cope with pain is determined by the preparation. Those who have prepared for a natural childbirth are more tolerant of painful contractions because they have expected them. Those who are prepared for the detours of motherhood rebound more easily if they are expecting them.

When your hope is in the love of God, you will find strength no matter the storm.

Your true hope will turn a storm into a gentle rain shower.

Reflection Questions:

There are three different approaches to epidurals in labor. A) No epidural, B) Epidural at all costs, and C) Unsure. Which approach do you personally relate to the most, and why? How might your perspective on pain management in labor relate to your emotional pain tolerance in life? A) I want to process every pain I feel, B) I don't ever want to feel pain, or C) I am not sure.

Share your thoughts on the statement, "The ability to cope is determined by the preparation." How can preparing mentally and emotionally for the challenges of motherhood influence our ability to handle detours and difficult moments?

How can you strengthen your emotional pain tolerance? What do you think is holding you back from trusting God when you are disappointed? If there has been an area in your life that you have hidden from God, would you consider letting Him in? A counselor can help you discover why it is difficult to bounce back from painful circumstances. Pain layers upon itself if not resolved.

37 weeks

Learning to Delight in Your Children – God Delights In You

> *Take delight in the Lord, and he will give you the desires of your heart. Commit your way to the Lord; trust in him, and he will do this: He will make your righteous reward shine like the dawn, your vindication like the noonday sun. Be still before the Lord and wait patiently for him.*
>
> Psalm 37:4–7a, NIV

As soon as I walk into the room, I know the look. T.O.P (a.k.a. Tired of Pregnancy). Usually, she is leaning back on her arms that hold her up like tent pegs. There is no room for her to sit forward anymore. Her eyes do not have the expectant sparkle. They have the frustrated glint of annoyance. Because "this thing," the baby, has taken over the limited real estate in her body. It is no longer a cute bump - it is an alien that is threatening to rip her belly apart!

"I'm over it." And I get it. The finish line is so close, and yet so far. The last mile of any race is the hardest because it is about how we finish. Do we finish with delight or desperation?

The discomforts of early pregnancy and third trimester are different and yet very similar. The baby is getting in the way of your life, your sleep, and your diet. The call for sacrificial love only gets deeper as you mourn your first stretch mark (a.k.a. love tattoos) and the need for a diaper (for you, not for the baby). No one talks about how glamorous this part of pregnancy is. But we accept the call of this phase. Why? Because we know it is temporary. We delight in our children because of their potential.

But the need to delight in our children persists even when they come out of the womb. Even when they are not delightful. Even when they fail to reach their potential. Our children have good days, but they also have a lot of days when motherhood is disappointing if we are honest with ourselves.

There is also a T.O.M (Tired of Motherhood) that is true for mothers if they dare to admit it. We know the constant demand is worth it, just like carrying this baby is worth it. But there are days when the demand feels like it is too much.

The demand is too much when we expect ourselves to mold the perfect child. Delighting in them becomes work when we are focused on an outcome rather than the process. But when we delight in who they are without trying to change them, we are refilled.

Psalm 37:4 gives us a picture of delighting in God. This verse on a coffee cup gives us the false impression that we can get exactly what we want if we follow the right steps. But the Aramaic word, anag, translated as "delight," means "to be soft, delicate, dainty[26]."

> *To delight in God is to become moldable to His plan and His timing. When we are soft, His desires become our desires.*

To delight in our children is to be moldable to who they are. We may think that we are the potters of our children, but perhaps we need to be more pliable to them. Perhaps we need to mold ourselves to them.

Your pregnant body has molded to your baby. Your ribs literally cradle your baby's foot while he kicks you. But what if we applied the same principles to motherhood? What if we are pliable to our children's needs? If we are open to their needs (even when they are completely different from our own), we may see more change.

Can you keep your heart soft to God's plan and timing for your labor and delivery? Can you thank Him for the final touches He is molding into your child? If you already have children, can you be soft to the pre-programmed temperaments of your children? You don't have to change

---

[26] James Strong, "Hebrew and Chaldee Dictionary of the Old Testament," The New Strong's Exhaustive Concordance of the Bible (Nashville: T. Nelson, 1990), 6026.

them. When you're moldable to your children, they actually have the freedom to change more.

It doesn't mean that we don't protect our children. It doesn't mean we stand by silently when we know they are in danger or wrong. But it means we have great joy when we delight in who God has made them to be. When we wait for Him to finish their story, we can wait with a new patience. We can even find delight as we wait to see God do His work.

> **Reflection Questions:**
>
> *How can you shift your focus from trying to mold the perfect child to embracing the process and delighting in your children as they are?*
>
> *Explore your understanding of delighting in God. How can you cultivate a soft and moldable heart aligned with His plan and timing, both in your motherhood journey and other areas of life?*
>
> *Reflect on your own self-care and well-being as a mother. How can you ensure that you nurture yourself spiritually, emotionally, and physically to truly delight in your children? When we do not fill ourselves with the Spirit, it is easy to demand the role of the Spirit from our children.*

38 weeks
Letting Go – God Is Trustworthy

"I [Hannah] prayed for this child, and since the Lord gave me what I asked him for, I now give the boy to the Lord. For as long as he lives, he is given to the Lord." Then he worshiped the Lord there.

1 Samuel 1:27-28, NIV

When will this baby get here? The forty weeks are coming to a close, and if you are still pregnant, you may feel like a ticking time bomb. Some women try to start labor with their spicy bean burritos, speed walking, and castor oil concoctions. But please talk with your birth provider before trying anything to start labor, because there may be recommendations unique to your situation.

The last few weeks of pregnancy feel like forever. I wish we could hit the button for "Eject" as soon as the bun looks semi-done. But the crust is still caramelizing, so let us wait for the finishing touches!

The only one who knows the exact timing of labor is the one who designed it all. God's design for who is the boss? The baby.

Your baby is now in the driver's seat for the start of labor. Babies send a hormone called cortisol to their mommy's brain when they are ready. Your baby's adrenal glands have been maturing in the last few weeks to make cortisol. Cortisol adds the final touches to the baby's lung development by telling the lungs to make surfactant. Surfactant helps your baby's lungs breathe. At the same time, this surfactant also increases inflammation in the uterine wall[27]. The inflammation lifts

---

[27] Carole R. Mendelson, Alina P. Montalbano, and Lu Gao, "Fetal-to-Maternal Signaling in the Timing of Birth," The Journal of Steroid Biochemistry and Molecular Biology 170 (June 1, 2017): 19–27, https://doi.org/10.1016/j.jsbmb.2016.09.006.

the "brake," so the uterine fibers can begin contracting in an organized fashion to start labor.

So yes, your baby is driving before walking. Can you believe these children are the boss of us already?

Letting go of your plans for the timing of this momentous event is incredibly challenging. Some mothers have resigned themselves to this wait. Some mothers have already scheduled their induction or their c-section. But even if you know your baby's birthday, there are still more things to let go.

Motherhood is about learning to let go.

The moment your baby is handed to you, it feels like your baby is yours. For the last nine months, you have been physically connected to your baby by the pearly twine of the umbilical cord. The moment the cord is cut, your body lets go of your baby.

But the emotional and spiritual letting go of our children? This takes a lifetime to perfect. We love these little beings so much that we want to craft the perfect experience for them.

The challenge for the Christian mother is bringing her child back to the Lord. For He is the giver of our children, and we can loosen our grip on all the details.

When you love God more than your children:

> *You will see yourself as a steward of the good gift God has entrusted to you.*
> *You will see your child as an instrument of God's glory.*
> *And ultimately, motherhood will not be about you.*

In 1 Samuel 1, year after year, Hannah struggled with infertility. When she became pregnant, she carried Samuel with the understanding that he would never be truly hers. Like a surrogate mother, Hannah understood who this child belonged to from the very beginning. The child in her womb was the Lord's. Hannah carried her son for the Lord. She carried a pregnancy, breastfed her son, and weaned him—all while still being open-handed to God the entire time.

Hannah knew to whom Samuel belonged. Her sacrifice set her son apart for eternal purposes. Samuel was one of the most influential judges of his time. He was given the wisdom to choose the kings of Israel, including King Saul and King David.

What if we carried our children as if we were surrogate mothers? Knowing that our children are, in fact, the Lord's. The advent of reproductive technologies has allowed women to become surrogate carriers of a pregnancy for another woman. A surrogate mother carries a pregnancy knowing that the child in her womb is not ever truly hers. What if we were able to pray, *"God, this child is yours"* from the moment of conception?

This was my prayer during my first pregnancy, "God, this child is yours." I was a Christian romantic, remember? I didn't know that this answered prayer was going to include a special needs journey for my family. It just seemed like the right thing to pray for at the time. But this prayer posture from the very beginning of my motherhood experience was vital to my survival when she was given her diagnosis. When my world felt like it was falling apart, I knew my child was God's and not mine. This prayer changed my whole experience of picking up the aftermath of her diagnosis.

It is not too early (nor too late) to bring our children back to God, recognizing that they are not ours to begin with. Motherhood is not about us. It is about the glory of God. When we let go, He works in us and through us.

Every stage of parenting has its different joys and struggles. Each day is a new day to bring our children back to the temple. But like Hannah, we can trust that God loves our children even more than we do. He has a great purpose for them—if only we will let go!

Reflection Questions:

In what ways have you experienced letting go of your motherhood experience already? Reflect on moments when you had to release control or adjust your plans for your child's well-being.

Reflect on the story of Hannah from the Bible. How does her example of surrendering her son Samuel to God's purposes resonate with you? Are there aspects of her story that you can apply to your own journey as a mother?

Are you willing to pray, "God, my child is yours?" And would you be able to trust God with the implications of what this prayer means?

39 weeks

The Impostor Syndrome — God Knows The Truth

> *Then Jesus said, "Come to me, all of you who are weary and carry heavy burdens, and I will give you rest. Take my yoke upon you. Let me teach you, because I am humble and gentle at heart, and you will find rest for your souls. For my yoke is easy to bear, and the burden I give you is light."*
>
> Matthew 11:28–30, NLT

The truth is every mother doubts herself. Can I really do this mom thing? Am I going to be a good mom?

But this doubt is usually buried in a small box deep in a mother's soul. First of all, we don't have time to doubt. And second of all, this doubt conflicts with feminism. We are fed by a culture that says we can do it all. And yet, the guilt when we cannot do it all is universal in motherhood.

When we cannot do it all, we tend to cover our guilt by overcompensating. And thus, the Impostor Syndrome is born.

How often have you been tempted to fake it til you make it?

Impostor Syndrome leads to fake personas. We can become Impostor Christians. We can become Impostor Mothers. As long as our worth is being held up by how capable we are, we will miss the point of why Jesus came to this Earth.

But being an honest Self-doubter leads to a real person: Jesus, who pursues us even in our imperfect selves. When we are honest about doubt in our abilities, we find freedom in imperfect motherhood.

Doubt about our motherhood abilities keeps us in the right posture.

Why is self-doubt important for the Christian?

- *Self-doubt brings us to the right questions.*
  Who do we depend on? The default mode is to prove our capability by not needing anyone else. Doubt can be beautiful because it leads us back to our Creator. The conversion of a doubting mother to a trusting mother involves a dependence on a capable God.

- *Self-doubt confronts our limits.*
  We want to believe we are limitless. On some days, you will feel like you have mastered motherhood. But some days (most days), you may wonder if you were actually made for this job. The struggle is real. But God uses our motherhood limits to keep us attentive to His capabilities and less on our own.

- *Self-doubt is a soft ground for eternal vines.*
  When Eve began to wonder if God really knew what He was doing, she doubted the heart of God. Doubt was the reason pain entered the world. When Jesus crushed Satan at the cross, hope was given to every mother who doubted herself. Because one day, her fear of failure will no longer consume her in heaven. But on this Earth, facing failure is God's tender call for His children to find Him.

When you allow self-doubt in your motherhood, you will find freedom. It is beautiful when you can be yourself in front of a Holy God. He already knows who you truly are anyway. You don't need to be perfect to get God's approval. Jesus loves us not because of how good we are. He knows our sins and loves us anyway. You don't need to fear failure.

Personas are burdensome.

> *Jesus wants to carry this burden for you.*
> *Jesus wants to carry your motherhood.*

The motherhood journey is busy from day one. The fetus only continues to grow outside of the womb and has more demands every day. This motherhood thing gets hectic quickly and can be all-consuming. But

Jesus is not asking you to let go of every burden. Instead, He's asking you to let Him help you carry it. "Help me, child, so that I can help you."

The yoke in Matthew 11 is a wooden farming device that connects two oxen by their necks to pull a heavy load. Jesus offers to carry the bulk of the burden and let us carry a lighter load. He promises rest for the burden-carriers. But He also acknowledges that burden carriers will probably never let go, so He makes the load lighter instead. He still wants you to actively participate in your calling to motherhood.

Will you let Him help you carry your motherhood load? Will you let Him carry your fears? Will your heart be gentle and humble as He leads?

When we allow Jesus to lead the yoke, our load becomes lighter. Matthew 11 says that Jesus wants to teach us. He wants to give us rest.

Our children are at the mercy of God rather than at the mercy of every mistake we commit as parents. So don't be an impostor. Be an honest self-doubter, and you will deepen your faith in a capable God.

You can pray, *"Jesus, you carried the ultimate load on your back when you carried the cross. I don't need to carry the cross because of your great mercy. Now, as I walk through the different burdens of motherhood, you walk beside me. You carry the load that I cannot carry. So even if I am not enough, you are enough. Help me be an honest self-doubter so that I return to the cross's beauty each time. Thank you for giving me true rest."*

Reflection Questions:

Have I ever doubted my abilities as a mother? How can these doubts shape my understanding of my need for God's help?

Do I believe that Jesus is willing and able to help me carry the burdens of motherhood? Am I willing to let Him share the load with me?

Do I believe that my children's well-being ultimately rests in God's hands rather than solely on my efforts? How can I cultivate a greater trust in God's plans and purposes for my family?

40 weeks

On Being Held – God Holds Us

> *I love you, Lord, my strength. The Lord is my rock, my fortress and my deliverer; my God is my rock, in whom I take refuge, my shield and the horn of my salvation, my stronghold.*
>
> Psalm 18:1–3, NIV

When you're facing the task of pushing a baby out, it easily trumps all the other fears in your life. It's okay to be worried about how you will handle contractions. Perhaps your excitement is greater than your fear. But most of the time, exhaustion is greater than fear.

The last few weeks, it may get harder to find the mercies of God sustaining you because all you want is for your baby to stop dancing on your bladder! And the prodromal labor contractions are downright annoying!

God is working in these moments of exhaustion! Consider the amazing design of labor and delivery. The cervix is a "donut" made of connective tissue and collagen that changes in its water content the closer a woman gets to her due date. The cervix usually begins to thin out and opens during the last few weeks of pregnancy. The hole in the cervix opens up to one hundred times its normal diameter for a mother to begin pushing[28]!

---

[28] Kristin M. Myers et al., "The Mechanical Role of the Cervix in Pregnancy," Journal of Biomechanics 48, no. 9 (June 1, 2015): 1511–23, https://doi.org/10.1016/j.jbiomech.2015.02.065. This process can take weeks. So even when it feels like "nothing is happening," know that microscopic changes are happening!

The God who has made this process also knows your heart. He knows if you're scared. Labor is scary even when you have done everything to prepare.

But take heart, my friend - the snuggle will be worth the struggle. When contractions begin to get stronger, remember the One who holds you.

A pregnant mama is like a crab clinging to a rock in the middle of the ocean. The waves pummel over the crab. But somehow, the crab can hold on. She is not afraid of the relentless, powerful, and impossible waves.

The task of pushing a baby out may seem impossible. Wave after wave of contractions seem terrifying!

But in between each of the waves, in between each of your contractions, turn your eyes to the rock. The crab's eight legs tightly grip the rock because the rock has deep holes in its surface. As the crab leans into the rock's pockets, the ocean is no longer a place of fear but peace.

The crab is immovable, strong, and *held* by the rock.

In Psalm 18, King David describes God as a rock, a fortress that protects him. On this rock, David feels safe. When you are in labor with contractions crashing down on you, God is your fortress. You are safe with God.

God is the rock who holds onto you during labor and delivery.

His rock has many pockets:

- *He saves you with effective pain management if you want it, such as an epidural.* He gives you a break between contractions so that you can even deliver without an epidural should you desire natural childbirth.
- *He sustains your body even when you are not eating during labor.* When your body is in labor, you do not need any food because of the adrenaline response that shuts off your hunger. God sustains you during labor to have enough energy to do what He has created you to do.
- *He provides at least one compassionate caregiver during your*

birth experience. It is not always who you expect. But even if someone in the team does not understand you, there is always at least one caregiver who becomes the hands and feet of Jesus.

- *He protects your baby by providing a team that can respond to emergencies.* If you deliver in a hospital, there are medical staff who are trained to respond to emergencies in case your baby has trouble breathing or needs extra assistance after birth.

If you focus on the multiple pockets holding you, your peace will be magnified. Your faith will be greater than your fear.

God is your strength. He is your rock. He is your safety.

When your contractions start, my friend, remember who holds you!

Reflection Questions:

Have I focused more on the waves (challenges and difficulties) rather than the rock (God's strength and protection) in my life? How can I shift my focus to trust in God's faithfulness and provision?

In what ways have I experienced God's protection and provision in my pregnancy journey so far? How can I remind myself of these moments and find reassurance in God's ability to hold me during labor and delivery?

How can I surrender my fears and concerns about C-sections or other potential birth outcomes to God? Do I trust that He will protect and guide me through any circumstances that arise?

How can I actively remind myself that I am not alone during labor and delivery?

Part IV
Labor and Delivery

We have just spent the last forty weeks growing in our relationship with God. Sometimes, things go perfectly during pregnancy. Sometimes, pregnancy is not what we expected. Labor and delivery are no different.

You may have comforted yourself by eyeing reliable global population growth. Centuries of women have already made it to the other side and have even come back for more! But honestly, this truth doesn't really make the first contraction pain seem any less scary.

As you prepare for this eviction, a critical mental shift needs to occur. While we know possible detours can occur, we also need to believe that the miracle of birth is in the hands of God.

One of the most significant mental states of making it through the labor marathon is believing *it is possible.*

> *It is possible for your body to birth a baby. God has made you for this. It is possible for you to get through the pain. One contraction at a time.*

Birth has been designed by an incredibly brilliant creator.

Did you know that even paraplegics with spinal cord injuries can give birth vaginally[29]?

How comforting is it to know that even without the physical effort of being able to control your birthing muscles, God has already designed a uterus that is strong enough to push a baby without a mother's help?

We need to believe that the miracle of birth is possible in our bodies.

And at the same time, we need to balance this belief with a realistic one.

The journey of the baby through the birth canal can take longer than you think it will. Or the journey can be so fast you don't even make it to the hospital! Like God, babies have their own timetables. Some babies need to be rescued from the womb. So, if your baby chooses the

---

[29] Molly Khalili et al., "Pregnancy, Delivery, and Neonatal Outcomes among Women with Spinal Cord Injury in Sweden 1997–2015: A Population-based Cohort Study," Acta Obstetricia Et Gynecologica Scandinavica 101, no. 11 (August 28, 2022): 1282–90, https://doi.org/10.1111/aogs.14440.

cesarean bypass, it is still okay! If your provider believes that your baby is stressed during labor, then let the birth plan go. Your medical team wants to give you a healthy baby to hold in your arms. Most providers want you to have a meaningful birth experience. Sometimes, detours from the birth plan are needed.

If your birth plans fall through, you don't have to feel like a failure. You still have a beautiful birth story because it is your story.

You are going to be a mother—by vaginal birth or by cesarean:

A mother who is willing to lay her life down for her child.
A mother whose love is greater than her fear.
A mother whose story is unique to her.

My friend, you are giving the greatest gift to any human being, regardless of how it happens.

You are giving life.

You do not need to prove yourself to anyone, especially yourself. It's going to be beautiful!

Chapter 1

Born—Again Sanctification

(Link to a diagram on the cardinal movements of labor and delivery.)

Before we get into the nitty-gritty details about childbirth, let's feed our souls with the beauty that is about to unfold. Yes, birth is painful. But purposeful pain can be endured.

There is a prize at the end that allows women to face one of the scariest moments of their lives. Baby girl is worth it. Little guy is worth waiting for.

Understanding the journey of a baby through the birth canal is an important part of understanding what to expect in labor. The baby needs to go through a process of rotating in such a way that the easiest diameters fit through the narrowest parts. Most babies follow this path to a vaginal delivery, but not all babies can complete the journey as they should.

Many variables affect a baby's path. Is the baby too big to fit through the tunnel? Is the tunnel too narrow? Is the baby stuck in the wrong position? Are contractions strong enough?

The distance from womb to delivery is roughly the length of an adult's hand. And yet, it can be the longest distance in the world—especially for a tired mama on the third day of her labor induction.

As a baby journeys through the birth canal, his movements are purposeful. If he does not tuck his chin into his chest at the right time, he will become trapped in the birth canal. Birth mechanics are simple in theory, but one missed movement may be the difference between a vaginal delivery and the need for a c-section. The journey from the womb to the world is both beautiful and broken.

Similarly, the Christian's journey from the womb to the tomb is both beautiful and broken. Christians consider themselves "born again" when they accept the gift of Jesus for salvation and eternal life. But sanctification, or being made like Jesus, means identifying with Jesus even in His suffering. Sanctification requires a cost. The Christian undergoes "sanctifying postures" that can either sour or deepen her relationship with God.

Let's go over the different birth movements a baby makes through the birth canal and parallel these movements to the "sanctifying postures" of the Christian.

1. ***Engagement:*** The baby descends into the pelvis and chooses to "engage" in the birth process.
   When going through seasons of suffering, we choose whether or not we will engage with God. We can try to "fix" problems on our own, or we can engage in conversation with God. We must ask ourselves if He is trustworthy enough to carry our burdens.

2. ***(Neck) Flexion:*** The baby's chin is tucked into his chest, looking down at his feet. His head is cradled by the pelvic muscles.
   When we suffer, our faces are downcast. We tend to focus inward. We can spend time wallowing, but then we must ask ourselves who we worship more. Suffering reveals the lies we believe and the idols that we trust.

3. ***Internal Rotation:*** The baby rotates into the position allowing the narrow part of his head to proceed under the pubic bone.

The beginning of our sanctification is when we turn away from ourselves and turn toward God. Suffering gives us the perspective of how small our worlds are relative to God's world.

4. **Extension:** The baby extends his head with eyes up to the sky as he begins crowning.
   We must look up to Jesus as we choose to trust Him again and again. Only when we keep our eyes upward will we see Him providing for our needs.

5. **External Rotation:** After his head has emerged, the baby rotates his head outward, looking around his new world.
   A posture that is now focused outward and upward can now bless others outside of ourselves.

6. **Expulsion/Delivery of Shoulders and Body:** The baby is placed skin-to-skin on his mother's chest.
   Relief and peace flood the room. We are given a new peace because of our pain. Our crosses have a new purpose.

When a baby misses a step in birth movements, labor is prolonged. Obstetricians call the obstructed process "labor dystocia." Suffering lasts longer, and more interventions are needed, including possibly a cesarean. But if the obstetrician can help facilitate these movements by making contractions stronger or rotating the baby's position, a vaginal delivery may still be possible.

When Christians suffer, we spend a different amount of time in each stage of sanctification. At times, we can become stalled in one of the postures, experiencing a "sanctification dystocia." We can become embittered or disillusioned if we trust our emotions.

Emotions are beautifully God-given, but certain emotions can also slow our healing. We suffer longer when bitterness stalls our sanctification. We may excuse our addictions because we believe we are owed. We may surf the victim vortex that tells us it is everyone else's fault rather than our own. We may need help from professionals, ministry leaders, and others who have also experienced "sanctification dystocia." Ultimately, knowing Jesus is what delivers us from ourselves.

When you read the Bible to understand this tender hearted Savior, it will sanctify your emotions. The words of Jesus will meet you in those dark places so that you can "internally rotate" away from yourself. The hope of heaven will keep your head "extended," looking up to Jesus. A focus on an eternal kingdom will diffuse into the spheres of influence for which you "externally rotate." You will find yourself with a new holy purpose.

The shortest distances are often the most difficult ones to overcome. For a baby, an average of four inches can be the longest journey from the womb to the world. For the brokenhearted, a twelve-inch gap spans the distance from the head to the heart.

A Christian is sanctified when the crosses of motherhood help her identify with Jesus' story. God personalizes His gospel story for each of us. He wants to weave His story of redemption into ours.

Reflection Questions:

Think about a time that you "suffered." Most people think that suffering needs to be a catastrophic event, but "suffering" is akin to drowning. Drowning occurs at five inches or at five feet under water. Rather than comparing your degree of suffering to someone else to justify why you can call your struggle "suffering," think about a time that you have felt out of control. And let this be a moment that you ask yourself these questions and then reflect on the scripture that follows each of these questions:

What does my suffering teach me about Jesus? (Isaiah 53:3)

What does my suffering teach me about my sin? (Job 36:15)

Is God's plan better than mine? (Luke 22:42)

Is God's mercy enough for today's trial? (Lamentations 3:21–33)

How will God use my bruises for His ministry? (2 Corinthians 1:3–7)

Am I filled with the peace that surrounds the cross? (John 14:27)

Chapter 2

Labor and Delivery Expectations

This section of the book is different from the previous sections. I hope to help empower you with the truth of what actually happens in labor and delivery. Knowledge helps empower women to be less anxious about the unknown. There are so many sources of "truth" on social media that it is a dizzying time and place for women to find reliable information.

This part of the book is written from my professional experience and personal experiences as an obstetrician. Each physician and midwife has a different practice style, so I can only speak from my own experiences as an obstetrician who practices in a hospital. I am biased toward delivering in the hospital as I believe all deliveries are vulnerable to unexpected curveballs. Having immediate access to medical care in a hospital is lifesaving for mothers and their babies. I absolutely believe God is sovereign over birth. I also believe God can save mamas and babies through the hands of trained medical professionals.

We will go over labor and delivery in general terms, knowing that every woman's experience is her own. I will not be able to cover every detour that can occur in labor and delivery. Inductions or unique medical complications of pregnancy can cause unexpected birth experiences, and these detours are significant in your motherhood journey. Talk to your birth provider for questions specific to your pregnancy and birth experience. Even if your birth story turns out differently than you expect, I hope that the last forty weeks together have shown you that there is One who already holds all of the detours in His hand.

He will bring to completion the beauty that He has already started in your womb.

And I am certain that God, who began the good work within you, will continue his work until it is finally finished on the day when Christ Jesus returns.

Philippians 1:6, NLT

The Truth About Labor

Let's talk about the signs that labor may be approaching.

Over the last few weeks of pregnancy, you may experience "lightening" when the baby drops into your pelvis. You should feel like it is easier to take a deep breath, but it also feels like you are waddling more. Not all women experience this to have a vaginal delivery, and it is more commonly felt in women with their first baby.

An increase in vaginal discharge can signify that the cervix is dilating. Some women experience an increase in diarrhea a few days before their delivery. These symptoms are not diagnostic of labor nor absolutely predictive. Talk with your provider if you have these signs, as they usually have specific advice based on your symptoms. You may notice that your doctor is referring to your cervix as if it were an aging fruit. Is your cervix ripe yet?

A ripe cervix is already beginning to open and this means that there's a higher chance of a vaginal delivery once contractions begin. The cervix is the "donut" that flattens with contractions and stretches open. The hole of the donut, or inner circle, is measured in centimeters. The diameter of dilation is a subjective exam measured by your provider's fingers. Usually, for women with their first baby, the cervix is closed even at full term. For women who have already had babies, they may start with a more dilated cervix. Labor is official once contractions become regular and the cervix begins dilating.

When labor starts, it can be subtle. Contractions usually start off as back pain, abdominal tightening, or a similar feeling to menstrual cramps. False labor may also have painful contractions. But false contractions lessen in intensity and frequency with time. True labor involves contractions that increase in intensity and frequency with time. The distinction between true and false labor may not always be possible without a cervical exam from a healthcare provider.

Contractions are more likely to be "doing something" if you must breathe through them because they are so intense. If you can watch Netflix without flinching, then it is not labor. But once you have contractions every three to five minutes with increasingly greater intensity, you are likely in labor. Your provider will give you instructions about when to come to the hospital for evaluation.

Some labors start with your water breaking without contractions. Sometimes, the contractions start first, and the water does not break unless your doctor helps you. Your doctor or midwife may use an amnihook (which looks like a plastic knitting needle) to help break the water. Breaking water is painless as no nerve fibers are on the amniotic bag. However, contractions tend to get more intense and closer together once your water is broken, so keep this in mind for pain management!

When you are admitted to labor and delivery at the hospital, you will have two straps wrapped around your belly to monitor your labor. One strap monitors the baby's heart rate, and the other strap monitors how often you are contracting. Most of the time, labor can be managed by external monitors. Sometimes, there is a need for internal monitors that are placed inside the uterus to monitor the contractions and the baby's heart rate. It is not routine that internal monitors are needed. They can be helpful to monitor the baby if the outside monitors are not giving enough information to care for your baby safely.

The goal of the first phase of labor is for the cervix to open to ten centimeters in diameter. The diameter of the birth canal is roughly ten centimeters when there is no cervix felt around the baby's head. The medical lingo to describe this is "completely dilated" or "fully dilated." You will get cervical checks throughout labor to make sure that you are continuing to make progress. Sometimes, contractions can slow down, and to keep making progress, you may need a medication called Pitocin.

Pitocin is the name brand for the hormone oxytocin, a hormone released by your pituitary gland. Pitocin causes a release of calcium in your uterine muscles. The muscles at the top of the uterus pull up on the lower part of the uterus until the cervix opens completely. Imagine squeezing a Mentos candy out of its package, and you will understand what contractions are doing to your cervix. (sorry, Mentos will never look the same). If contractions are not strong enough, the cervix will not change. But if you let Pitocin supplement what your body is already trying to do, your suffering can be shortened. The pain may be more intense, but the labor will be shorter in duration. Talk with your medical team if you have concerns about Pitocin.

It is important to keep active, especially in labor. This causes contractions to get closer together. Repositioning and movement can help manage your pain. You may notice that your nurse may recommend certain positions for you to help the baby rotate into the right position for birth.

Sometimes, an epidural is important to help your pelvic muscles relax. When your pelvic floor relaxes, the baby can drop into the pelvis, and the cervix can dilate fully. One of the hardest parts of labor and delivery is knowing which muscles to relax and which ones to tense up. Your team should be able to help coach you with which muscles you need to use and which muscles you should relax.

The Truth About Pushing

Pushing a baby out takes a coordinated muscle dance. You will need to push during the second phase of labor when your cervix is completely dilated. Learning how to concentrate your energy on the "right" places of your body for effective pushing takes some time.

But let's simplify pushing.

If you know how to poop, you will know how to push. You use the same muscles to push out a baby. Even if you cannot feel your body with an epidural, you will still have control over your pushing muscles. And if you do not have an epidural, sometimes the pushing starts involuntarily before you are completely dilated. The nurses may coach you to relax so that you are pushing at the right times.

During pushing, the baby must move under the pubic bone so his or her head can "crown." Pick a spot between the intersection of the wall and the ceiling to focus on during your pushing. During this time, it may feel like you are pushing but not making progress. Most of the time, there is progress with each push, even if you do not feel like it is making a difference. Your baby's head has been designed to change its shape in order to fit through the birth canal (Don't worry, God takes care of coned heads). If your baby comes out with a conehead, do not be alarmed. The baby's head is very moldable, and by the next day, it reshapes into a more normal head shape.

When pushing the baby out, many women feel like they want to give up. But one of the mercies of this stage of labor is that there are usually breaks between each contraction. So, use each of these breaks to close your eyes, take a deep breath, and regroup your mojo before you go into the next push. Sometimes, music helps keep you focused. Make a "push playlist" on Spotify to keep you energized.

Pushing takes a lot of mental energy. Sometimes, maintaining mental energy is more challenging than maintaining physical stamina. You may feel like you cannot do it. You may feel trapped. The minutes may feel like hours. But you will make it! Remaining calm and focused is an important part of getting on top of the pain. Remind yourself that your Creator has made your body for this moment.

If you are getting annoyed at the process, channel that anger into your pushing. Tell that baby who is boss. (This might be your last time to get that word in. The baby believes that he or she is the boss after birth.)

Your baby's head may seem like the hardest part to deliver. Once the baby's head is delivered, the rest of the baby's body delivers quickly. On rare occasions, the baby's shoulders get stuck, which may necessitate your provider to use different maneuvers to get the baby out safely.

The Truth About Post-Delivery

Once the baby is delivered, the energy in the room shifts to the baby. Everyone surrounds the baby like the paparazzi! It's somewhat anticlimactic. You have done all the hard work, pushing with so much encouragement, and suddenly, the support shifts. It may feel like your cheerleading team has stopped cheering for you and has rushed the stage while you stay in the background. Sometimes, the baby can go directly to your chest for skin-to-skin contact. Sometimes, your baby needs more time to transition with the nursery nurses. It is not uncommon for babies to need help with the transition to their first breath. As they peek their heads out for the first time, sometimes their first breath is a gulp of amniotic fluid. They may require extra suctioning to clear their airway. They may look limp right after they are born, but usually, after five minutes, they are squirming around.

Your obstetrician or midwife will stay by your side after the baby is born. Sometimes, it can take up to thirty minutes before the placenta delivers. The placenta has a story too. She may grieve that she is no longer needed and hold on longer than you'd like. Even placentas have personalities. While you wait for your placenta to do her thing, there is plenty to keep you and your medical team busy! You will have your baby to hold and your provider may be repairing any vaginal tears with sutures.

Most women are terrified of vaginal tears. Yes, they do happen. Even with perineal massage, many factors can affect the extent of the tear. If the baby comes out with his arm in "carpe diem" fashion or is determined to come out looking at the ceiling, there are no fancy oils that can prevent a tear. Skin elasticity, pelvic bone shapes, and the baby's diameter all can affect the extent of a tear. But rest assured that the vulva is a very vascular area that will heal quickly. Even if women receive stitches, they dissolve by the six week visit. Most women are back to their normal exercise by two months postpartum.

Once the placenta is delivered, you will get a massage (be forewarned, it's not Swedish or Deep Tissue). It is a uterine massage, and it hurts! The massage helps your uterus stay firm so you do not have bleeding afterward. This is because sometimes a clot can form inside the uterus that does not allow the uterus to clamp down on itself. It's like a baseball glove with a baseball inside. If the ball is not removed, the glove cannot close. A clot may need to be removed with a uterine massage and an internal exam. When the uterus can "squeeze" on itself fully without the clot in the way, the bleeding decreases. This is why your medical team will be pushing on your belly, sometimes with more force than you would expect.

You may be too distracted by your beautiful baby to notice what's happening around you. Most mamas have an endorphin high that helps them focus on their excitement over the pain. But it's also not uncommon for mamas to need time to recover from the intensity of the delivery before holding their baby. You may need time to regroup and focus as your care provider assists your recovery. It's also a perfect time for daddy to get a turn to hold your precious child!

The Truth About Cesarean Sections

Your obstetrician wants you to have a vaginal delivery. The recovery is easier for women who have vaginal deliveries. But ultimately, a healthy mama and healthy baby are your healthcare provider's main priority. It is important that you believe your provider's intentions are for your good. Otherwise, it makes a very awkward and uncomfortable delivery experience. If you are having trouble trusting your care provider, having these discussions before labor and delivery is important.

There are many reasons for a c-section. Sometimes, cesareans are needed because the baby cannot tolerate labor. A cesarean is needed to rescue the baby. Sometimes, a cesarean is needed if the cervix stops dilating. This is more common when the baby is looking toward the ceiling instead of the floor (the baby is "posterior"). When the baby's head is not pressing against the entire cervix, the cervix stops dilating. Sometimes, a cesarean is needed if the baby is stuck in the birth canal. If this is the case, your baby and your body require rescue.

Your child may have another plan for how he or she will enter the world. God can make a safe detour to deliver your baby by cesarean.

When a cesarean is indicated, some mothers are visibly disappointed and frustrated. It can be incredibly frustrating, especially if they have been following all of the medical team's instructions for position changes and laboring for hours. We have a certain idea of what our births will look like. It is not easy to let that go.

Sometimes a vaginal delivery is not possible without significant complications. A cesarean may be the mercy of God, who is trying to protect us. Laying down our lives for our children is the very picture of

Jesus on the cross. We let go of our plans for the good of someone else. Your sacrificial love is a beautiful gift you are giving your child.

While there is usually time to discuss the procedure, emergent situations may necessitate an urgent cesarean delivery. If you have an epidural, you can be awake for the cesarean. However, if you do not have an epidural, you may need general anesthesia, which means you will be asleep while the baby is born.

During a c-section, your arms are strapped to arm boards, and your body is held by a "seatbelt" on the bed. Your skin will be tested before surgery to ensure you are numb. You should not feel any sharp pain, but you may feel the pressure of your obstetrician pushing on your belly when the baby is delivered. Vomiting is not an uncommon experience during cesarean delivery, and the anesthesiologist has medications to help if needed.

After delivery, the baby is taken to a warmer for evaluation by the nursing team and pediatrician. Babies born by cesarean may have more amniotic fluid in their lungs. The nurses suction the baby's airways to remove this extra fluid. Sometimes, the babies need to go to the nursery for extra oxygen as they transition to breathing on their own. Babies born by cesarean also may have more fluid in their ears and may fail their initial hearing tests. Talk to your pediatrician if you have any concerns.

In a cesarean, it can feel very anticlimactic when your doctor delivers your baby, and you do not get immediate skin-to-skin contact. After the baby is delivered, the baby is moved to the warmer instead of your chest. But it is still going to be okay. You can still bond with your baby in the recovery room. You can still do skin-to-skin in the recovery room. You can still breastfeed even after a cesarean.

Cesareans are the exit path for one out of every three babies that are born in the United States[30].

A C-section ejection is still a beautiful birth.

---

[30] "Total Cesarean Deliveries by Maternal Race: United States, 2019-2021 Average," March of Dimes | PeriStats, Accessed 8/1/2023, https://www.marchofdimes.org/peristats/data?lev=1&obj=1*=99&slev=1&stop=355&top=8.

Without access to a cesarean, women can labor for days with their baby trapped in their pelvis. Not only does this increase the chance of damage to their baby's brain, but there can be unnecessary harm to their pelvic muscles. Fistulas (an abnormal connection between the bladder and vagina) are complications of prolonged labor when a cesarean is inaccessible.

Access to hospital care and collaboration with your medical team is an important part of having a healthy birth story.

The Truth About Pain Management

The pain experience of labor, delivery, and postpartum is different for all. We expect pain in pregnancy. We expect pains during labor and delivery. But we rarely talk about postpartum pain. We will briefly review some of the different times to expect pain and how to advocate for yourself in these moments.

Many women make plans for their pain management before experiencing the pain of a contraction. However, a woman in pain is usually in a different state of mind. The intensity of labor is very difficult to describe to someone who has not experienced it before.

There are also non-medication routes for pain management. Although we will not be going into any detail in this book, if you are interested in understanding more about this, look up information on the Gate Control Theory. In short, the brain interprets pain differently if other sensory inputs are happening simultaneously. The nerve fibers that carry information about contraction pain differ from those that carry information about vibration. By having both signals simultaneously, the vibration pain signal may "close" the gate for the sharp contraction pain signal to reach the brain[31]. For example, water immersion in a tub can help the brain interpret the contractions as less painful. Also, in early labor, squeezing a plastic comb before a contraction begins may decrease the severity of contraction pain that the brain can process.

---

[31] Lorne M. Mendell, "Constructing and Deconstructing the Gate Theory of Pain," Pain 155, no. 2 (February 1, 2014): 210–16, https://doi.org/10.1016/j.pain.2013.12.010.

In early labor, women can usually walk and bounce on a ball. Some women have back labor (contractions feel like back pain) if the baby is facing posteriorly. For those who are interested in pain medication, intravenous (IV) pain medications are usually an option in early labor. IV pain medications are given through a catheter that is placed into your vein. Narcotics are given based on the doctor's experience and preference. But as contractions get closer together and more intense, the IV pain medications will be less effective in taking the edge off the pain. Usually, an epidural is the most effective option for pain management. At about eight to ten centimeters, when a woman is "transitioning," it becomes difficult to sit still for an epidural. It is important to understand that medications and epidurals given at the right time can help you have a more pleasant birth experience—your care team will help you determine when is the best time for you and your baby.

According to a study on 17 million women who birthed from 2009 to 2015, 65–76% of women got an epidural during labor[32]. While it is true that women have delivered without epidurals for millennia, our merciful and loving God gave us a multitude of options for pain management that we can choose from without shame.

Sometimes, women associate epidurals as a weakness in their armor. But sometimes, epidurals are really important for labor progress. When your body is stressed from pain, cortisol, the stress hormone, is roaring through your body. This causes your pelvic floor to tighten up, narrowing the path for the baby to drop into the pelvis. Many times, after an epidural, the baby can descend easier and faster through the birth canal[33].

---

[32] Alexander J. Butwick, Cynthia A. Wong, and Nan Guo, "Maternal Body Mass Index and Use of Labor Neuraxial Analgesia," Anesthesiology 129, no. 3 (September 1, 2018): 448–58, https://doi.org/10.1097/aln.0000000000002322.

[33] Michael H. Walter, Harald Abele, and Claudia F. Plappert, "The Role of Oxytocin and the Effect of Stress during Childbirth: Neurobiological Basics and Implications for Mother and Child," Frontiers in Endocrinology 12 (October 27, 2021), https://doi.org/10.3389/fendo.2021.742236.

Not all epidurals are created equal. Sometimes, the epidural "doesn't work" nor provides the level of numbness that you may expect. Many variables, like an individual's anatomical differences, can affect an epidural's effectiveness. Your delivery team can help troubleshoot if needed. The pain medication for an epidural doesn't "run out," as the cartridge can be replaced. The medicine runs continuously into your back through a small tube.

If you get an epidural, you may still feel the pressure building with each contraction, but it will no longer be a sharp pain. The relief women feel after an epidural is almost instantaneous. It feels like floating on a cloud after an unrelenting thunderstorm. Your legs will feel numb and weak. It is normal if you cannot move your legs after an epidural. With an epidural, you will likely have a urinary catheter placed in your bladder since you will not be able to control your bladder. Once you have an epidural in place, you will not be able to walk around.

Although the sharp pain will be gone after an epidural, women feel more pressure as the baby descends into the pelvis. An epidural usually numbs the skin when the baby's head and body are being delivered. In some cases, it does not take away all of the sensation.

The "Ring of Fire" is the burning pain from the skin of the vulva that stretches around the baby's head when the baby is crowning. Epidurals usually take this pain away. But for those without an epidural, this burning pain is usually the moment that most women want to back away and stop pushing. But at this moment, picture a tiger jumping through a flaming hoop at the circus—push into the pain and through the pain—and the baby will be here!

After the baby is delivered, you may need a repair for a vaginal laceration. This involves a needle to inject the local anesthetic. Lidocaine can remove the feeling of sharpness, but you may still feel the tugging of the suture. If you need stitches, it is usually a suture that will dissolve by the time you see your provider at your six-week postpartum visit.

Most women focus so much effort on preparing for labor and delivery that they forget about the pain postpartum (see The Truth on Postpartum)! But the recovery after a delivery persists into the first few weeks as mamas heal from their stitches. Sometimes, sitz baths help dissolve the sutures faster if your provider recommends them.

As you recover, breastfeeding awaits.

The Truth About Breastfeeding

Many women have a desire to breastfeed. Breastmilk is a nectar full of nutrients, antibodies, and fatty acids that are gentle on a baby's gut. Obviously, it is cost-effective. There are also multiple health benefits to breastfeeding. Breastfeeding is recommended by the American Academy of Pediatrics due to its benefits in decreasing ear infections, SIDS (sudden infant death syndrome), and childhood obesity, to name a few[34].

However, there can be unexpected barriers to breastfeeding. The top two reasons that women stop breastfeeding are fatigue from feeding or inadequate milk supply[35]. Your care team can help you with your baby's latch to help you have more efficient feedings while you are in the hospital. Milk supply issues are not always clear until after you leave the hospital. You can always talk to an outpatient lactation consultant if you have supply issues.

The first few days after birth, you will make nutrient-rich nectar called colostrum. It looks like a cloudy gold liquid. It may seem like the baby is not getting enough fluids initially. But the baby's stomach is small (the size of a marble!), and the baby does not need much fluid to be hydrated. Your care team will help you count wet diapers to ensure the baby is well hydrated.

God has designed a unique supply-and-demand system for breast milk production. As the baby continues to suckle, this signals your brain to convert colostrum into milk[36].

---

[34] "Breastfeeding Overview," Accessed 9/4/2023, https://www.aap.org/en/patient-care/breastfeeding/breastfeeding-overview/.

[35] Christine Brown et al., "Factors Influencing the Reasons Why Mothers Stop Breastfeeding," Canadian Journal of Public Health 105, no. 3 (May 1, 2014): e179–85, https://doi.org/10.17269/cjph.105.4244.

[36] Felix Jozsa, "Anatomy, Colostrum," StatPearls - NCBI Bookshelf, February 5, 2023, https://www.ncbi.nlm.nih.gov/books/NBK513256/.

Often, your milk does not come in while you are in the hospital and does not change until a few days after delivery. You will find yourself more thirsty over the first few days after delivery. The water in your body is flooding the breast tissue. Think of breasts as a frozen concentrate flooded with water to make juice. The colostrum becomes "diluted" into milk. Your breasts may feel hard when your milk comes in. Engorgement can be painful because of the swelling of your breast tissue. Talk to your lactation consultant for ideas of what you can do to decrease your pain from breast engorgement if this affects your ability to breastfeed.

For some women, breastfeeding has different seasons of barriers. You may find that some feeds go well while others do not go well at all. Don't be discouraged when not all feeds are ideal. Breastfeeding is a dynamic learning curve. The demands change as the baby grows. Your baby's latch can change from week to week. What works today may not work tomorrow, and vice versa. Breastfeeding can be a ninja obstacle course!

Breastfeeding can be challenging for women regardless of how the baby is delivered. For women who have trouble breastfeeding after a cesarean, some women wonder if it is the cesarean that has impacted their breastfeeding success. If women have long labors leading up to the cesarean their breastfeeding experience may be affected by exhaustion. Lactation consultants can help you as you work through the first few days after your delivery. Talk to your provider if you have trouble with the baby's latch or milk supply.

Remember that God knows what your baby needs. He is a creative designer. As your baby demands more milk, the breasts make more milk (and sometimes too much)! If breastfeeding does not work out, God has also provided a worthy alternative food source. Breastfeeding is good for the baby but not always good for every mom. He is merciful in providing ways for babies to thrive even on formula.

The Truth About Postpartum Pain

Hopefully, you will take the time to marvel at the wondrous creation in front of you as you tickle the feet that have been kicking you for the last

Labor and Delivery Expectations

forty weeks. May the wonder of your child cover the not-so-glamorous parts of postpartum. The postpartum experience is a euphoric blur. But honestly, this part is going to pass quickly. The early morning hangouts will be over before you know it.

Postpartum pain is different for everyone. Sometimes, you may have contraction pains again as you begin breastfeeding. God uses the same hormone, oxytocin, to release milk and contract the uterus. For women who have had children before, this cramping tends to be worse. These contractions prevent you from having postpartum hemorrhage by shrinking the uterus down to its original size. The cramping is protective, even though it may not feel good! Talk with your medical team if your pain is not being managed well.

Your postpartum nurses will help you manage pain from any laceration or incision. After a cesarean, you may need narcotics for the first few days. For those who have had a cesarean, your medical team will likely remove your bandage the first day after surgery. For those who have had a vaginal delivery, an ice pack is very important to help decrease swelling. Taking pain medications on a schedule can facilitate a faster recovery. Pain medications work better for both recoveries before the discomfort becomes too painful. Once the pain escalates to a certain level, it takes longer for the pain medications to work.

If you are experiencing nipple pain from breastfeeding, talk with a lactation consultant. Nipples are made in all shapes and sizes. If a latch is not deep enough, nipple pain can escalate quickly. Nurses can help you find the correct latch. While some initial discomfort is okay, breastfeeding should not hurt. If nursing causes pain, it may mean that the baby is not latched on correctly. You should get assistance from a lactation consultant as soon as possible.

Postpartum is an exhausting time for new parents. It is a sacred time only for you and your true village. It is okay to set boundaries so you can prioritize rest. There are already so many interruptions for a new mother. Medical staff will interrupt your sleep (in addition to your little one who knows exactly when you've just fallen asleep). Give yourself permission to protect your peace.

Most families stay in the hospital one to two days after a vaginal delivery and two to four days after a cesarean. During this time, there is a lot of support available for you. Nurses help you stay on top of pain management. A pediatrician makes sure your baby is growing. A lactation nurse helps you find a comfortable latch for breastfeeding. And there is a glorious button that will call a nurse to take your baby to the nursery if you need a break! Hospitals are encouraging rooming-in for newborns to improve the chances of breastfeeding success. But if you are reaching a point of exhaustion, it's okay to use the nursery for a break. You need to leave the hospital with some reserve in your energy tank. Accepting the help of a nursery does not make you a weaker mom. Help makes you a rested and resilient mom. For women who have prolonged labor, you may need more time to recover in the hospital (with the baby in the nursery) before going home.

And then they will tell you that you're ready to go home. And as you walk slowly out of the postpartum wing and get into your car, it all becomes real. The door closes. The weight of responsibility is both exciting and terrifying. There is no nurse call bell. No one to tell you that you are doing it correctly. No one tells you that you are doing it incorrectly. It is a mix of excitement and silence in this car ride home.

But you are going to be great at this. Why? Because you are the perfect parents for your child. God has custom-picked each child for his or her mother. He has equipped you to care for this little baby in ways you don't even realize yet. You do not go alone. You go with God.

Welcome to the next chapter of your life.

Myths About Labor and Delivery

I would like to debunk some of the myths that women believe on social media and answer some of them in general terms.

Myth #1: "When my water breaks, there will be a big gush, followed by a birthing head."

Reality: While water breaking can lead to a faster delivery, it is rare for a baby to arrive right after Niagara Falls. Unlike the movies, you need your water to break with contractions to have a torpedo birth. Usually, there is time to go to the hospital once the water breaks. But if you have birthed a child before, the tunnel is already open. It may not take many contractions for your cervix to be completely open. Call your provider's office when your water breaks because they may have different instructions for you based on your pregnancy.

Myth #2: "Water breaking is a dramatic waterfall."

Reality: Most of the time, water breaking is unmistakable. But there are times when a slow amniotic fluid leak is possible. It is important to talk to your provider if you constantly feel wet.

Myth #3: "Labor starts with strong contractions."

Reality: Most contractions start as mild and irregular. With time, the contractions become more strong and regular. Strong contractions are the effective ones that change your cervix. A changing cervical exam is your ticket to admission to Labor and Delivery.

Myth #4: "I won't know if I am experiencing a real contraction."

Reality: If contractions were represented by punctuation, a Braxton-Hicks contraction is like a question mark. A true contraction is an exclamation mark. It has a beginning, middle (most intense), and end. For the musicians, think of a contraction as having a crescendo and then a decrescendo. A true contraction is usually unmistakable. Some women describe a contraction as menstrual cramps, a charley horse, or intense back pain.

Myth #5: "The recovery from a cesarean is more painful than a vaginal birth."

Reality: Recovery is easier after a vaginal delivery than a c-section. Less pain medication is needed after a vaginal delivery (although most women are not using narcotics a week after their c-section). But honestly, both exits are painful. Both exits have a recovery process. For vaginal deliveries, different degrees of vaginal tears require a different amount of stitches. Sometimes a vaginal delivery can even be a more painful recovery than a cesarean incision. Most women are surprised by the mobility they have after a cesarean. They are able to move better than they may have expected due to the many pain management options that anesthesiologists offer.

Myth #6: "If I get an epidural, my labor will slow down, and I will have a higher chance of a cesarean."

Reality: A 2018 meta-analysis showed that epidurals do not increase the risk of cesarean delivery[37].

However, it may take longer to push a baby out with an epidural compared to someone who does not have an epidural. Sometimes, it may take longer to get the hang of pushing without feeling the contractions. If your contractions become more infrequent after receiving an epidural, you may need Pitocin. Regular contractions are important to keep the momentum going to change your cervix.

Myth #7: "Pitocin contractions hurt more than regular contractions."

Reality: This is somewhat true. Effective contractions should hurt. Your cervix is changing. If you need Pitocin, chances are your contractions are not strong enough to make a difference in your progress. Pitocin adds gas to the engine, and there is a sudden boost of energy to the uterine muscles. Stronger contractions mean more painful contractions. If the contractions are too frequent, the amount of Pitocin can be decreased.

Myth #8: "I need to eat during labor to have energy."

Reality: When your body is in a stressed state of labor, your hunger drive will be a lower priority. Your body is in a fight-or-flight mode. Your brain will be focused on getting through contractions rather than filling your stomach. Many women feel nauseous in labor as intense pain causes nausea. A diet of clear liquids in labor is recommended because eating food can cause problems during intubation (putting a breathing tube in) if an emergency cesarean is needed. You will not get dehydrated in labor because you can drink clear fluids and receive intravenous (IV) fluids during labor.

---

[37] Millicent Anim- Somuah et al., "Epidural versus Non-Epidural or No Analgesia for Pain Management in Labour," The Cochrane Library 2018, no. 5 (May 21, 2018), https://doi.org/10.1002/14651858.cd000331.pub4.

Labor and Delivery Expectations

Myth #9: "The doctor will cut me a new one."

Reality: Routine episiotomies are no longer done at every delivery. Talk with your provider to understand practice styles. Episiotomies are no longer indicated unless your baby is in distress and requires a faster delivery.

Myth #10: "The placenta always delivers after delivery."

Reality: Sometimes, it can take up to thirty minutes after the birth for the placenta to deliver. If the placenta does not detach, surgery (dilation and curettage, i.e., "D and C") is needed to remove all of the pieces of the placenta.

Myth #11: "I may get the 'shakes' after delivery because I'm cold."

Reality: Most of the shivering after a delivery is related to an endorphin and adrenaline release. Your body has gone through an incredible amount of stress, and it takes time for your mind and body to connect again. The shaking will pass. I often tell my patients to stick their tongue to the roof of their mouth as this gives them something to focus on so that the shakes do not bother them as much.

Myth #12: "Breastfeeding is natural."

Reality: Yes, the milk is natural. But the act of breastfeeding is not always natural. Some feedings go well, and it feels like, "Aha! I've got it!" And then some other feedings do not go well at all. During the first twenty-four hours, the baby is often sleepy and uninterested in feeding. But as the baby becomes more awake, the demand for feedings increases. For some women, breastfeeding is seamless. But for many women, breastfeeding has more barriers than they expect.

Myth #13: "My breast milk will come in right after I deliver."

Reality: Breastmilk can take twenty-four to forty-eight hours to come in. When the baby is put to the breast for the first time after delivery, the baby is receiving colostrum. Colostrum is called "liquid gold," as it is rich with antibodies that help your baby's immune system.

Myth #14: "I will love breastfeeding."

Reality: Not all women love breastfeeding. Breastfeeding can affect a woman's self-worth (more on this to come). Breastfeeding is a continuance of laying down your body for your child. Some women think it is worth it, especially if it comes easily for them. But for the women who are running into every obstacle, beware of letting breastfeeding define your worth as a mother.

Lactation consultants, obstetricians, and pediatricians can help you find the best plan for you and your child. Your pediatrician will recommend breastfeeding. But if you find that your mental health is suffering as a result of breastfeeding, you will need to be honest with yourself and your medical team. If you are having trouble bonding with your baby because of breastfeeding, then you may need to take a step back.

Myth #15: "I am not at risk of postpartum depression because I have a good support system."

Reality: A recent study identified previous depression, current depression and anxiety, and low partner support as key risk factors[38].

But the risk factors I have observed for postpartum depression are when:

1. Mamas do not feel in control of their breastfeeding experience.
2. Women have had a birth experience they regret.
3. Women have a baby that is difficult to soothe.
4. Mamas are not getting a break from the constant demand.

A big identity change happens when you have a baby. Even with the best support system, mothers have an instinctual pressure to feed and train their young. Sometimes, there are blatant reasons for postpartum depression (admission to the neonatal intensive care unit, a colicky baby, etc.). Sometimes, there are no obvious reasons for postpartum depression. Even with the best support system, perfect sleeping baby, and easy breastfeeding experience, postpartum depression still happens.

We will discuss more of the changes that are happening to your mother's soul in the postpartum section.

---

[38] Teri Pearlstein et al., "Postpartum Depression," American Journal of Obstetrics and Gynecology 200, no. 4 (April 1, 2009): 357–64, https://doi.org/10.1016/j.ajog.2008.11.033.

Chapter 3
QR Codes for Bible Verses from Pregnancy and Postpartum Devotions

Labor and delivery can be a marathon. Every woman needs something different to keep them focused during their labor. If you enjoy meditating on scripture, the following QR code will lead you to scriptures from each of the devotions in this book. You can reference these Bible verses from your smartphone while in labor or postpartum.

Bible Verses From The Pregnancy Devotions

Bible Verses From The Postpartum Devotions

Part V

Postpartum

I hope your birth experience was perfect and you had everything you hoped for. It is the mercy of God when a woman has her dream delivery.

But in my experience, over 50% of the mothers are surprised by how their birth experience has unfolded. Some are pleasantly surprised. Some are completely in shock with what has just happened to them.

The endorphins of the day wear off, and the reality sets in. This little baby is no longer the passive recipient of nutrients. Feeding, changing, and soothing a baby are a lot of work. It's rewarding work but still more work than most mamas expect.

It is normal to feel like the whole birth experience was surreal. Time bends in labor and delivery. Days feel like hours, and hours feel like days. This is especially true if you have had a long induction or prolonged labor. In that case, you are probably still trying to understand what happened during your delivery. It's okay. The truth is many things will not make sense at this moment.

But you will find your answers as you regain some of your sanity and humanity. Even in the moments that don't make sense, God is not surprised by your delivery experience. He was present during it all, and He is still present today.

Becoming a mother helps us understand God's love for us.
How did you feel when you looked at your child for the first time?

That first look of love is exactly how God looks at you.
Precious. Perfect. Worthy of your best.
In that moment, you forget all of the nausea, back pain, and even the labor. Because it has all been worth it. And in that moment, you make a silent vow to do anything and everything to protect this little person who has been entrusted to you.

But have you ever considered all your hopes and dreams for your child? God actually has these hopes for you, too. He will use your motherhood journey with all of its triumphs and failures for your good and His glory.

Even when you know God, the first few weeks can be full of fears. It is a lonely experience at times. Some of you may be single mothers. Some of you may have an emotionally unavailable partner. And even with the most supportive partner, he still can't help you breastfeed. Mothers carry the load for the beginning of a newborn's life. It's a biological truth.

Not only have you birthed a new child, but you have birthed other children who will go home with you from the hospital. Their names are Guilt and Self-doubt. They linger when the house is quiet. They are present when we are half-asleep and most vulnerable to the attack of irrational fears that come our way.

And so we need a Defender who tells us who we truly are. Jesus carries our guilt and self-doubt. He loves us despite our motherhood failures. And thankfully, God holds together what we cannot.

So, over the next few weeks, we will explore how God does just that. I get it - you don't have much time. The baby is here!

This next section will be daily devotions with practical tips to deepen your walk with the Lord amid the great transitions of motherhood. Each devotion is followed by a prayer you can use during common newborn mommy moments. And if you do not have time, you can meditate on the scripture and pray the one sentence daily prayer throughout your day.

Week One

The Mommy Expectations Redo

I had to change my expectations for motherhood.

My newborn experience was more extreme than normal, so I do not want to cause unnecessary fear for any of you who have just delivered your baby. But I share my story so you can understand where these postpartum devotions come from.

When my first baby was handed to me, she did not stop shrieking. I remember the newborn nursery nurses taking her away for only ten minutes before bringing her back to me because she was not able to be soothed. We couldn't use the newborn nursery because she continually cried. I thought I was going through normal newborn exhaustion. Now, I know that it was because my daughter had uncomfortable sensory issues.

By the time I brought my first newborn home, my expectations for motherhood were completely shattered. She was my perfect bundle of joy, but at the same time, I could not catch a break in my recovery. I felt numb toward her. I felt incapable as a mother.

The rush of postpartum hormones brought me anxiety about whether I was doing enough or not doing something correctly. We tried every remedy and swaddle for a colicky baby. We would go through eating and soothing cycles for hours at a time. When I finallly could get her to latch, she would spit up and scream herself to sleep, only to wake up thirty minutes later to repeat the same cycle. I had no idea what was normal anymore. It felt like my life was crumbling. I was at the bottom of its pit.

Breastfeeding was one of the hardest things I had done in my life. I found myself dreading breastfeeding. Breastfeeding was not bonding me to my beautiful daughter. I had counseled many women on how breastfeeding was natural and best for the baby. But when I was the one dealing with breastfeeding pain, jaundice, mastitis, and a colicky baby, I found breastfeeding more suffocating than I could have ever imagined.

I did not have risk factors for postpartum depression, but the dark days I experienced in postpartum depression were scary. There were days I did not want to be a mama anymore because it was so hard. I missed my previous predictable life. My postpartum depression evolved into anxiety as I had a hard time letting anyone take care of my baby. I was incredibly sensitive to the "helpful suggestions on my parenting." It was so humbling to feel inadequate. I always prided myself as someone who could help people. But I could not help my little baby, who was struggling to eat.

But in His great mercy, God comforted me. He changed my heart about motherhood. He began by purging my pride. It was incredibly humbling to feel inadequate when I had spent so much time in medical education learning to become adequate. And yet, I needed to empty myself so He could fill me.

Without the struggle of my postpartum days, I would have been a very self-assured mother. I would have prided myself on my successes and asked God to bless my plans as an afterthought.

I started motherhood with plans to teach my daughter. But my journey of parenthood has been my daughter teaching me. Only God could have changed my heart during these dark days. He used this dark place to illuminate what was true in my life. Motherhood was about Him, not about me. My children were His, not mine. My children were safest in the center of His will. I just needed to give up my control.

My postpartum depression lifted after about eight weeks. I gave into the chaotic season of newborn nurturing and let go of my perfect house.

Postpartum depression was just the first sacrifice of my motherhood altar. When He called me to be a special needs mother, I needed to give even more of my plans to God. But because I had learned to trust Him in the early days, the relationship of trust was already there. So many lessons in the early days of postpartum became stepping stones for the next season of challenges with my children. He equipped me with the skills needed to become a special needs mother.

By the time I had my second child, God had changed my expectations and purpose in motherhood. If you have children at home, you are likely already a seasoned, realistic mother. While some things will still be difficult in the newborn period, you won't be as overwhelmed. I did not have postpartum depression after my second pregnancy. But I still had the emotional highs and lows in the postpartum period. Postpartum is full of feels even if you're in a stable place.

If you feel like you are drowning, I see you. Please tell your loved ones, healthcare providers, and trusted friends. If you ever feel like you want to hurt yourself or your baby in this hazy newborn period, please get help. Being honest with yourself and those who love you is crucial to helping you succeed in motherhood. Not all mamas have such extreme emotions postpartum. Still, if you are one of the women who can relate, I hope you will be encouraged over the next few weeks as we study God's Word together.

I am truly happy for you if you have had your dream birth experience. But will you pray for the mama struggling in motherhood today? We all have different valleys at different times. Today, some mamas are in the darkest days of their motherhood. Let us lift each other up, praying for God's goodness to be clear for even the woman in the murky mire.

Becoming a mother is a new identity for the soul. As we get through these weeks together, may you find an identity in Christ that makes all the difference in keeping you rooted.

Day 1: Feeling Like A Failure - God Is For Your Good

It's official! You are a parent! I hope you are madly in love with your little person and enjoying the snuggles! I also hope you can focus on everything that went well in your birth experience. But this isn't the case for everyone.

Somewhere along the way, we have convinced ourselves that a woman's strength is based on her ability to have an unmedicated childbirth. Or that if we need a cesarean, we have failed as women. Or if we have delivered a premature child, there is something wrong with our bodies.

If this is you, the feeling of failure may cast a shadow on your first day with your child. If your baby needs extra time in the neonatal intensive care unit or requires more transitional care, it does not mean that you have failed.

However, the feeling of failure is very hard to rationalize in the surge of postpartum emotions.

The truth is a lot of women feel disappointed in their birth experience.

Disappointed with their birth team.

Disappointed with themselves.

Some women feel like their body has betrayed them.

We want someone and something to blame. The playback of what we have done (or not have done) is on replay. It's okay to be disappointed, but we must be cautious about letting this replay of events paralyze us.

Today, let's meditate on how God uses our disappointment for good. Sometimes, disappointment is our reality check. Let's focus on how God has provided for our birth experiences, for there are always mercies laced around disappointments. We can focus on all of the things that went wrong, or we can focus on everything that went right. We can be honest with God about our disappointments. For He already knows our discouraged souls.

> *Why are you cast down, O my soul, and why are you in turmoil within me? Hope in God; for I shall again praise him, my salvation and my God.* *Psalm 42:5*

Sometimes, you need to literally speak the truth out loud to your soul. The soul is susceptible to guilty feelings and self-doubt. But you can speak loudly to your soul to drown out the other voices:

> *Soul, why am I so discouraged about my delivery experience? Why am I in such turmoil? My hope is in God. I will still praise Him even if everything turns out differently than expected. God rescued me from pregnancy yesterday. What a gift!*

Ask God to redefine in what and in whom you place your hope.
Is your hope defined by your success or His mercy?
Is your hope in a full-term delivery or in His mercy to sustain a premature infant?

When you realize what you have been saved from, the Savior becomes even more precious. You will be able to praise Him even when you're disappointed.

There are mercies in your birth experience if you ask God to help you see them.

A Prayer of Praise When You Snuggle Your Little One:

Jesus, thank you for delivering me yesterday.
Even if my delivery was not what I expected, you are my hope.
You love me not because of how well I perform.
You saved me because you are loving and good.
Thank you for the mercies in my delivery.
In Jesus' name, Amen.

A Quick Prayer For Today:

> *Jesus, help me to see your mercies.*

Day 2: When They Come Out Differently - God Is Trustworthy

Most babies look like their daddies when they're born. It doesn't seem fair to women after all the struggles of pregnancy and delivery! But add some hair, thin out those cheeks, and they will begin to look like you in no time, right?

The first twenty-four hours are a honeymoon period for parents and their newborn. Most of them start out life cooing quietly with an easy temperament. But it is on the second day of life that babies become more demanding. (They want you to fall in love with them first before they let their true colors show.)

But what if the baby is not like anything you expected? What if you have a premature baby that needs the help of a NICU while your empty arms ache? What if your baby will not cooperate with breastfeeding? What if you feel the panic rising as you wonder whether or not you were made to do this?

Your baby may become more demanding today and may even begin cluster feeding when it seems like no amount of milk is enough. If you feel overwhelmed when the baby glares at you like you should know what you're doing, it's okay. Just because you birthed your child does not mean that you know everything about your child right away.

There is a learning curve to figure out how to soothe your child. There is a learning curve for maneuvering getting out of bed. There is a learning curve for breastfeeding.

Most women are not pros at breastfeeding right away. Most women wonder, "How do I know if the baby is getting enough?" or "How do I know if the baby needs to be woken up to eat?" Sometimes there are clear answers, and sometimes there are not. Your care team will know how to direct you. But the pressure to know all the answers can be intense when you're alone with your baby, trying to figure it out. In these quiet (or not-so-quiet) moments, ask God to give you wisdom on what to do. Put the crying baby down in the bassinet, walk away, and take a deep breath before coming back. Sometimes, when you can calm down, the answers become clearer.

Trust your God-given instincts. Even if you don't know everything yet, you have studied this little being more than anyone else has. You are an expert for your child. You're going to figure it out - especially if you trust the Lord with this new precious piece of your heart.

Trust in the Lord with all your heart
and lean not on your own understanding;
in all your ways submit to him,

and he will make your paths straight.
Do not be wise in your own eyes;
fear the Lord and shun evil.
This will bring health to your body
and nourishment to your bones.   *Proverbs 3:5–8, NIV*

You don't need to be the wisest mother on day two. You only need to trust the Lord with your heart. He will make a crooked path straight.

A Prayer During A Feeding:
God, I trust you with breastfeeding my child. *Even though it doesn't always seem to go well from my standpoint.* *I know that you will straighten my mommy path.* *I do not need to figure it all out because I trust you.* *You will bring health to my body as I recover because I fear you. I love you.* *In Jesus' name, Amen.*

A Quick Prayer for Today:

> *Jesus, help me to be okay with not knowing all the answers.*

Day 3: Running on Empty - God Fills Us

I hope that you are finding time for rest. The excitement of all the visitors and new responsibilities can sometimes be overwhelming. And if you are going home to the demands of other children, pets, and now this newborn - rest may be low on the list of priorities.

I hope that you continue to have endorphins bathing your heart. But most of the time, the endorphins become harder to feel twenty-four hours after birth. If you have experienced zombie walking, the panic may start to rise.

It's okay to wonder if you are going to make it. You will make it.

The Bible promises care for mothers.

> *He will feed his flock like a shepherd.*
> *He will carry the lambs in his arms,*

> *holding them close to his heart.*
> *He will gently lead the **mother sheep with their young**.*
>
> Isaiah 40:11, NLT, emphasis added

Close your eyes and picture a gentle shepherd who holds a sheep close to his heart.

You are His treasured mother sheep who is with her young.

As you feed your child, God feeds you.

As you carry your child, God carries you in His arms.

He gently cares for the mama lambs who are with their young.

In this postpartum haze, He is holding you close to His heart. He will lead you. He will show you what you need to do next. Don't think too far beyond the next feeding - just live in the sweet moment of tenderness.

Bad days are followed by good ones. Bad feedings are followed by good ones. Remember, tomorrow is another day when His mercies will be enough. If you rest in Him, He gives you the strength to get back up again.

A Prayer For When You Have A Crying Baby:
Jesus, you are the Good Shepherd.   *Hold me close the way I hold my child.*   *Because I am lost in this mothering thing and need your help.*   *You will lead me if I ask.*   *Give me wisdom to know what my child needs.*   *In Jesus' name, Amen.*

Quick Prayer for Today:

Jesus, hold me close.

Day 4: Breastfeeding Idols - God Provides For Our Children

You may feel like you've got this breastfeeding thing down, or you may feel like breastfeeding is the hardest thing you have ever done. If breastfeeding is not going as smoothly as you had hoped, focus on your small wins.

Newborns teach us to live in two-hour increments. And in each of these increments, there are small wins.

Each little thing you figure out—which position works best, what soothes your baby—adds up over time. You are learning a growing human's habits that change daily. It isn't easy! Although it may seem like little progress from feed to feed, you will be surprised by how much more you know about this little person a week from now.

The pressure to produce milk and provide enough for the baby can be terrifying. Sometimes, we have the mercy of an easy breastfeeding experience. But most women wonder if they are doing it correctly with their first babies.

You will know you are breastfeeding correctly if the baby is content after feeding and continues to grow. You can count the number of wet diapers, how many poops, etc. But if you're a numbers person, beware of how this can become obsessive. You may feel like life is now measured in ounces rather than minutes.

If you focus on the big picture rather than each feed, you will find you are making progress. As you see your pediatrician for the baby's weight check-ins, you will see how much is going right.

But sometimes, feedings are not going right despite your best efforts. The desire to breastfeed may become obsessive. Sometimes, breastfeeding becomes about a mama's pride. If breastfeeding is proving something to yourself in your motherhood, you may need to ask what you are gaining and what you are losing by continuing to breastfeed. Sometimes, breastfeeding barriers can prevent mamas from bonding with their children.

We tend to define breastfeeding success quantitatively, usually by the baby's increasing weight gain. However, breastfeeding success should also be qualitative. One of the main purposes of breastfeeding is to strengthen the bond between mother and child. If this bond is getting weaker from breastfeeding, talk with your medical team about whether or not this is the only way to feed your child. Many breastfeeding barriers improve by two weeks. If you find at two weeks old that breastfeeding is destroying your spirit, take the time to reflect on Matthew 6.

Jesus knows we worry about feeding our children.

That is why on the Sermon on the Mount, He said:

> *"That is why I tell you not to worry about everyday life—whether you have enough food and drink or enough clothes to wear. Isn't life more than food and your body more than clothing? Look at the birds. They don't plant, harvest, or store food in barns, for your Heavenly Father feeds them. And aren't you far more valuable to him than they are? Can all your worries add a single moment to your life?"*
>
> Matthew 6:25–27, NLT

Baby birds may not have reflux, feeding, or latch issues. But the baby birds rest peacefully in their nest. Mama bird does not worry about the next meal. There is nowhere to store extra worms, anyway. She knows that God will provide the next meal for her babies. If God ensures that each baby bird gets enough, then God will definitely ensure your little one has enough too.

Your child is more valuable than the birds of the air.
God is the provider of enough milk for your baby.
God is the provider of enough formula for your baby.

We can worry about our baby's growth, but our worries do not add an ounce to their weight. On the other hand, a prayer of trust adds peace to our day.
And then, when you finally relax, the milk truly starts to flow!
He loves birds, but you'd better believe He loves you more!

A Prayer During A Feeding:

Jesus, provide enough milk for my baby today.
If it isn't from me, let me trust that you are providing nutrients for my baby in other ways, and it's okay. You know what my baby needs.
Help me to trust you. Amen.

Quick Prayer for Today:

Jesus, help me to trust you.

Day 5: Relying On Manna - God Knows Our Needs

Everything about the first few days of survival is about living in three-hour increments. Sleep, diaper change, eat. Repeat. The night-day reversal is a time vortex.

At times, it can feel like this pattern is never-ending. But it will end. The quicker you give in to sleeplessness and cluster feeds, the easier time you will have, enjoying all the beautiful things that are happening in front of you. The newborn period is about living in the moment.

Some days feel like a wilderness. Unknown and uncertain schedules can be very dysregulating for a mama who is used to having her day planned out. This lack of control in postpartum schedules is a big adjustment.

It is also a wilderness down there—from your vaginal tear to your cesarean scar— if you have dared to look at what lurks under. But it will all heal because God has created your body to be elastic and resilient. It takes a few weeks for your body to regenerate your nerves, muscles, and skin cells. Usually, by the time you see your doctor at six weeks, you will be almost back to normal.

There was a wilderness in the Bible. The Israelites wandered the desert for forty years while trying to find the Promised Land. Although they received God's daily provision, this was not enough for them. They were focused on what they did not have. They complained about life being better when they were slaves.

And yet, God continued to provide for their needs during this journey. He gave them a cloud to shield them from the sun and a fire to follow at nighttime. He provided a daily provision of manna, a bread that rained down from heaven. It was enough bread to sustain them for only one day at a time.

> *Some gathered a lot, some a little. When they measured it by quarts, the person who gathered a lot had no surplus, and the person who gathered a little had no shortage. Each gathered as much as he needed to eat.*
>
> *Exodus 16:17b–18, CSB*

He provided just enough food for the day. Not too much and not too little. Just enough. If the Israelites tried to store up the bread, worms got into the bread.

He provides enough nutrients for your baby today. Not too much and not too little.
There is no need to store up a milk supply right now.
There is no need for a predictable schedule.

There is only need for dependence.
Like your baby depends on you for the next feed, your Heavenly Father provides just what you need hour by hour. Enough sleep. Enough milk. In the wilderness, He provides just enough. In this daily dependence, you will find freedom to let go of yourself.

Prayer during a Nighttime Feed:
Jesus, you are enough for me. *Multiply the hours of my sleep so that it is enough.* *You provide exactly what I need for the moment.* *Help me let go of control. Amen.*

Quick Prayer:

Jesus, help me to let go.

Day 6: Letting Go Of Perfectionism - God Gives Us A New Song

If your baby still has a different schedule than yours, it's completely normal. I know those eight hours of uninterrupted sleep sound really good right now. But remember all those frequent awakenings from your bladder during your third trimester? Your body was trained during pregnancy to deal with sleep interruption! Waking up to a hungry baby (thank God, they're cute!) is probably better than waking up to a full bladder, right?

But sometimes, this phase can feel never-ending. There is a desire to go through this phase as quickly as possible. Where is the fast forward button, right? But in those slow hours of nighttime, take a moment to reflect on how your baby is already changing every day. You may already see the baby having more awake and fussy hours during the day.

For us perfectionists, this period can be absolutely tortuous when we have a feeding that goes well and a feeding that goes terribly. If you like to be in control of your time and schedule, the newborn period is difficult! But if you have already let go of perfectionism, you are one of the lucky ones who can enjoy every minute.

Women who have it all together easily believe that they are the reason everything is going well. But honestly, our wins are the mercies of God.

Sleep deprivation can do funny things to a mother's emotions. If you find yourself thinking in the extremes of "never, ever, always" start examining if you are having what psychologists call black-and-white thinking[39].

Check your thoughts. Do you ever think . . .

> *I will never figure this breastfeeding out.*
> *I am a failure because I cannot ever figure out how to soothe my baby.*
> *I am always going to have sleepless nights.*
> *It's my fault that my baby has colic.*

If your thinking is going down this path, be honest with yourself and those around you. Black-and-white thinking can be a sign of postpartum anxiety and postpartum depression. Black-and-white thinking typically causes you to interpret everything as good or bad. Instead of having a balanced view, everything feels ten times worse than it truly is.

---

[39] Summer Beretsky, "How Does Black-and-White Thinking Affect Your Mood and Behavior?," Psych Central, April 24, 2023, https://psychcentral.com/health/how-does-black-and-white-thinking-impact-us.

If you are having these extreme thoughts, reflect on this passage:

I waited patiently for the Lord to help me,
and he turned to me and heard my cry.
He lifted me out of the pit of despair,
out of the mud and the mire.

Psalm 40:1–2, NLT

> You can pray: *God, I am in a pit. I am despairing. I am crying.*

He set my feet on solid ground
and steadied me as I walked along.
He has given me a new song to sing,
a hymn of praise to our God.

Psalm 40:2–3, NLT

> You can pray: *God, steady my feet so I have somewhere to stand and not feel like I am drowning. Give me a new song to sing because the only song that's going through my mind right now is "Loser."*

"Many will see what he has done and be amazed. They will put their trust in the Lord"

Psalm 40:3, NLT

> You can pray: *God, you are doing something amazing in my heart. Let my mama journey be about you so that others put their trust in you.*

Do you feel like you are in a never-ending pit of blowouts and spit-up? It's okay. But we must get back to the solid truth: He gives us a place to stand in the pit. He steadies us even when we are sleep-deprived. He gives us a new song to sing. Have you tried singing worship songs while you rock your baby? When you lift your voice to sing, your focus changes. As you relax, your baby also relaxes. Sing to God, and you will be amazed at how it will change your spirit.

You do not need to be a perfect mother.

You need to be an imperfect child of God, dependent on His grace.

> **A Prayer for the Imperfect Mother:**
> *God, I am a perfectly imperfect mother.*
> *I don't have it all figured out, but you know what we need.*
> *Help me wait patiently for you to help me.*
> *Lift me out of my pit so that I have a new song of worship to sing.*
> *Help me to trust you.*
> *Amen.*

A Quick Prayer for Today:

God, help me to praise you.

Day 7: Postpartum Blues Or Depression? - God's Perfect Power

While postpartum blues are very common in up to 85% of women with a depressed mood the first week, [40] postpartum depression is different. Postpartum depression lasts longer with more severe symptoms. Postpartum depression occurs in one in seven women.

There are many hormonal changes going on, from an increase in your stress hormone cortisol to lower hormonal levels of progesterone and estrogen. All the ups and downs of hormones, along with sleep deprivation, can truly affect a woman's ability to cope with the exhaustion of motherhood[41].

Postpartum depression is defined as having at least five of the following symptoms according to the Diagnostic and Statistical Manual of

---

[40] Temitope Omoladun Okunola et al., "Postnatal Blues: A Mirage or Reality," Journal of Affective Disorders Reports, September 1, 2021, 100237, https://doi.org/10.1016/j.jadr.2021.100237.

[41] Crystal Edler Schiller, Samantha Meltzer- Brody, and David R. Rubinow, "The Role of Reproductive Hormones in Postpartum Depression," CNS Spectrums 20, no. 1 (September 29, 2014): 48–59, https://doi.org/10.1017/s1092852914000480.

Mental Disorders (DSM–5)[42]

- Depressed mood (subjective or observed) most of the day
- Loss of interest or pleasure most of the day
- Not sleeping or sleeping too much
- Easily agitated
- Feeling worthless or guilty
- Loss of energy or fatigue
- Recurrent thoughts of death
- Trouble concentrating
- Change in weight or appetite

Some women have all of the symptoms and some women only have a few of these symptoms. The symptoms can change from day to day with some days better or worse than others.

If you have postpartum depression, you are still a good mother.

Postpartum depression is not a measure of your love for your child.

You can love your child and still have postpartum depression.

It is important to note here that postpartum depression can happen to anybody. The pressures of newborn feeding fall squarely on a mother, especially if she is breastfeeding. Even with a supportive village, mamas feel an incredible weight to keep their newborn alive. Being a mama can actually be quite lonely.

In those quiet hours of the night when your support system is asleep, do you have thoughts like:

> *I am not doing enough.*
> *I should be able to figure this out and I can't.*
> *I feel trapped.*
> *I am so weak.*

Sometimes, you know these kinds of thoughts are irrational. But at other times, these thoughts may be confused with truth.

---

[42] (American Psychiatric Association. (2013). *Diagnostic and statistical manual of mental disorders* (5th ed.). Arlington, VA: Author):

If your ability to determine what is true is becoming more difficult, you need to tell someone. Your village may notice this change in you but not know how to tell you. It is important to tell a health provider who can help connect you to a counselor and discuss if medications may be helpful.

If you feel like you want to hurt yourself or your baby because it is too difficult, please be honest with yourself and go to the emergency room. Mothers who end up on the news hurting their children are not bad people. They are depleted. They feel "trapped" and need to know there is hope.

We all are susceptible to postpartum depression[43]. And why wouldn't we be? Our bodies have just gone through an incredible amount of change. The hormones that help with breastfeeding also prevent us from "going back to normal."

We expect to get our bodies back after pregnancy, yet the demand keeps on going. We expect our energy to improve after delivery, but it keeps getting drained instead. The pressure to maintain another life outside of our body is a new terrifying anxiety.

God knows that you may be hanging by a thread. But guess what? It's okay to feel weak. When you know Jesus, you're allowed to feel weak. His power is made perfect in our weakness.

> ...*So, to keep me from becoming proud, I was given a thorn in my flesh, a messenger from Satan to torment me and keep me from becoming proud.*
> *Three different times, I begged the Lord to take it away. Each time, He said, 'My grace is all you need. My power works best in weakness.' So now I am glad to boast about my weaknesses so that the power of Christ can work through me. That's why I take pleasure in my weaknesses and in the insults, hardships, persecutions, and troubles I suffer for Christ. For when I am weak, then I am strong.*
> *2 Corinthians 12:7–10, NLT*

---

[43] Saba Mughal, "Postpartum Depression," StatPearls - NCBI Bookshelf, October 7, 2022, https://www.ncbi.nlm.nih.gov/books/NBK519070/.

The Mommy Expectations Redo

The postpartum time is a special time of communion with God because, in our inadequacies, we find that He provides for us. His power is made perfect in our weakness.

But if you are having difficulty seeing this truth, tell someone. If you would rather stay in bed than care for your baby, or if you are having a hard time seeing the good, you could be dealing with postpartum depression.

You are stronger than you think you are. But it's also okay to be weaker than you want to be. It takes courage to admit your limitations. It takes strength to admit you need help.

Be strong and courageous, my friend. Get help. It takes the support of a village to raise a baby, and it takes the support of an army to raise a mama.

Prayer During a Weepy Mama Moment:
Jesus, I feel weak.   *You are strong.*   *Carry my child because I cannot.*   *Your power is made perfect in my weakness.*   *Let your grace be all I need. Amen.*

A Quick Prayer for Today:

Jesus, be strong for me today.

Week 2

Battling Discouragement

No one ever told me it was going to be this hard.

The mamas around me left out an important detail: childbirth was the easiest part!

Postpartum? That part was left out of the story.

Probably because many mothers black out the newborn part of their motherhood experiences.

Why?

Because, similar to pregnancy, we know all the work is worth it. But while we are living it, the nights are long. The days are long. Who even knows what time of day it is anymore?

I don't know about you, but I had the impression that newborns slept all of the time before I became a mother myself. I also thought that they would feed and go right back to sleep. I didn't know anything about cluster feedings. I didn't know they needed so much bouncing and burping to be comfortable. I didn't know that I would be obsessed with every little detail about my child and the pressure to keep her alive.

My second baby was much easier than my first during the postpartum period. But honestly, all newborns are difficult in their own ways.

My second child had colic while breastfeeding as well because she had multiple food allergies (that we did not know about at that time). She began rejecting my breast milk and screaming while I desperately tried to feed her with what I thought was best.

On one of my desperate days, I remember going to the post office. I had ordered a booty trumpet to relieve my baby's gas and constipation. My package got lost during a busy holiday season. That small funnel was my lifeline to sleep. And when the sweet lady at the post office could not find it, I went ballistic. Literally, I went postal at the post office. It was not my finest moment as a human being. But when you have a lady standing between you and your sanity, you want to climb on top of her desk and scream at the top of your lungs.

I needed help! That booty trumpet was essential to my mental health. Why wouldn't the lady want to go the extra mile to help me? I could barely make it to the post office with this screaming baby.

The poor lady shrugged apologetically. This crazy mama was losing her mind.

Sometimes, this newborn experience can make you feel like you are going crazy.

Our worlds are crashing while the rest of the world still orbits casually around its axis.

The highs are the highest you may have ever felt.

And the lows are the lowest you may have ever felt.

It is hard, but it does pass. I promise.

I did not get my baby booty trumpet that day. I left the post office discouraged. Yet when I finally got the booty trumpet, the flimsy plastic did not even work. Those five-star reviews had lied to me! I just had to accept my fussy baby the way she was. As she got older, it became clear her fussiness was the result of multiple food allergies.

Caring for an allergy kid, we learned to give her what she needs rather than what she wants. In my mommy's discomfort, God gave me what I needed rather than what I wanted.

I learned to live in my discomfort. My new normal was not having everything turn out exactly as I planned. When I let go, I began to see the little mercies God sent to encourage me daily.

It's okay to be discouraged during this part of the journey. The discouragement that mamas face is real. God will meet you in the most tender places of your heart. As you grow through the discomforts of your mommy journey, you will see the goodness of God. He is doing a good work in you.

Day 1: God's Mercy In Zoloft - God Helps Us

Sometimes, there are situations that can make postpartum emotions more extreme. For example, the financial stress of maternity leave, an emotionally unavailable partner, or health issues with your newborn. Some emotions are temporary and related to your situation. But if you find yourself dealing with postpartum depression, it is important to ask for help.

There is a stigma associated with medicines that can affect our brains. Many Christians believe that if you know Jesus, you should not struggle with depression or anxiety. But honestly, that's just not true. Our bodies are broken from the fall in the Garden of Eden. Our minds can be as sick as our bodies. Jesus did not come to heal the healthy but to heal the sick (Luke 5:31–32).

The sick know they are in need of a savior. In the book of John, a blind man came up to Jesus for healing of his ailment. Jesus took mud into His hands, spit into it, and rubbed the salve onto the blind man's eyes. He instructed the man to go wash his eyes in the pool of Siloam. It was not until the man completed all the medical treatments that he was able to see. There are many instances of Jesus doing miracles by touch alone. But in this particular instance, He gave the blind man a prescription. Jesus used medicinal elements from His creation to heal this man's ailment (John 9).

Sometimes, the ailment is a physical illness. Sometimes, the ailment is an emotional one, like postpartum depression. Postpartum depression and postpartum anxiety are true medical ailments that are not just fleeting emotions. Any ailment that prevents us from seeing the goodness of God may need Jesus' salve to heal us.

Medications are elements of creation that Jesus uses to heal ailments. Sometimes, mamas need "Vitamin Z" (Zoloft) to see God's love clearly again. * Jesus has many ways He rescues His creation. Sometimes, His help is the mercy of Zoloft. The medications in this drug class, selective serotonin reuptake inhibitors, do not change your personality (or make you into a Pollyanna). Medications give you a floor to stand on so you can get back up. The need for medication is not a lack of faith. Medications are for the humble who realize they need God's mercy.

There is no magic pill that takes away depression. Anxiety can cloud the brain and muddy the truth. God has made medications to help us see the truth more clearly through the postpartum haze. These medications help us see God's faithfulness and goodness more clearly.

Honestly, you may also need the Zoloft because everyone else around you won't take it! Sometimes, Zoloft helps you have extra grace for others so you don't take things so personally. You may find it easier to forgive when your mind is not so consumed with what you are owed.

Zoloft and other medications are not for everyone. I usually encourage postpartum mamas to get fresh outdoor air and Vitamin D from sunlight[44].

A new context can give women their strength for the next feeding. The sunlight also helps with the circadian rhythm, which is disrupted by a newborn's schedule. Running one errand a day without their baby can give them some semblance of their "old" lives. A counselor can help you find where your thought patterns may be getting stuck.

Above all else, pray for God to give you strength. Pray for Him to give you a heart for your child. If you still want to run away from being a mama, be honest with yourself. And then be honest with God. He already knows, anyway.

The healing begins when you no longer have to hide.

Ask yourself if you believe these truths:

> *You are blessed beyond all measure.*
> *You have been chosen.*
> *You were made for your child—and your child was made for you.*

If you're having a hard time seeing these truths, ask yourself what you need to see the truth. If there is a disconnect between what you know and how you feel, it is okay to get help.

---

[44] Parvin Abedi et al., "The Relationship between Vitamin D and Postpartum Depression in Reproductive-Aged Iranian Women," Journal of Medicine and Life 11, no. 4 (October 1, 2018): 286–92, https://doi.org/10.25122/jml-2018-0038.

*For I have chosen you
and will not throw you away.
Don't be afraid, for I am with you.
Don't be discouraged, for I am your God.
I will strengthen you and help you.
I will hold you up with my victorious right hand.*

Isaiah 41:9–10, NLT

A Prayer For A Moody Mama:

*Jesus, I am afraid this feeling will never end.
I am discouraged and need your help.
Strengthen me. Help me.
Hold me up with your right hand. Amen.*

A Quick Prayer Today:

Jesus, hold me up with your tender hand.

*There are many types of medications that are similar to Zoloft (generic name is Sertraline) that your provider may prescribe. Zoloft is not the only medication that is effective in treating postpartum depression, and your providers may recommend different medications based on their experiences and preferences. The reference "Vitamin Z" is a literary tool and not a medical recommendation nor a medical term.

Day 2: Asking for Help - God Is Already There

The truth is no one can care for your baby like you can. There may be very few people you trust to care for your child.

But sometimes, your mommy anxiety can get in the way. Postpartum anxiety is also a real emotional roller coaster that many mamas experience.

Anxiety gets in the way if you believe:

*No one else can take care of my baby.
I do not want to be a burden on anyone, so I will not ask for help.
I'm so overwhelmed I don't even know how to ask for help.*

I need to be with my baby every second of the day because something bad is going to happen.

It's okay to feel these feelings. This is the normal postpartum mommy brain. Remember, your brain has physically changed in the areas of defensiveness. You have developed maternal protective instincts. But be aware if your anxieties escalate to the point that:

You cannot fall asleep because you are anxious about missing the baby's needs.

You are irritable with the relationships that do not revolve around your baby.

You are isolating yourself because you think that no one else understands.

You don't want to be a mother anymore because the anxiety is so physically uncomfortable.

Your loved ones may tell you that your anxiety is normal. While anxiety is normal, your experience of postpartum blues and anxiety is unique to you. If the anxiety is paralyzing you, it's okay to admit the struggle. And then get help. Similar to postpartum depression, postpartum anxiety benefits from medications as well. Ultimately, there is no magic pill that takes away the anxiety completely.

Because anxiety is also a spiritual issue. Who is in control?

Who do you trust to keep your children safe? Is it God or yourself?

In these moments, you must ask who holds your days and nights. Who is watching over your baby while you rest? Where does your help come from? The Bible says that:

> *I look up to the mountains—*
> *does my help come from there?*
> *My help comes from the Lord,*
> *who made heaven and earth!*
>
> *Psalm 121:1–2, NLT*

The God who made the heavens and the Earth also knows your baby's every coo and whimper. God wants to help you.

He will not let you stumble;
the one who watches over you will not slumber.
Indeed, he who watches over Israel
never slumbers or sleeps.

Psalm 121:3–4, NLT

He never sleeps! He is better than any baby monitor.

The Lord himself watches over you!
The Lord stands beside you as your protective shade.
The sun will not harm you by day,
nor the moon at night.
The Lord keeps you from all harm
and watches over your life.
The Lord keeps watch over you as you come and go,
both now and forever.

Psalm 121:5–8, NLT

Who has your back?

God does. He does not have day/night reversal. He is awake with you in the middle of the night. And although He may not be physically changing a diaper with you, He can give you the strength to endure the blowouts. He sees your sleepless nights, giving you enough energy for the next thing that you need to do. He is your help.

> **A Prayer For An Anxious Mama:**
>
> *Jesus, you watch over me and my family wherever I go.*
> *You stand beside me even at nighttime and do not ever sleep.*
> *You will not let me stumble.*
> *You are my help.*
> *I do not need to worry because you already know everything. Amen.*

A Quick Prayer for Today:

Jesus, help me not worry about tomorrow, for you are already there.

Day 3: Warring With Self-Doubt - God Has Called You

Do you believe you were made for motherhood? Some days, the calling is clear. On other days, it can feel like a hot mess.

Remembering your *why* will help you keep going.

I pray that the snuggles cause you to fall in love with your baby all over again, even when they are cranky. I pray that the "work" of caring for a newborn does not get in the way of the beauty that is happening before your eyes. Right now, the work may seem one-sided. But by two months old, most babies will start smiling back at you. The first smile makes all the work worth it. This smile is the first "thank you" for the last eleven months of work!

But until that moment, it's okay to doubt your abilities and ask yourself if you were made for this. You're living the same day on repeat. While the monotony has its sweet moments, your brain may start to feel like mush. Adult conversations may seem a distant memory. Do you only speak goo-goo-ga-ga now?

Remember that child, Self-Doubt, who also climbed into the backseat when you brought your baby home from the hospital? Self-Doubt wants you to believe you are not made to be a mother. Or even worse, He tells you you are not worthy of being this child's mother.

Nehemiah had an impossible task in front of him. He was rebuilding the wall around the city of Jerusalem while there was opposition on every side. The wall was crucial to his city's protection and value. But it seemed impossible. Outsiders criticized and threatened Nehemiah's plan. His people almost left the project because they were afraid. Yet somehow, Nehemiah never wavered. He remained confident in his task.

How did Nehemiah not struggle with self-doubt?

- **Nehemiah knew his calling was from God.**

    Nehemiah had a vision of what he was supposed to do for Jerusalem. He did not let opposition, self-doubt, or doubt from others get in the way of his calling. Nehemiah 2:4-5, NIV says, "Then I prayed to the God of heaven, and I answered the king, "If it pleases the king and if your servant has found favor in his sight, let him send me to the city in Judah where my ancestors are buried so that I can rebuild it."

God called you to be a mother. When Self-Doubt says you are not worthy of being a mama, remember who has called you. Keeping focused on the current task will help you overcome discouragement.

- **Nehemiah was not building the wall to please everyone else.**

    Nehemiah 5:15, NIV says, "Out of reverence for God, I did not act like that. Instead, I devoted myself to the work on this wall." Nehemiah knew who the boss was. He kept focused on the task at hand.

    When Self-Doubt says you are selfish for taking a longer maternity leave, remember you are building the foundation for your child. You do not need to worry about being a good employee. You are replaceable at the office but not replaceable at home.

- **Nehemiah delegated his tasks.** (Nehemiah 3) Building the wall took many specialists who were experts in their area—the Fish Gate, the Fountain Gate, and the Dung Gate. Many tasks needed to be delegated to get the job done.

When Self-Doubt says you should be doing more, delegate the household tasks to someone else. You are trying to build a "wall" when you're raising a baby. You don't need to do it all alone.

With discipline and consistency, Self-Doubt's voice will get quieter and less influential.

Remembering your purpose, your true boss, and utilizing your village will keep you focused on what is true. The "wall" of motherhood will be built. When God is your confidence, the enemy loses interest in discouraging you.

> *So the wall was completed on the twenty-fifth of Elul, in fifty-two days. When all our enemies heard about this, all the surrounding*

nations were afraid and lost their self-confidence because they realized that this work had been done with the help of our God.
Nehemiah 6:15–16, NIV

My friend, the work of your motherhood is being done with the help of God.

A Prayer In A Moment of Self-Doubt:
Jesus, you are all I need. *You have called me to build up my children.* *You are my boss and the one I want to please the most.* *Thank you for your merciful provision in what I cannot do on my own for my children.* *Please let truth trump self-doubt today. Amen.*

A Quick Prayer for Today:

God, let me listen to only what you say about me.

Day 4: Surprising Grief - God Is A Compassionate Father

The euphoria of having a baby is real. There are so many exciting new moments—sibling meet-cutes, a newly decorated nursery for the homecoming, and a palpable energy in the house.

But there are surprising griefs as well.

Relationships undoubtedly change forever. The previous youngest siblings are now the older ones who face their "dethronement." The spouses play second fiddle, and suddenly, there are at least three in the marriage. Mothers and in-laws move in to help, sharing not only space but also their opinions.

Or perhaps you are grieving relationships that are no longer present that you expected to be here. Have you lost your mother to death or an estranged relationship? The feelings of abandonment can be surprisingly triggered in postpartum because someone is missing in the celebration of this milestone in your life. Or if your mother has abandoned you, the betrayal seems unfathomable when you hold your precious child. The relationship triggers are incredibly strong amid all the postpartum hormones.

Or do you have grief related to missing your life before children? It probably was a lot less complicated. You had guaranteed sleep. Life revolved around whatever you wanted to do, not on a feeding and diapering schedule.

Or do you have grief about what you thought your family would look like after the baby arrived? Has the father of your child left you to fend for yourself when you are most vulnerable? We have ideals about how things will look when we get home from the hospital. We have a picture of who will be there and the rosy relationships that should know exactly what we need. But the reality is many relationships fracture under pressure.

If you have been abandoned by the world, you have not been abandoned by God.

You can tell God about these griefs. Tell him what you wish it would be. Ask Him to help you see how He fills those broken places. And then reflect on the compassion of God to meet you at these tender places.

If you have felt abandoned in these postpartum weeks:

The Lord is like a father to his children,
tender and compassionate to those who fear him.
For he knows how weak we are;
he remembers we are only dust.

Psalm 103:13–14, NLT

Your Heavenly Father is tender like you are with your child.
He shows compassion on you when you are at your wits' end.
You don't have to be strong in front of Him.
He is with you.

> **A Prayer For The Surprising Griefs:**
>
> *Jesus, I am blessed, but sometimes I still grieve what no longer is or what I thought it would be. I know you are a Father who loves me and does not abandon me. You let me grieve. Amen*

A Quick Prayer for Today:

Help me see how you fill my broken heart.

Day 5: Comparing To Yourself - God Measures Differently

Does it look like there is someone else who is doing a better job at motherhood than you are? Some women make motherhood look easy. Glamorous. Perfect.

It's easy to believe this is the norm.

If you want to be discouraged when you're not feeling great about yourself, sign onto social media, read tabloids about celebrity parents, go to a group breastfeeding class, or eat that gallon of ice cream (I've been there, done that). The worst thing to do when feeling insecure about your parenting is to compare yourself to other mothers. On the outside, it often seems like everyone else has it figured out. But if you peel back the layers, most mamas are struggling—especially if they want to do a good job in parenting.

Mamas are sinners who have birthed children who are sinners, but we often do not want the world to know that. Instead, we want our children to reflect our successful parenting. But sometimes, even with the best parenting, your children may fall short compared to everyone else's children.

In these moments, we need to ask the right questions:
What is your standard of success? Is it a sleeping baby? Is it a baby who can already hold her head up high during tummy time? Is it a baby that dominates the growth curve?

Most mothers use quantitative measures to define their success.

However, a Christian mother's standard of success is measured differently. Her success is not relative to others. She compares herself... to herself. Instead of looking around, she needs to look within herself.

The true questions for your parenting success are:
Have you given God your most tightly held parts of your heart?
How have the fruits of the Spirit grown in you?

The fruits of the Spirit grow best in the soil of struggle. Often, these fruits do not bloom until our expectations of ourselves are dashed. It's okay to struggle because there will be a sweeter fruit when we draw to God in these places.

> *But the fruit of the Spirit is love, joy, peace, patience, kindness, goodness, faithfulness, gentleness, and self-control"*
>
> Galatians 5:22–23, NLT

You are not the same person compared to the pregnant woman who read this book two weeks ago. God uses this newborn time to purge us of our selfishness. When the Spirit works in you, the fruits of the newborn mother are vibrant:

He fills us with sacrificial **love** on a sleepless night.
He gives a new **joy** when our children are content after a feed.
We have true **peace** when we entrust our precious children to His care.
We have more **patience** after hours of bouncing with a crying baby.
We have more **kindness** toward those who are also struggling with parenthood.
We want to make our world full of **goodness** because our children are now living in it.
We want to be more **faithful** to God as we recognize the vulnerability of parenthood.
We learn how to be **gentle** with a fragile, sleeping newborn.
He gives us **self-control** with others as we function on less.

Let these changes in your Spirit be the most important in your postpartum story. We are the mirrors of a greater story. In postpartum and for the rest of motherhood, the fruits will continue to grow. Some seasons will be harder than others for fruit to flourish. And sometimes, the harvest will be strikingly obvious. Let postpartum be a time when you see your growth as a Christian as the most important thing. Does your postpartum story reflect the Holy Spirit in your life?

A Prayer For The Mama Who Wants To Be Like Everyone Else:
Jesus, change the way I measure my motherhood success. Let the change be in me. Protect me from comparison to others so that I will not be discouraged. Let the fruits of the Spirit be my true success. Help me to continue to grow through even the uncomfortable places of being a mama so that I may look back and see the blossoms of postpartum. Amen.

A Quick Prayer for the Day:

Jesus, fill me with the fruits of the Spirit today.

Day 6: Fearing Worst Case Scenarios - God Is Merciful

As a mother, my soul is in a constant battle. I want to trust God with my precious children. But as soon as I give my children up to God, I take them back and stuff them into my pocket, hoping He isn't looking. Because surely, I know what they need better than He does. Does this sound familiar?

When my children are in my pocket, motherhood is about me. I am under pressure to do more and be more. I fear that my children will suffer because of my failures. I am anxious about all the things that can go wrong around them and for them. I started fearing worst-case scenarios.

Fearing all of the worst-case scenarios can become paralyzing. Are you always worried about SIDS? Are you worried about your baby's growth? When I enter this place of "extreme-thought mothering," my mind thinks in extremes. I find myself thinking more about the worst-case scenarios for my children and how I can prevent them.

But when I bring my children to God, I find freedom (after the initial gulp when I let go).

One of the most uncomfortable things about motherhood is that it teaches us about our sin. Sin is when we worship our loved ones more than Him. Our children are worthy, but are they worship-worthy? The taller the pedestal our children are placed on, the higher the stakes if something happens to them. When we worship our children, our fears grow into extreme thoughts.

The Bible does not promise our children will always be safe. The Bible promises that Jesus' love will always be able to find us in the worst-case scenarios of this life.

> *Neither death nor life, neither angels nor demons, nor our fears for today nor our worries about tomorrow—not even the powers of hell can separate us from God's love. No power in the sky above or in the earth below—indeed, nothing in all creation will ever be able to separate us from the love of God that is revealed in Christ Jesus our Lord.*   Romans 8:38–39, NLT

The Bible says God's love will be enough even in our worst-case scenarios.

All of our worries, uncertainties, and anxieties are covered by a Savior who is already holding us for tomorrow's pain. You can rest assured that this same God has written every day of your child's life while woven in your womb (Psalm 139:16).

It's okay to worry about SIDS. It's okay to worry about your baby's growth. It's okay to worry about if you are doing this motherhood thing correctly. The truth is anxiety about worst-case scenarios never truly goes away - it just morphs with the season of motherhood. But if God is on your pedestal, your worst-case scenarios will be redefined.

His love will be enough no matter what happens in your motherhood story.

A Prayer For The Anxious Mama:
Jesus, help me to love you the most. Help me to trust you to carry my children. Nothing separates me from your love. I love my baby so much, but I know you love him/her more. Help me to trust that your love will be enough even in my worst-case scenarios. Amen.

A Quick Prayer for Today:

Jesus, I want to trust you with my worst fears.

Day 7: Lamenting For The Overwhelmed Mama - God Knows Our Colic Too

The newborn period is a time of so many emotions. The highest of highs and the lowest of lows. Even if you do not consider yourself an emotional person, sleep deprivation can begin to play with your mind. Motherhood opens women to emotions they may have never experienced before.

Even if you are not feeling all the emotions, your baby is likely full of big feelings. Hangry? Too hot? Too cold? Too tired? When they aren't happy, the whole house knows about it.

Sometimes, you may want to complain, too. You may want to whine. You may want to shout. Go ahead. If newborn wailing is allowed, so is a mother's lament.

Lamenting is important because emotions speak louder than truth until they are lamented. Then, the emotions are quieted as they are covered with truth. Like any deep relationship, you can be honest with God.

The Bible gives mamas a blueprint on how to lament. The Psalms, written by David, are full of honesty with God. David writes lamenting psalms from a place of overwhelming exhaustion.

First, the psalmist speaks out of emotion -

> *My God, my God, why have you abandoned me?*
> *Why are you so far from my deliverance*
> *and from my words of groaning?*
> *My God, I cry by day, but you do not answer,*
> *by night, yet I have no rest.*
>
> Psalm 22:1–2, CSB

But then, the psalmist remembers God's provision in the past.

> *It was you who brought me out of the womb,*
> *making me secure at my mother's breast.*

> *I was given over to you at birth;*
> *you have been my God from my mother's womb.*
>
> Psalm 22:9–10, CSB

Then, the psalmist ends with affirming truth and worship.

> *For he has not despised or abhorred*
> *the torment of the oppressed.*
> *He did not hide his face from him*
> *but listened when he cried to him for help.*
> *I will give praise in the great assembly*
> *because of you;*
> *I will fulfill my vows*
> *before those who fear you.*
> *The humble will eat and be satisfied;*
> *those who seek the Lord will praise him.*
> *May your hearts live forever!*
>
> Psalm 22:24–26, CSB

David begins with an emotional reaction to his trial and ends with a grateful heart.

You can hear the change of heart as the psalmist declares truth over emotion. His emotion follows his mind shift. He is able to praise God after he gets over himself.

We can use these psalms to help us lament our motherhood journeys when they deviate from the norm.

Is your baby dealing with colic?
Talk to God about your frustrations, and then choose if you will trust Him.

Is your baby not gaining weight?
Grieve breastfeeding if you need to, then choose if you believe He is faithful. Thank God for providing other ways to feed your baby.

Has your partner checked out on you?
Tell God about your hurt, and then choose if you believe God is strong enough to help you. Worship God for being a present Father.

Lament so that you can listen to the love of God.

Battling Discouragement

When you lament in a "healthy way," lament will lead you to worship.

But if you begin lamenting in an "unhealthy way," lament can become grumbling. We must guard our hearts against the victim vortex. Our honesty should end with worship.

If you have difficulty getting to a place of worship, get help. Ultimately, our lament should lead to a posture change and a deeper trust. If you find that your emotional venting is causing you to be further from God, you may need to seek the counsel of someone who has walked through the valleys of faith longer than you have. God would rather you wrestle than walk away.

> **A Prayer For The Lamenting Mother:**
>
> *Jesus, this is harder than I thought it would be. Sometimes, you feel far away. But I know you are not. You are with me. I praise you for how you are providing in the little ways I cannot even see. I praise you for your goodness and faithfulness to me. Amen.*

A Quick Prayer for Today:

Jesus, this is hard. Help me see your love for me today.

Week 3

Saying Hello To Guilt

I was so good at parenting . . . until I became a parent. Surely, those parents were doing it all wrong. I would do it better when it was my turn.

But after I became a mama, I realized how much I could not do. Guilt moved in. Because I had expectations of myself that I could not fulfill. I was the Type A personality who thought she could fix everything. But with my newborn, I couldn't fix everything.

Hello, Guilt. Goodbye, Self-Righteousness.

My postpartum experience humbled me to the core.
I could not help my child, who was screaming with each feed.
I felt intense guilt that my body was failing at what it was supposed to do for my beautiful daughter. I could not fix her pain or soothe her with breastfeeding.

As the desperation grew, it was very hard for me to be alone.
Any "villagers" willing to enter this pillage zone were a godsend.
Yet my anxiety also did not let anyone else care for my child.

My mother moved in for the first six weeks after my first baby's birth. We stepped on each other's toes often. We offended one another often. And we forgave one another often. The house felt small when we expanded from two to four overnight. However, my mother was essential to my survival during the newborn period. I would not have made it through my first newborn experience without her.

My mother's love language was advice-giving, and I was learning how to be resilient. My sensitive mommy heart needed to grow a thicker skin. I was also learning the balance of being teachable while establishing my identity as a mama.

But in the quiet places of the night, the voice of guilt would tell me what I was doing wrong. It was the voice of an accuser who told me I was not made for this. We can hear the words of guilt telling us what we should be doing better.

But the word of God does not guilt mothers. The Bible is full of tenderness and freedom for the guilt-ridden postpartum mother. God desires to turn our guilt into a dependence on Him. We are not giving up when we remove the pressure to fix our children. Instead, we are giving up our children to God. A rough postpartum period can foster humility rather than pride.

The cross usually becomes more important in this postpartum period because Christian mothers have a place where they can lay their burdens down, especially when things do not follow according to plan. When we lay our plans and dreams on the cross, we do not need to be everything for our children. We do not need to worry about messing them up. We do not need to fear if we are doing the right thing. God already knows what is going to happen. We are free to parent by prayer.

So hello, humility. Goodbye, pride. Only Christ can turn our guilt into humility. Our lives are no longer about what we accomplish. Instead, our motherhood journeys are about what He has already accomplished for us.

Day 1: Forgiving Ourselves - God Chose Us

Sometimes, our greatest offenders are ourselves.

During the last two weeks, you have developed a rhythm for feeding your child. If breastfeeding has not worked out, a mother's guilt can be very intense. Do you have guilt about what you expect your body to be able to do?

No amount of papayas, milk cookies, or mother's tea will change the body God has given you. You can buy nipple shields and every five-star reviewed product to improve your chances, but your breasts may have another plan.

It's also okay to admit that you do not like breastfeeding. Not all mothers love it. Breastfeeding can be unnatural for some mothers. Some mothers even feel more depressed during breastfeeding. The pressure to produce and maintain the milk supply is exhausting.

Running into multiple forks in the road while breastfeeding is not uncommon. You may run into mastitis or a nipple yeast infection. There is a "Goldilocks Breastfeeding Complex" that is a challenge of too much or too little milk. Finding the "just right" balance of breast milk is not always easy.

The normal breastfeeding experience is often two steps forward followed by one step backward. The process is dynamic as your milk supply and baby's demand change.

But when breastfeeding does not work out, women experience intense guilt. There is pressure to give our children the "best head start." But the desire to breastfeed can become obsessive. We can become blinded by the breastfeeding idol.

If this is your story, beware of guilt, who whispers in your ear that you are a failure.
Guilt tells you that you did not try hard enough.
The Accuser is an expert at making you feel little.

In these moments, it is important to cling to the truth of God's Word. When you know Jesus, you know you have been chosen for the mission of motherhood.

Saying Hello To Guilt

Since God chose you to be the holy people he loves, you must clothe yourselves with tenderhearted mercy, kindness, humility, gentleness, and patience. Colossians 3:12, NLT

You have been chosen to be part of His holy people that He loves.

We are not perfect mothers. We can be angry with ourselves that we aren't getting it right, or we can extend grace to ourselves by saying that we are trying our best.

Clothe yourself with mercy, kindness, humility, gentleness, and patience towards others today. But then look in the mirror because the wearer of these virtues needs to extend them to herself as well. Have you extended mercy to yourself today? Kindness to yourself? Humility is when you recognize you may not have all the answers. Gentleness with your Spirit? Patience with yourself even when you fail?

Or have you focused only on what you are not doing right?

There are always things we can do better in motherhood. But there are also many things you are already doing well. For the failures of motherhood that have already occurred (and will still occur), God has already forgiven you! Thankfully, the blood shed on the cross has no expiration date for forgiveness!

Forgiving ourselves gives us freedom from perfection. We become reliant on the grace of God instead of our own achievements.

Have you tried your best in this thing called motherhood?
If yes, show guilt to the door and slam it behind him.
Then look to Jesus, who died to conquer guilt. Jesus' death and resurrection protect you so that the Accuser cannot have a hold on you.

Jesus loves you, not because of your success.
Jesus loves you in spite of your failures.
Jesus loves you, even when your best is not good enough.
Because the truth is, if not today, we will fail our children sometime in the future.
We are not perfect mothers.

How we process our early motherhood challenges will continue to build on later moments of motherhood.

If we are hard on ourselves, our children are more likely to be hard on themselves. If we forgive ourselves, they will forgive themselves as well.

You are the perfectly imperfect mother of your child. Whether you are breastfeeding or formula-feeding, your love is more important than your motherhood success. Our children do not need perfect mothers as much as they need humble mothers.

> **A Prayer For "The Mother Who Can't Get It Right":**
> *Jesus, forgive me for not being able to get this mothering job right all the time. But I know you will not leave me at this moment. You extend mercy and kindness to me. You are patient with me. Even when I cannot get it right, you are still enough. Thank you for being sovereign over what feels like my inadequacies as a mother. Amen.*

A Quick Prayer for Today:

Jesus, help me do my best, and then I give you the rest.

Day 2: Forgiving Others - God Forgives Us

Since God chose you to be the holy people he loves, you must clothe yourselves with tenderhearted mercy, kindness, humility, gentleness, and patience. Make allowance for each other's faults, and forgive anyone who offends you. Remember, the Lord forgave you, so you must forgive others. Above all, clothe yourselves with love, which binds us all together in perfect harmony. And let the peace that comes from Christ rule in your hearts. For as members of one body, you are called to live in peace. And always be thankful.

Colossians 3:12–15, NLT

Sleep deprivation is a pressure cooker for emotions and broken relationships.

A sleep-deprived brain goes into survival mode. When you are barely surviving, fuses shorten. Everything feels like a big deal. Words feel more jagged than intended. Grudges form thicker walls than before. Our survival brains close off relationships rather than build them.

But on this island of babydom, I pray you keep the dock open.

There will be relationships that will disgust you in this period. People who do not get it. People who talk about things that they do not understand. It can be draining when you are already empty. Before you respond with anger, recognize if your tank to be refilled.

After a good nap, the nerves are less raw. After a meal, the mind thinks more clearly. After you rest and your stomach is full, would you reconsider the relationships that need forgiveness? Forgiveness does not mean you need to be boundary-free. Forgiveness means that you are releasing your grudge so that you can be freed. If you want to be freed from guilt in your relationships, consider whether you should forgive because Jesus said so. (Matthew 18:21–22)

When the jets have cooled, ask yourself the real questions.

What are you losing by not extending forgiveness?
What can you gain by extending forgiveness?

Focusing on the offense usually causes us to miss out on relationships that still have good in them. When we step back, we see whether the grudge is worth it.

If you are a Christian, God has chosen you to be a holy people, according to Colossians 3:12–15. He asks you to forgive those who have offended you. Then, He demonstrates what this looks like by saying yes to the cross. Instead of telling the haters what He was owed, He stayed silent. Jesus knew God was the ultimate judge.

When we remember the debt we have been forgiven, God changes our hearts.

We do not forgive others for being the "better person" or for the sake of the new baby.

We forgive because Jesus said so.

You can fan the flame of unforgiveness by replaying the injustice. Or you can worship God's mercy toward you. Reflecting on what Jesus did at the cross for you ultimately spurs your heart for supernatural forgiveness.

Forgiveness is not kneeling to be a doormat. Forgiveness is kneeling at the altar of worship, where we let God be the judge. When we let go of what we are owed, we will be freed.

> **A Prayer for the Mama Who Has Been Owed:**
>
> *Jesus, I feel like I am owed more in this relationship with _____. And yet you were owed more respect, and you forgave those who treated you unfairly. You went to the cross because you had compassion for me. Help me to clothe myself with compassion for others even when it is difficult. Help me forgive the debt owed to me as you have forgiven me. Let your peace surround me. Amen.*

A Quick Prayer for Today:

Jesus, justice is yours and yours only.

Day 3: The Art Of Boundaries - God Knows Our Limits

There is always a generational gap between grandparents and parents in how we raise our children. What worked for one generation is now no longer the standard. For example, babies slept on their tummies a generation ago, but now pediatricians are recommending babies sleep on their backs to prevent SIDS[45].

The current generation of parents is Google-educated. Grandparents, on the other hand, did not have the same cautionary tape around their babies. What worked for one generation is now considered risky parenting by the other.

There is a desire for adult children to please their parents while growing into their own family. However, getting their approval is not always possible. All the well-meaning input can get overwhelming. And when sleep-deprived, the most well-intentioned advice can feel critical.

---

[45] Rachel Y. Moon et al., "Sleep-Related Infant Deaths: Updated 2022 Recommendations for Reducing Infant Deaths in the Sleep Environment," Pediatrics 150, no. 1 (June 21, 2022), https://doi.org/10.1542/peds.2022-057990.

Everyone may have an opinion, but your and your spouse's opinions matter the most. You have carried this child from implantation to the Baby Bjorn. You are an expert on your baby. Having studied hours of every grunt and burp, you know what your child needs. You are raising a different child from the ones your parents raised.

The village is necessary. And yet, the village can also drive new parents crazy. A true village will not make the newborn experience about themselves. A true village will lift you up so that you can succeed. If you are surrounded by a village that makes you feel worse after they "help," you may need to establish healthy boundaries.

A boundary is kindness if it allows you to be a better version of yourself in the relationship. Boundaries are guardrails for peaceful relationships.

In Proverbs 4, there is a warning and a call.

> *Guard your **heart** above all else,*
> *for it is the source of life.*
> *Don't let your **mouth** speak dishonestly,*
> *and don't let your lips talk deviously.*
> *Let your **eyes** look forward;*
> *fix your gaze straight ahead.*
> *Carefully consider the path for your **feet**,*
> *and all your ways will be established.*
> *Don't turn to the right or to the left;*
> *keep your feet away from evil.*
> Proverbs 4:23–27, CSB (emphasis added)

Four body parts lead to the stumble: the heart, the mouth, the eyes, and the feet. We choose how long we will feel. We choose what we will say. We choose what we will see. We choose where we will go. This proverb calls us to guard our hearts by being aware of the different body parts that lead to the stumble.

You may need relationship boundaries to guard your heart. Like protective guardrails, boundaries keep your feet on the path so you do not sin. Sometimes, a boundary is a physical separation. And sometimes, it is an emotional one. Some boundaries need to be extreme and some boundaries can be measured wisely.

Boundaries can be guardrails rather than walls. Guardrails will filter what to keep out and what to let go. The proverb we just discussed is part of a father's advice to his son. There is incredible wisdom in the generations before us. The generations before us usually have a heart of concern rather than criticism.

What feels like criticism may be their expression of love. New parents can preserve their relationships by acknowledging their advice-givers. Learning to say, "Thank you for your suggestion, I will think about it," will save you a lot of drama. Filter out what you need, and then move on.

You are responsible for how much their advice will affect your mother's soul. So let the good in and then make a guardrail for what needs to stay out.

Guard your heart because it is the source of your life.

> **A Prayer For The Criticized Mama:**
>
> *Jesus, I'm already feeling insecure about my parenting. Yet you have called me to be my child's mother. Help me to have the wisdom to know how to humbly filter the advice that comes my way. If there are boundaries I need to set, show me how to navigate these relationships wisely. Amen.*

A Quick Prayer for Today:

Jesus, guard my heart.

Day 4: Self-Care Is Selfless - God Wants To Feeds Our Roots

Breastfeeding mothers guzzle gallons of water each day. No matter how much she drinks, the thirst demand can be incredibly powerful. Your body is craving all of this water in order to make milk. You will need to drink sixteen cups of water a day[46]!

---

[46] "Nursing Your Baby — What You Eat and Drink Matters," Accessed 8/4/23, https://www.eatright.org/health/pregnancy/breastfeeding-and-formula/nursing-your-baby-what-you-eat-and-drink-matters#:~:text=Keep%20Hydrated,time%20you%20breastfeed%20your%20baby.

If you do not take the time to hydrate, you may find that your breastmilk supply lessens. You cannot make breast milk unless you water yourself first.

Self-care is selfless. We have spent so much time talking about the sacrificial love of motherhood. Thankfully, God acknowledges that we are humans with limits. Refilling is important for the survival of the constant demand of a newborn. As your newborn becomes more aware and spends more time awake, their naps are now time for you to engage in self-care.

The rhythms we obsess about for our newborns should be the same rhythm of self-care for mamas. Sleep, eat, and play. Have you done these three things for yourself today?

Sleep: Take a nap when the baby sleeps.
Eat: Order food so you don't have to cook.
Play: Take a walk, sit outside, listen to music (that doesn't sound like a lullaby), sit with your spouse, and do not talk about the baby. Play with something that is not baby-related.

Sleeping, eating, and playing are all self-care.
Self-care is selfless.
Self-care is necessary for the best version of mama to keep showing up.

One of the most important ways to practice self-care is with soul care.

Spend time praying and meditating at 2:00 a.m. God is awake with you. He is a good listener. Resetting your mind will help you focus on the beauty of what is happening around you. You will have a clearer mind to meditate on Scripture as you feed your baby.

You can fill others only when you have been filled yourself. In Jeremiah, the rooted mother has taken time to water her roots:

> *But blessed are those who trust in the Lord*
> *and have made the Lord their hope and confidence.*
> *They are like trees planted along a riverbank,*
> *with roots that reach deep into the water.*
> *Such trees are not bothered by the heat*
> *or worried by long months of drought.*

*Their leaves stay green,
and they never stop producing fruit.*

Jeremiah 17:7–8, NLT

When I meet a mother unbothered by hard days, it is because she has been well-watered. She has taken the time to deepen her roots in Scripture so she has perspective when the storm comes. She is a well-rested, well-watered tree.

But as mothers, we get lost in the details easily. Self-care is an important part of helping us step back so we can see the whole picture. Our perspectives change when we practice self-care.

Refill yourself today so that you have more to give.

A Prayer For The Thirsty Mother:
Jesus, thank you for giving me time to be watered today. Feed my roots so that I can be firmly planted, not bothered by the heat or droughts of motherhood. Help me to always stay fruitful with you as my source. Amen.

A Quick Prayer for Today:

Jesus, fill me today.

Day 5: Trusting Others With Your Baby - God Knows Your Baby The Best

Part of letting go of motherhood is letting others nurture your child along with you. The motherhood protective instinct is very strong in the first few weeks. You know your baby the best, and it is not easy to let someone else care for your baby.

But the truth is, it is beautiful when our children have multiple caregivers that pour into them throughout their lives. We cannot be all things for our children at all times. In the village of motherhood, when we do not understand our children, another person often will.

You alone have the role of biological mother. You are irreplaceable. But there is beauty when you also let others into your children's lives. You may have heard of baby Moses floating down the Nile to be picked up by Pharaoh's daughter.

> *The woman became pregnant and gave birth to a son; when she saw that he was beautiful, she hid him for three months. But when she could no longer hide him, she got a papyrus basket for him and coated it with asphalt and pitch. She placed the child in it and set it among the reeds by the bank of the Nile. Then, his sister stood at a distance in order to see what would happen to him.*
> Exodus 2:2–4, CSB

But how often do we think about Moses's mother, Jochebed? She was an incredibly clever and intelligent woman. She hid her baby to protect Moses from infanticide for three months! Can you imagine hiding a newborn for three months?

Jochebed took a risk by asking someone else to care for her son when she could not protect him. Jochebed knew Moses needed another "mother" to protect him. She crafted a papyrus basket that floated down the Nile into the arms of Pharaoh's daughter. Jochebed recruited the daughter of her enemy to care for her son! Talk about faith! Pharaoh's daughter could have easily ordered Moses's death right away. But God had a different plan. When Pharaoh's daughter saw Moses, she had compassion for him. Instead of seeing him as the enemy, she adopted Moses as her own.

It must not have been easy for Jochebed to let go of her son at that moment.

One of the most beautiful parts of this story is that when Pharaoh's daughter adopted Moses, she recruited Jochebed to be his nursemaid. In essence, after Jochebed let another mother into Moses's life, she was able to experience the fullness of God's provision. Imagine the sweetness of this open adoption.

Sometimes, we do not want to let go of the most precious thing in our lives, like our children. Guilt makes us believe that we need to do it all. Guilt says how dare we let someone else do it. But the true village that surrounds our children wants to help. You can bless your village by letting them care for your baby.

> **A Prayer For The Insular Mom:**
> *Jesus, I am having a hard time letting others into my life. I want to be able to do it all, but I cannot be all for my child. Let me cherish the village you have sent to help me and see it as a gift rather than a threat. Free me from the guilt of doing it all for my children. Amen.*

A Quick Prayer for Today:

Jesus, let me trust others to help me.

Day 6: Everyone Needs More of You - God Rejoices Over Us

One of the hardest parts of the postpartum period is feeling like you are never enough. Twenty-four hours does not seem like enough time in the day, yet the minutes feel like hours. Everyone wants more of you—your baby, your spouse, and your messy kitchen.

They are all telling you that you are not enough.

Guilt has moved in. Before children, guilt was not as heavy. But after children, it feels like many more people are counting on you. The pie has been sliced into smaller slivers - and everyone wants a piece!

Listen to how guilt speaks to you. Guilt is a great deceiver who tells you everything you should be doing and then tells you everything you should not do. Pay attention to your self-talk to see if *"should-be"* statements are destroying your soul.

Does this sound familiar? "I *should be* spending more time with my other children." "I *should be* cooking more and cleaning my house." "I *shouldn't be* so tired when I have so much help." "I *should not* be tired when I stay home all day."

Guilt tells us we need to do more to be worthy. Guilt is the great Accuser of Lies. He twists lies to sound like the truth. How did Jesus respond to the Accuser? Jesus answered with an abrupt, "Get behind me, Satan" (Matthew 16:23). Sometimes we have to say "Get behind me" out loud. If you are paralyzed by the *"should be"* today, tell the

Accuser to get behind you.

In these dark moments, God does not need more of you. He loves you not because of how well you perform as a mother or wife. He loves you not because of how joyfully you wash your bottles.

When you have those days where the guilt tells you that you are unlovable. Respond with Zephaniah 3:17, NLT:

> *For the Lord your God is living among you. He is a mighty savior. He will take delight in you with gladness. With his love, he will calm all your fears. He will rejoice over you with joyful songs.*

God delights in you.

Like a father who sings a lullaby to his child, He rejoices over you.

A Prayer During A Mama "Should-be" Moment
Jesus, I have so many things that I feel like I should be doing for my child. Sometimes, I can do it, and many times, I cannot. But you offer me freedom from guilt. You delight in me with gladness and calm my fears. Amen.

A Quick Prayer for the Day:

> *Jesus, thank you for not holding guilt over my head.*

Day 7: The "Good" Christian Mother - God Embraces Us At Our Worst

Do you feel pressure to be a "good" Christian mother in these newborn days?

Are you spending time in the Bible to feed your soul, or are your thoughts more like this:

I'm too tired to pray. I would rather sleep than read the Bible or this weird "Woven" devotion book.

I've been there. It's tough to focus on our souls when the demand to keep another being alive is so heavy. My quiet time with God during my newborn days was one or two-word prayers rather than in-depth

Scripture study. Structured quiet time in the Bible was too difficult.

But God knows. He is not a policeman telling you what you are doing wrong with your prayer life. He is not angry with you for taking a break from serving the children's ministry because He knows you need to rest. He is a tender Father who will keep you company during your midnight feedings.

God knows your exhaustion and doesn't need lip service right now. He does not need you to have it all together for Him. We may want to put a beautiful bow on postpartum and post about it on social media. But what happens before and after that perfect picture is real life.

Real life is chaotic. Real life is hard.

In the hard, we need to remember that our performance as a "good Christian" does not define our relationship with God. The reason we obey isn't because of obligation. The reason we obey is because we love God, the Father, who first loved us.

Remember the story of the prodigal son in Luke 15:11–24? A man had two sons. His youngest son asked for an early inheritance and went bankrupt partying. The son hit rock bottom when his "friends" abandoned him. He was eating from the troughs of pigs when it dawned on him that his father's servants were eating better than he was. He made a plan to ask his father for forgiveness. You can imagine the stench of the pig, his face caked with mud when he stumbled home. He was embarrassed, ashamed, and felt unworthy.

> *So he returned home to his father. And while he was still a long way off, his father saw him coming. Filled with love and compassion, he ran to his son, embraced him, and kissed him (Luke 15:20, NLT).*

The father embraced his son. "He was lost, but now he is found" (Luke 15:32 NLT). It wasn't his son's loveliness that caused the father to embrace him. It was his son's repentance that brought the father to compassion. Jesus finishes the story by telling the people about how God welcomes those who are aware of their debt into His kingdom.

Guilt tells you that you are failing as a Christian. But God is not asking for you to be a perfect Christian. He is asking you to be a daughter dependent on His sacrifice on the cross. Your loveliness is not in your works as much as it is in your soft heart. As motherhood brings out your awareness of a need for Jesus even more, your love for Him will grow as well.

It is a relief that we do not need to post our best selfie for God. We may not smell like pigs (or do we?), but we can be ourselves in front of a Holy God. We can "post" our disheveled hair without makeup, spit-up tie-dyed shirts—and still be beautiful in His sight.

> **A Prayer For The Mama Who Doesn't Have It All Together:**
> *Jesus, thank you for relieving me from the pressure to be perfect as a mother and perfect as a Christian. Following you doesn't mean that I have it all together. It means I understand the cost you paid to love me the way you do. Let me be my true self with you. Amen.*

A Quick Prayer for Today:

Jesus, help me not get wrapped up in performance.

Week 4

Re-defining Your Identity

I found the postpartum experience to be numbing for my identity. I was someone who had all the answers for everyone else, but when it was my turn to be pregnant and postpartum, I didn't have all the answers anymore.

Everyone always asks me what it was like to be a pregnant OBGYN. It was terrifying because I knew all the things that could go wrong. But I also believed the lie that although medical complications happened to my patients, they wouldn't happen to me. Somehow, I thought residency would prepare me for the sleepless nights of having a newborn. I also believed I would have an easy breastfeeding experience because I knew all the textbook answers to every question. But when it was my turn to implement the techniques I had walked other women through, none of them worked for me. I had been confident in my identity as a physician, but my "brand" fell apart when I could not help my own children.

I felt betrayed by all the books on parenting that did not apply to my situation. My education had not prepared me for my motherhood journey. I felt like a foreigner in my own body. It was not the body I was proud of when I walked down the aisle in my wedding dress. I was never going to be able to get back there again.

It became clear that my identity before children had been self-centered and self-reliant.

Motherhood helped me see that life was no longer about me.

I also struggled with God, as this was the first time I truly felt helpless in my life. There was no answer for my children based on my diligence or resourcefulness. For many years, I had loved God. But I did not know what it meant for me to need Him desperately. Jesus had not been my lifeline until I had my children. And that was humbling for a Christian who thought she had already figured it out.

After I became a mother, my life was not about achieving a good Christian life. My life was about becoming a dependent daughter in the kingdom of God.

So many things changed the moment I had my children. My relationship with my spouse, with others, and with God. My significant relationships became deeper. I had to distance myself from some of the people who no longer understood me.

Many times in the first year of my baby's life, I did not know who I was anymore. I no longer had time for all the things I liked to do before children. I lost myself in the motherhood journey—especially during the first year.

I had a different experience than most. I was raising a special needs newborn and did not realize it at the time. The months of impossible feedings turned into years of therapies and medical appointments. I gave up parts of my career to be the best mama I could be. I became isolated in a life that very few can understand. But I gained so many more eternal, deeper things. I continue to advocate for my daughter and will do so for the rest of my life. It is humbling, but it is beautiful.

God used my broken self-sufficiency to prepare me for something more. He redeemed my broken heart by the perfectly imperfect fruit of my womb.

I have always believed having children is the best thing ever, regardless of the hard experience. It took time for me to find myself again amid the baby bottles, spit-up, and laundry. But when I found myself again, my soul was richer and deeper.

It is okay to lose yourself in the beginning. It is only natural when you love someone else so much. But as you get pieces of your sanity back, I pray that you find yourself again. I pray you find time for the little joys that make you who you are. Your children are important, but you are important too. They are more joyous when you are more joyous.

Let's spend the next week going over the identity changes that happen for a woman postpartum. You can find yourself again in your new normal.

Day 1: Mommy Still Looks Pregnant - God Redefines Beauty

I was looking forward to the postpartum body bounce-back. I anticipated that after the delivery of my children, all the swelling, gelato, and cellulite would be delivered along with my placenta. Instead, after my baby, placenta, and amniotic fluid were delivered, I didn't lose the forty pounds I had gained during pregnancy. I still looked pregnant after I delivered. Although breastfeeding helped the calorie burn, it was always the last ten pounds I could never lose.

Some mothers have a great metabolism, and breastfeeding is a great treadmill for weight loss. But some mamas never get back to their pre-baby body. If you already didn't feel great about your body before having children, chances are that feeling doesn't improve after childbirth. If you felt great about your body before having children but can't get back there, it's really tough! Your doctor may have some suggestions for weight loss once it is safe to resume exercise. Sometimes, a pelvic floor therapist can be a helpful as you recover postpartum.

At your preconception visit, did anyone talk about prolapse? Did anyone tell you about the hemorrhoids that are here to stay? Or the stretch marks that have no recoil? Or that you should wear a pad before you jump on a trampoline?!

We expect our bodies to change during pregnancy, but we often don't think about the changes mamas experience afterward.

A baby bump is normal even when you're postpartum. The uterus may be shrinking in size, but your skin has already been stretched out. After the baby arrives, the belly skin drapes lazily like a deflated hot-air balloon. No wonder moms wear high-waisted jeans!

Even though our babies are worth it, we can still feel gross. God already knows. He does not let our bodies go through change without having a plan to give us a heart change as well. As we spend more time with God, He can change how we feel about ourselves. A true metamorphosis is on the way!

How do we convince ourselves that we are still beautiful when we don't feel beautiful?

- **By valuing valor over vanity.**

  Your body has gone through a battle. No matter how strong the warrior is, there are always wounds in battle. There will be some casualties to your body when you have children. Warriors do not have time for plastic surgery and trainers. They focus on the cause. Warriors fight for a cause, laying down their lives for the cause. It is always easier when you need to be brave for someone else. Your children teach you valor over vanity.

- **By being aware of the lies around us.**

  The world tells us that beauty must look a certain way. If we all had trainers, nannies, and personal chefs with unlimited money and time, we would all be able to look better than pre-children! However, since this is not the case, we need to have realistic expectations for the body bounce-back.

- **By defining beauty and how God sees it.**

  "But the LORD said to Samuel, 'Do not consider his appearance or his height, for I have rejected him. The LORD does not look at the things people look at. People look at the outward appearance, but the LORD looks at the heart.'" (1 Samuel 16:7, NIV).

  Ask God how He sees you. Because beauty is defined by who God says we are.

- **By managing our stress appropriately.**

  Do you hide in the pantry with your cookie friends when the children are out of control? When food is a comfort for anxiety, it becomes a crutch. Finding ways to diffuse stress through physical activity, appropriate diets, and getting a break from childcare will help you find other ways to manage than stress eating. You will feel better mentally when you make good choices for your body.

- **By surrounding yourself with soul sisters who not only commiserate but also motivate.**

Your tribe can help you focus on the true beauty that lies inside you. Seek the relationships that build up your soul. Be this kind of friend to someone else. Find the mama in the trenches with you. Encourage her inward beauty as she cares for her children. Find the mama who needs to hear that her valor is something you admire. When you focus on making another mama feel beautiful, you will feel beautiful yourself. That is how true beauty works.

On that note, you are an amazing warrior for your children. Your faithfulness to God that you express as a mother is beautiful. Your motherhood makeover is simply stunning, darling!

And now, I feel like a supermodel.

A Prayer For The Mama Who Needs To Feel Beautiful Again:
Jesus, I don't feel comfortable in my body. But I know these wounds are worth it. Help me to see beauty the way you see it. Help me focus on my health over an exact number on the scale. Give me ways to cope with my stress other than snacking. I pray that you would help me feel beautiful because you made me. Help me see myself the way that you see me. Amen.

A Quick Prayer for Today:

Jesus, let my heart be truly beautiful.

Day 2: Mixed-Emotions Mommy - God Knows How We Feel

The baby is now the star of the show. Everyone else has now been placed on the back burner, including yourself. All the phone calls from the family are to talk with the baby, and not to talk with you. Everyone's asking, "How is the baby doing?" But few of the phone calls are to ask how you are coping with this transition to motherhood. When I ask my patients two weeks postpartum how they are coping with becoming a mama, the waterworks flow more often than not.

Women feel guilty when they feel sad. Their baby is perfect. It is all worth it. So why is there still a heaviness that looms?

Because mamas feel abandoned. All the extra adoring attention you might have received during pregnancy has now been transferred to someone else.

You may ask the question quietly, How about me?

The identity of a postpartum mother is now a milky cow, a graffiti of spit-up, and a laundry machine. Even when we love our children, there is an identity crisis for most women.

The whole experience is really confusing for a postpartum mother. How can we love someone so much yet feel so lost sometimes? How can we spend our whole day trying to get our babies back to sleep, yet we can't wait for them to wake up once they are asleep?

Welcome to the new motherhood identity that has coexistent, mixed emotions. Many emotions will coexist in motherhood. Bitter and sweet. Sorrowful and rejoicing.

These co-existent emotions are also a part of the Christian experience. Paul says:

> *Rather, as servants of God, we commend ourselves in every way: in great endurance; in troubles, hardships and distresses . . .* ***sorrowful, yet always rejoicing; poor, yet making many rich; having nothing, and yet possessing everything*** *(2 Corinthians 6:4,10, NIV emphasis added).*

The concurrent contrast of emotions in motherhood is often confusing. And yet, this should not surprise us because the cross is a place of coexistent emotions. When Jesus died on the hill in Calvary, there were many contrasts in that moment. Justice and injustice. Hatred and love. Punishment and redemption.

Motherhood is full of mixed emotions because there is a constant dying to yourself for the good of someone else. As you go through different seasons of dying to yourself in motherhood, it's okay to have coexistent sorrow and rejoicing.

If you are in a place of sorrow today and wondering, "How about me?" reflect on the truths of Psalm 56.

You keep track of all my sorrows. You have collected all my tears in your bottle. You have recorded each one in your book (Psalm 56:8, NLT).

God keeps track of your sorrow. He has seen every tear you have ever cried when you were a newborn. He has seen every tear you have cried as a mother. You are not a mother in the shadows but a mama whose tears are held carefully. Tenderly. Intentionally.

By the time mamas return to see me at their six-week postpartum visit, most have accepted this new identity of mixed emotions. Their joy overshadows the sorrow more days than not. This balance shifts in different proportions throughout different seasons. If you are experiencing more sorrow than joy at six weeks postpartum, you may be dealing with longer-term depression. It is important to get help.

A Prayer For The Mama Who Is Having Confusing Emotions:
Jesus, my emotions are all over the place. I love my baby, but I also resent being a mom because it is just so hard. God, you know my sorrows. You are not surprised by them. Instead, you know every tear I shed for myself and others. I praise you because you always remember me. As I learn how to navigate this new normal, it fills me with joy. Amen.

A Quick Prayer for Today:

Jesus, let my joy be stronger than my sorrow today.

Day 3: Daddy's Identity Crisis - God Loves Him Too

We just talked about how the baby is now the star of the show. On the red carpet, you're the baby's manager, following closely with the diaper bag. But somewhere straggling behind you both is a daddy who is also trying to find his place.

Daddies have an identity crisis, just like mommies.

Becoming a father is full of mixed emotions for men. They may have always wanted to be a daddy. Or they may have feared becoming like the father they had (or didn't have). They may have never held a baby before. Although they may be completely ecstatic about becoming a father, they are often unaware of their own grieving process. He now plays second fiddle to the baby. Your relationship has changed overnight. If he does not bond with the baby, it makes a very uncomfortable dynamic for mamas.

Fathers may have trouble bonding with the baby because they cannot soothe their newborn without breastfeeding. Men can feel helpless with a crying baby. Some men begin to shut down when they feel useless. If you are struggling emotionally with postpartum depression, men may feel even more helpless. Men also go through postpartum depression as well. If they feel powerless, they may check out emotionally. Their distance only compounds the postpartum depression.

The reality is, during this haze of postpartum, your spouse still needs your admiration and love. The postpartum time is your chance to encourage fathers to become real men.

Maintaining and protecting relationships with your spouse must become intentional. While the intensity of the newborn season is unique, the demands of parenthood continue with each season. Intentional encouragement for one other is important in each parenting stage to keep a stable home for your children.

> *But encourage each other daily, while it is still called today so that none of you is hardened by sin's deception (Hebrews 3:13, CSB).*

When you see your husband trying to be present, you can be an encourager. Encourage him daily so that he is not deceived by the lies that tell him he deserves better.

You can tell him that he is adequate as a father when you leave the baby with him while you go to the grocery store. He may be scared the first few times you leave him with the baby, but it will give him a chance to bond with the baby. Your baby is resilient after the "freak-out" when you leave. Until you give him the opportunity to figure it out, he will think of parenting as your job only.

You can tell him he is useful when you give him concrete ways to help you. Not all men have the intuition to know exactly how to help. You can encourage them to change the baby's diaper even if they don't do it correctly. You can choose to show grace even when you know you can do it better.

You can tell him he is important to you when you spend time with him, even when you have a never-ending task list. He needs to know he is still significant in your eyes.

The more we recognize the changes daddies also go through postpartum, the more they will keep showing up. The more we let daddies connect with their babies, the more they participate. The more we pray for them, the more we relinquish our impossible expectations.

The postpartum time isn't easy for daddies, either. He needs encouragement too. When you encourage him, he will be more likely to encourage you.

A Prayer For the Mama Whose Baby Is The Only Thing That Matters:
Jesus, this baby is a blessing, but my spouse is also important. Help me encourage him so that he knows he is still important to me. Help me let go of control so my spouse can thrive as a daddy. Let me be a daily blessing to my husband. Amen.

A Quick Prayer for Today:

Jesus, let me be an encouragement to my spouse today.

Day 4: Spouse Identity Crisis - God is Love

As relationships change after children arrive on the scene, the true colors of each parent reveal themselves. Two sinners have different approaches to raising children. Conflict is inevitable, right? As these relationships change, it can be very destabilizing for your identity.

Your love will be tested after children. Lovers must become partners that can divide labor. Teamwork becomes essential to a successful marriage. You will find your marriage vows both tested and strengthened after children.

The Bible gives us a measuring stick for how to love (and how to be loved) in 1 Corinthians.

> *Love is patient and kind. Love is not jealous or boastful or proud or rude. It does not demand its own way. It is not irritable, and it keeps no record of being wronged. It does not rejoice about injustice but rejoices whenever the truth wins out. Love never gives up, never loses faith, is always hopeful, and endures through every circumstance.*
>
> *1 Corinthians 13:4–7, NLT*

What does this love look like between two people during the postpartum crazy?

- **True love wants to relieve the load of the other.**

    Is there an area where you can be more patient with him because his weight is heavy?
    Is there something he can do that would make your life easier? If he wasn't a mind reader before children, he probably is still not a mind reader. He will likely respond better if you have clear tasks identifying how to be helpful.

- **True love forgives short tempers.** Do you give grace even when he doesn't "deserve" it? Does he recognize that you are sometimes acting out from being overwhelmed? Love does not keep a record of wrongs (even when it feels good to hold that record over his head).

- **True love cherishes one another at the other's worst.** Do you let him sleep even when it's his turn (and vice versa)? Does he give you a break when you need one? Serving one another takes a humble spirit on both sides.

The call for true love in marriage goes both ways. Both parties are called to love one another, especially when they are sleep-deprived, short-tempered, and at their worst. Most couples are not in the best place to extend true love in the 1 Corinthians style when they bring a newborn home. It takes a few weeks to find the rhythms that help one another. If your spouse gives you true love, reciprocated respect is not difficult.

Some couples never get to this place. If you find that your relationship is becoming a power struggle, pay attention. It is never okay for him to mistreat you. Abuse can be active harm or withholding love for the purpose of manipulation. Postpartum women are particularly vulnerable to abuse. They are often reliant on men for finances and their health insurance. But a truly loving man does not take advantage of a woman's vulnerability nor make this experience about himself. The apostle Paul talks about a husband who gives himself up for his wife as Christ does for the church (Ephesians 5:25). True love is sacrificial. While the Bible speaks of forgiveness, there is no place that the Bible says to tolerate abuse. Extending forgiveness for a mistake is not the same as enabling the behavioral patterns of an abuser. If you are in this latter situation, please tell someone and get help.

Ultimately, there is no perfect marriage. Even a supportive spouse falls short. He cannot fix everything you will go through as a mother. The true love you need at times is not from a human. True love is from God.

Your Heavenly Father is not keeping a record of your wrongs once you have asked for forgiveness. He does not give up on you even when you fail. His love endures through every circumstance. He gives you true love even when no one else is around.

You are loved, my friend.

A Prayer for the Mama Who Desires True Love

Jesus, you are my true love. I pray that you give me wisdom on how to love my husband today. Help him be the best father that he can be. And even if I do not have a husband, I pray that you would love me the way my heart craves. Amen.

A Quick Prayer for Today:

Jesus, thank you for your true love.

Day 5: Multi-tasking Mommy - God Wants Our Attention

One of the new mommy skills to master is learning how to prioritize the multiple tasks you have in a day. There are only twenty-four hours in the day. So, if we divide the time for each task in the day, we have

2.746 seconds per task! This isn't logistically possible for any mama, right? And so, ladies, the multi-tasker is born.

We can breast-pump hands-free while we cook dinner and answer our work calls on our AirPods. The children are running around us like a moth to the flame of the stove. But that's no problem - because our bodies have the agility of an octopus. There's a hangry tantrum going on in the other room. The toys have been dumped out again. The peanut gallery is whispering into our ear that *it's our fault our children are melting down. We started dinner too late.*

So maybe the food is burned, and that wet spot (I haven't smelled it yet) doesn't get mopped up?! It's just a day in the life of a mother!

Can we really do it all?
Some days are better than others.
But eventually, we crash unless we multi-task wisely.

The Bible tells of the story of Mary and Martha in Luke 10. Mary was sitting at Jesus' feet, spending time recharging with her Savior. Martha was busying herself with all the preparations. She wanted to make everything perfect for Jesus that day. You can imagine that Martha was banging the pots, trying to get her sister's attention, who was not helping. Martha's annoyance grew as her sister focused only on listening to Jesus.

Resentment finally hit its peak. Martha was getting more and more irritated. Martha asked Jesus to tell Mary to help her. Jesus responds, *"Martha, Martha,' the Lord answered, 'you are worried and upset about many things, but few things are needed—or indeed only one. Mary has chosen what is better, and it will not be taken away from her.'" (Luke 10:41–42, NIV)*

Jesus was not upset at Martha's intention to be hospitable. He was more concerned about how Martha's multi-tasking was affecting her Spirit.

Even in the presence of Jesus, Martha was more worried about her task list than Christ himself.

Martha would not have been worried about many things if she had taken the time to organize her tasks before Jesus arrived. Her mind would have been more clear to spend time with her Savior.

You can sit with Jesus when you multi-task wisely.

The wise multi-tasking mommy:

- **Believes in intentional space for margins:** Getting anywhere will take two times longer than it used to take. Account for the blowouts and outfit changes that will need to occur before you need to be somewhere.
- **Believes that organization is kindness:** Planning out your meals ahead of time and writing your tasks for the week will allow you to delegate. Ask your helpers to assist with non-breastfeeding tasks. If you are not organized, ask a friend with the gift of organization to help you. (Trust me, organizers love this kind of thing.)
- **Believes in self-care:** Find someone to watch your children weekly if you have the finances. Or trade childcare with a family you trust. You need time to organize and prioritize what is important. Use this self-care time to organize your tasks. Spend time in the Bible and prayer, and meet for coffee with a friend who lets you be yourself. Exercise so that you get the good endorphins when your provider says it's okay to resume exercise. Rebuilding muscle mass is very important after going through pregnancy. The stronger you feel physically, the stronger you feel mentally.

When you multi-task wisely, you can sit at the feet of Jesus without wondering what is next on your list.

You will be more patient with your children's dramatic tantrums. You will be less annoyed when your child needs another clothing change. You will be able to slow down without stressing out. And in this stillness, even hear Jesus speak.

A Prayer For A Multi-tasking Mama:

> *Jesus, I don't want to be worried or upset by many things. Help me to multi-task wisely so that I can hear you more clearly. Help me find time to organize. Show me how to organize so that I can spend time recharging. Make space in my schedule so that I can give grace. I want to choose what is better. Amen.*

A Quick Prayer for Today:

Jesus, clear my mind so that I can hear you speak.

Day 6: Lonely Mommy - God Understands Loneliness

The camaraderie of new mothers is beautiful. But it can become difficult if your baby is on a different path from everyone else. When your newborn experience differs from your friend's, you may feel like you're missing out.

Why is her baby sleeping so well, and mine is not?
Why does her baby breastfeed and mine does not?
Why is my baby having all the problems, and everyone else's seems so easy?

Mamas are sensitive to being different from one another during early motherhood. We want to do everything right to keep our children as "normal" as possible. But it can be extremely isolating when our children do not follow the norm. It may feel like we're shivering in the cold while looking through a frosted window. Inside, a party of mothers are laughing by a warm fire while they bounce their Gerber babies on their laps.

The isolation is real when you have a different story than everyone else.

I was on a different newborn journey with my baby. She was feeding on a different schedule than my friends' babies. I felt like the only mama who was dealing with reflux. It felt like no one could help me. The gap widened as my daughter fell behind her developmental milestones. My baby sat alone at playdates while the other babies walked around her. I felt so alone.

But in this place of loneliness, someone else was outside with me. His name was Jesus. He was also different from those inside the party. Jesus looked at me tenderly and gave me a place of belonging. He understood how I felt.

My isolation helped me know Jesus more.

> *He was despised and rejected by mankind,*
> *a man of suffering and familiar with pain.*
> *Like one from whom people hide their faces*
> *he was despised, and we held him in low esteem.*
> *Surely, he took up our pain*
> *and bore our suffering,*
> *yet we considered him punished by God,*
> *stricken by him and afflicted.*
> *But he was pierced for our transgressions,*
> *he was crushed for our iniquities;*
> *the punishment that brought us peace was on him,*
> *and by his wounds, we are healed.*
>
> *Isaiah 53:3–5, NIV*

Jesus was not like everyone else.
In fact, Jesus endured a purposeful isolation.

His isolation would help him identify with the suffering of his people. (Hebrews 4:15) His isolation would heal those with deep wounds. (Isaiah 53:5) His isolation would bring us peace when we accept Him. (John 14:27)

All of our children will experience isolation in some way. It is an inevitable rite of passage in humanity to not always fit in. God uses isolation for our good and His glory. He took up our pain on the cross so that we would have hope when we were alone.

It is okay to wonder why God gave you a different plan than everyone else. He loves you still. Next time you feel left out of the party, look around you. Jesus is there. He will show you the other mothers who are also shivering beside you. You will see mothers that you would not have seen before. And it will not feel so lonely.

It's okay if your story is different from everyone else's. Your identity is not based on how well you fit in. Your identity is based on who Jesus says you are. He says you were worth His wounds.

> **A Prayer For The Mama Who Does Not Fit In:**
>
> *Jesus, you were rejected at the cross. The isolation I feel pales in comparison to that. But you felt this loneliness at the cross, so you could understand my pain. You have a plan for my children, and even if it differs from the one I would have written, I trust you to heal my wounds. Thank you for being pierced for me so that my pain now has a purpose. Amen.*

A Quick Prayer for Today:

Jesus, help me see you next to me.

Day 7: Enduring Rhythms - God Is At The Finish Line

Have you settled into your new life rhythms? The "eat, play, sleep" cycle is on repeat and dictates the entire household's schedule. There is comfort in this rhythm. The intensity of the newborn rhythm is temporary. But rhythms continue with each motherhood season—packing lunches, school pickups, sports practice. These different rhythms set the course for each family.

Rhythms are important. But when we rely on rhythms, we can become complacent and numb.

Some consequences of the numbness do not show up for decades. Many spouses no longer know one another after their children move out of the house. Some children have everything they want but no relationship with their parents. Often it isn't until life falls apart that God is invited back into the home.

Practicing enduring rhythms will protect the relationships that matter the most to us.

An enduring rhythm is the intentional pursuit of a mother to prioritize the most important relationships in her life.

A mama with enduring rhythms:

- **Pursues her husband to understand how he is doing.** Prioritizing time to affirm his values helps him become a better husband. Praying for him daily helps him become a better father.

- **Shepherds her children's hearts more than their behavior.** Jesus saw the sin but also saw the person. While we need to teach and correct our children, we must value their honesty over perfect answers.

- **Guards her time with God so that she has wisdom in the balance of correction and listening.** We need to set time aside to parent by prayer and let go of what is His.

A mama with these enduring rhythms will have more stamina in the race of motherhood.

> *Therefore, since we also have such a large cloud of witnesses surrounding us, let us lay aside every hindrance and the sin that so easily ensnares us. Let us run with endurance the race that lies before us, keeping our eyes on Jesus, the pioneer and perfecter of our faith. For the joy that lay before him, he endured the cross, despising the shame, and sat down at the right hand of the throne of God.*
>
> *Hebrews 12:1–2, CSB*

There will be hard days in this motherhood endurance race, but you do not run alone. Jesus is at the finish line. Even when you fall, you will have the perseverance to get back up and continue.

He has woven your motherhood journey with purpose. His purpose. His *good* purpose.

I can't wait to hear how your story unfolds!

Until then, I'll see you on the course.

> **A Prayer For A Mama Who Is Getting Complacent:**
>
> *Jesus, help me manage my time so that I can spend time on what is most important. Help me to keep my eyes on you. I want to run this race with endurance and away from the sin that so easily entangles me. Give me wisdom to know how to pursue my spouse and children in deeper ways. Amen.*

A Quick Prayer for Today:

Jesus, give me endurance for the race to which you have called me.

Part VI
Epilogue

Congratulations! You have already been pregnant, you are lactating, or you are running after your feral munchkins. You are living the great calling of motherhood. I hope you are having the time of your life!

As we have seen over the last few months together, becoming a mother is so much more than the physical strains and body aches. The soul of the mother grows and evolves with each season of her children's lives. Every mother has a different story but the same aches as you do.

You may be surprised by the degree of emotions that now course through your veins after holding your child for the first time. I pray that your dreams, emotions, and fears have been held in check by focusing on the Creator of your child. God is faithful even in unexpected outcomes. He is a balm to our anxious souls. He alone holds the future.

If you still fear, it's okay. But then ask yourself why.
Fear says *what if.* Faith says *even if.*

When the most vulnerable part of your heart is on the line, trusting God's goodness is vital to your resilience. If you trust God's plan is good, then you will have incredible peace even if your motherhood journey is different from what you expected.

There are so many beautiful, rewarding moments of motherhood. And there are also many shadowed crosses. But among these crosses is gospel hope for all of us. God sanctifies women through motherhood. We empty ourselves and allow Him to fill us. We see our need for a Savior in a new way. The tenderness of God reaches us on lonely days. The provision of God protects us in our most vulnerable places.

Galatians says it best:

> *My old self has been crucified with Christ. It is no longer I who live, but Christ lives in me. So, I live in this earthly body by trusting in the Son of God, who loved me and gave himself for me.*
>
> Galatians 2:20, NLT

Motherhood causes us to no longer live for ourselves. Some days of motherhood feel like we are carrying a very heavy cross. But in this sanctification, we are truly freed. We can do the routine, the mundane, and the hard because Christ lives in us. We are not alone in motherhood. We are lifted by the power of Christ, who understood the cross and then conquered it.

If you do not have a relationship with Jesus Christ, you only need to ask Him to come into your life. There are many things to live for in this life, but living for Jesus will help you find hope in life's darkest places. As you dig deeper into what the Bible says about Him, you will see the incredible plan of how your motherhood journey fits into this broken world. You will see eternity through a new lens when your mother's heart encounters pain.

From the moment that you were woven in your mother's womb,
God knew every single day you would live as a child
He knew every day you would live as a mother.
He knew every tear you would cry,
He knew every crack of your broken heart,
And He said, "The story isn't over."
I will break myself so that she will know she is loved.
I will go through the brokenness of being human
So that she will know that I understand her.
I will stay on the cross,
So that she knows I will never leave her.
I will raise from the dead,
So that she knows nothing is outside of my power.
I will go to heaven,
So that she knows where she is going when she follows me.
She is secure. I am with her always.
He holds you in His hand, mama.

> *Peace I leave with you; my peace I give to you. Not as the world gives do I give to you. Let not your hearts be troubled, neither let them be afraid. John 14:27, ESV*

Dear Mama -
I would love to hear from you.
Subscribe to Woven Motherhood for updates and freebies!
Follow the QR code below.
On this journey with you,

Rachelle Keng
AUTHOR | OBGYN | MOTHER

https://www.rachellekeng.com/contact
https://www.instagram.com/rachelle.keng/
https://www.facebook.com/rachelle.keng

Check out The Woven Motherhood Podcast with stories of mothers who have experienced hope in their unconventional motherhood journeys.

https://anchor.fm/wovenmotherhood

Part VII
Acknowledgments

It takes a village to raise a child and it takes a village to write a book. This book was written in fifteen minute increments while stranded in airports, waiting in school pick-up lines, and amidst the fragrance of burnt dinners.

My loving husband, Mike, took the brunt of the household duties while supporting me to write this book amidst our childrens' many requests. He has believed in me even when I was discouraged as a mother and an author. He is my best friend, rock, and soulmate. I am forever grateful.

My mother, Rita Huang, a psychologist and author herself, dedicated her life to helping others find hope. She told me in her dying days that I would write a book that would be a "light." I wish she could see her answered prayers in this project. My father, Raywin Huang, taught me to "try my best and let God take care of the rest." I am blessed they poured so much prayer and unconditional love into me as a young child.

My family (Ritchie, Grace, Karis, Elia, and Isobel) and my in-laws (Rudy, Grace, Russell, Caroline, Annalise, Sydney, and Cora) have always supported my projects.

My mentors and colleagues made me into the physician that I am today (Drs. Rajiv Rangrass, Yuvelle McFarland, Anne Echeverri, and Bob Stager). I have had the most amazing work families at Saint Joseph Mercy Hospital, Kaiser Permanente, Cleveland Clinic Hillcrest, Sentara Martha Jefferson Hospital, Jefferson OBGYN, and Lifespring.

My patients taught me so much about the vulnerabilities of being women. Their story is also my story. I am honored to be a part of women's lives as they become mothers.

I am grateful to the Bible teachings of Nancy Guthrie, who taught me how to grieve with hope; John Piper, who helped me value the sovereignty of God; and Tim Keller, who taught me to see the gospel in every story of the Bible.

The publishing team at Hope*Books was the perfect publisher. My team: Brian Dixon, Krissy Nelson, Molly Wilcox, Amber Burnett, Hope Dover, Kati Benton, Charity Johnston, and the design/marketing team at Hope*Media. And last but not least, my developmental editor,

Acknowledgments

Abby Mcdonald. You all squeezed more out of me than I thought was possible. The OG 2022 Hope*Books Author Cohort are my people! Thank you for believing in my book!

There are many friends who contributed their ideas, prayer, and support of this project throughout the years - Erika Brandenstein, MD; Kim Briehl, RN; Gena Carazzana, RN; Peter Rothschild, MD; Liz Wann; Ruth Graham; Morgan Bettinger, Michelle Little PT, DPT, OCS at Women in Motion Physical Therapy; Shelby Dean; Penny Merrel, CLC; Kristin Morgan, LPC, PMH-C; Jacob and Brittney Dunn; Andrea Asher, RN; Don and Nancy Fong, MD; Christina Chen, MD; Ruth Scully; Shirley Lehigh; Elizabeth Eldredge, RN; Heidi Curnette, RN; Erin Muller, RN; Leslie Beaster, RN; Carole Eichler, RN; Mary Eldredge, LSW; Rachel Mitchell; Jill Halseth; Elizabeth Sinclair; Rachel Perry; Esther Makowski, NP; Patty Chan, NP; Therese and Phillip Shuffer, MD; Beverly Lam; Pastor Dale and Hannah Fields; Dao and Alicia Nguyen, PhD; Carol Pantuch; Kathy Hassell; Rebecca Medina Stewart; Pastor Gary and Lillian House; Pastor Rob and Susie Pochek; Pastor Keith and Lisa Goad; Peggy Rudnick; Felicia Aldinger; Rachel Fahrenbach; Maria Webb, Doris Wong, Sally Nisley, Sheila Richardson, Nancy Ryalls, Angela Anger, MD, Sheila Wallace, Berta Sanchez and the many other friends who taught me their lessons of motherhood.

My trustworthy nanny, Rebecca "Bex" Simmerman, who took stellar care of my children so that I could write without guilt.

My children, Maleia and Anya. Becoming your mother is the best gift I have ever received. Every bump in the road is worth it and I would do it all over again. You have been my greatest teacher and my greatest joy. Love you both forever and always.

To God be the Glory.